The Marches of Wales

You are holding a reproduction of an original work that is in the public domain in the United States of America, and possibly other countries. You may freely copy and distribute this work as no entity (individual or corporate) has a copyright on the body of the work. This book may contain prior copyright references, and library stamps (as most of these works were scanned from library copies). These have been scanned and retained as part of the historical artifact.

This book may have occasional imperfections such as missing or blurred pages, poor pictures, errant marks, etc. that were either part of the original artifact, or were introduced by the scanning process. We believe this work is culturally important, and despite the imperfections, have elected to bring it back into print as part of our continuing commitment to the preservation of printed works worldwide. We appreciate your understanding of the imperfections in the preservation process, and hope you enjoy this valuable book.

THE MARCHES OF WALES

ARMS OF THE MORTIMERS.

LADY BRILLIANA HARLEY.
From the Painting by Sir Peter Lely.

THE MARCH
OF WALES

Notes and Impressions
Welsh Borders, from
Sea to the ...

By CHARLES A. ...

Author ...
...

With One Illustrated and ...
Sketch ... the Author ... four ...

LONDON: CHAPMAN & HALL, LD.
1894

LADY BRILLIANA HARLEY.
From the Picture
by Sir Peter Lely.

THE · MARCHES
OF · WALES

Notes and Impressions on the Welsh Borders, from the Severn Sea to the Sands o' Dee

By CHARLES G. HARPER

Author of "The Brighton Road," "From Paddington to Penzance," etc., etc., etc.

With One Hundred and Fourteen Illustrations, from Sketches by the Author and from Old-time Portraits

LONDON: CHAPMAN & HALL, LTD.
1894

TO JAMES PENDEREL-BRODHURST, ESQ.

My Dear Mr. Penderel-Brodhurst,

I inscribe this book to you, not because you have any especial acquaintance with the line of country of which it treats, nor, indeed, that your antiquarian sympathies have crystallized into an enthusiasm for the history of the Marches of Wales, beyond the lively interest which the story of the borders has, and should have, for the Englishman whose interest in politics and political geography goes back beyond the merely Parliamentary squabbles of this little day. The Wrekin, it is true, comes within the horizon of your Staffordshire home, but you are no Salopian for all that. Yet I claim you for that county, if only by reason of your seventeenth-century forbears, the Penderels of Boscobel, who performed such service to King and State when, after Worcester fight, they concealed the royal fugitive at Boscobel, just within the Shropshire borders. That is one reason for my dedicating this book to yourself; but not the chiefest. No: it is rather upon grounds more personal to myself that I dedicate this book to you, for you can (perhaps more than any other) understand why this is not—as I could wish it had been—a pure History of the Marches, rather than a series of historical doses administered in the guise of a touring book—the unpalatable dryness of historical facts sweetened, so far as my ability lay, by an engaging popular treatment.

But I have cause for disquiet. I read reviews and see how commonly the art of criticism is mistaken rather as the opportunity for fault-finding than the due exercise of appreciation. I see the extraordinary fallacy trumpeted about that an artist can have no proper sense of language, nor a literary man that of form or colour; so it seems a sure thing that, in one or other of the two media in which I work, this book will be judged of lacking properly workmanlike qualities. Alas! I also have my doubts in this instance, although well assured of the legitimacy of the practice by which an author may become his own illustrator, and vice versâ. For good or ill (I myself may not choose the epithet) the day of the artist-author is at hand; it pleases me, therefore, to consider that I am (ah! that First Person Singular) one of the earliest of that new race who have invaded the most conservative precincts of the Press, armed with Pen and Pencil, and have thence won to the library shelf.

Thus, my friend, you shall see how it comes that I dedicate this book to you who are peculiarly well-acquaint with these doubly-equipped adventurers. I do it with no little trepidation, for, clearly, you who have so excellent a taste must readily discover that particular medium (if only one) in which I lack, and, through me, my book. How then shall I better appease you than by the assurance that I offer you (such as it is) of my best?

Yours very truly,
CHARLES G. HARPER.

LONDON,
September, 1894.

Preface

LET me say at once that herein is no attempt at a history of the Marches of Wales. That history is not yet written, and probably never will be, for the ways of the English with the Britons, and of the Normans with the Welsh are too confused and involved,—so tangled and altogether so complex —that a proper exposition of them at this length of time is impossible. The numberless feuds and forays, the obscure pillagings and burnings, of these old-time disturbed borderlands are not for telling in their entirety, neither can anyone fix the ever-shifting frontiers between Wales and England before the final creation of the Principality and the settlement of the shires. But the episodes of a bygone state of politics and society that have survived such wholesale destructions of records as the burning of the historical manuscripts in the libraries of Raglan and Brampton Bryan Castles are moving with all the rush and force of those extremely physical times, and I have endeavoured to recall, between the somewhat uneventful chronicles of a walking tour, such of them as befell at the places we passed on our journey from the Severn estuary to where the Dee flows into salt water between sandy shores.

This is no consistent panegyric of pedestrian pleasures. Walking is a pleasant means to a healthful holiday, but it is not free from the annoyances of travel that accompany other methods of progression, and I, for one, cannot understand

Preface.

why it should be an accepted convention with the writers of touring works that they should ever be in a steadfastly good humour through all the mishaps of their touring; as though they relished their trials and inconveniences. Take, then, this record, seen through spectacles both rose-coloured and neutral-tinted; nor blame me for that skies are sometimes dark and ourselves footsore, and therefore in an unreceptive frame of mind.

CHARLES G. HARPER.

List of Illustrations

Lady Brilliana Harley	*Frontispiece*
Map	PAGE XV
Baptistry, Chepstow Church	5
Henry Marten	9
Chepstow Castle	13
Caldicot Castle	27
Carved Stone, Caldicot Castle	30
,, ,, ,, ,,	30
Window, Caldicot Castle	31
Saint Arvans	32
Tintern Abbey	35
"A cat of demoniac aspect"	38
"Trustful gaze—good Bingo"	39
"O Moon, look gently on this wicked world"	40
Chapel Hill Church	47
Barbados Hill, Tintern	49
Tombstone, St. Arvans	52
Epitaph, Tintern Parva	53
Epitaph, Mitchel Troy	54
"Transpontine Drama"	55
Tombstone, Chapel Hill	56
Epitaph, Llandogo	56
"The Picturesque"	60
Raglan Castle	63
Badge, Raglan Castle	65
Fireback, Raglan Castle	66
Henry Somerset, First Marquis of Worcester	67
"Owls"	81
Roadside Stocks, Portskewett	84
An old Sundial, Saint Ann's	85

List of Illustrations.

	PAGE
Lady Probert's Sundial	87
An old Doorway, Trelleck	89
Churchyard Cross, Trelleck	90
Monnow Gate, Monmouth	93
Henry V.	97
Sign of the White Swan, Monmouth	100
John Kemble's Grave	103
Pembridge Castle	105
The Monnow below Skenfrith	108
Skenfrith	111
Chimney, Grosmont Castle	113
Grosmont	114
Grosmont Castle : Evening	115
Announcement of a local Tea-fight	120
Rural Postman	122
White Castle	125
John à Kent	129
"Some Life at Pontrilas"	130
Carven Head, Ewyas Harold	131
The Golden Valley Trout	138
Urishay Castle	141
Carven Head, Eardisley	145
Pembridge Belfry	152
"This pious but unfortunate benefactor"	159
Waterspout, Leominster	162
,, ,,	163
,, ,,	164
Edward IV.	177
Brampton Bryan Castle	183
Ludlow Castle from the Quarry : Evening	187
The Keep, Ludlow Castle	197
Ludford Bridge and the Clee Hills	211
Broad Gate, Ludlow	215
Window, Ludlow Castle	220
Ludlow Castle, 1789	221
Sir Henry Sidney	223
Casket containing the heart of Sir Henry Sidney	226
Mortimer's Tower	228
Charles Gerard, Earl of Macclesfield	229
Miserere, Saint Lawrence's, Ludlow	233
,, ,, ,, ,,	233
The Reader's House	234
The Country Shop	235
Bromfield	242
Stokesay Castle	243

List of Illustrations.

Cottage Tablets :—	PAGE
Dorrington	255
Old Furnace	257
Trelleck Grange	258
Sloop Inn, Llandogo	258
The George, Tintern	259
Coedithel Farm	260
New Inn, Brockweir	260
Monnow Street, Monmouth	261
Welsh Newton Farm	261
"Louis Napoleon"	264
The Barber's Shop	265
Old Shop	268
,, ,,	269
Shrewsbury Castle	273
Wyle Cop	275
The Refectory Pulpit	276
A River in the Marches	299
Somewhat hard of hearing	302
"Looks of fire and hate"	303
Whittington Castle	313
A suggestion for unconventional Tourists	317
The Village Concert	319
William	321
The Lady of the Weather	329
Dissent	344
"Obviously unsophisticated"	350
Caergwyrle	351
"Unkempt roadway"	353
Hawarden Castle	357
"Physique of the Suffolk punch"	365
The Convention of Opéra Bouffe	366
"Sea-gulls"	367

Decorations and Tail-pieces by the Author.

WORKS BY THE SAME AUTHOR.

ENGLISH PEN ARTISTS OF TO-DAY: Examples of their work, with some Criticisms and, Appreciations. Super royal 4to, £3 3s. net.

THE BRIGHTON ROAD: Old Times and New on a Classic Highway. With 95 Illustrations by the Author and from old prints. Demy 8vo, 16s.

FROM PADDINGTON TO PENZANCE: The Record of a Summer Tramp. With 105 Illustrations by the Author. Demy 8vo, 16s.

A PRACTICAL HANDBOOK OF DRAWING FOR MODERN METHODS OF REPRODUCTION. Illustrated by the Author and Others. Demy 8vo, 7s. 6d.

REVOLTED WOMAN: Past, Present and to Come. Illustrated by the Author and from Old-time portraits. Demy 8vo., 5s. net.

THE PORTSMOUTH ROAD: Annals of an Ancient Turnpike. With 100 Illustrations by the Author and from other sources. Demy 8vo. [*In the Press.*

I.

WE had taken train from Bristol. In this third-class compartment were two other passengers, and all the way they talked of things electrical—of ohms, and volts; currents, and accumulators; the one giving, the other in receipt of, information. It subsequently appeared that our fellow-travellers were the Vicar of Chepstow and the resident engineer at the Severn Tunnel Pumping Station.

The train had passed Pilning. The vicar pulled up the carriage window and we plunged into the darkness of a lengthy tunnel, emerging thence in some three minutes, to come, as the night shut down, to the windy platforms, dimly lit with oil-lamps, of the Severn Tunnel Junction.

We were strangers, and when we were come again into daylight from beneath the Severn, directed an inquiring glance at those two. The vicar caught that look of wistfulness, and answered it as though it had been a spoken word. "Yes," said he, "that is the Severn Tunnel."

You see, he was used to such dumb inquiries. For the Severn Tunnel bulks large in the mind's eye of all them that have read of the years of work that go to make the story of this great achievement; and he knew well the look of disappointment that always sits blankly upon the faces of strangers who expect an effect of grandeur, of impressiveness, in this passage-way beneath the Severn sea. For, indeed, the Severn Tunnel is not physically impressive. Its story is thrilling; but to them that know (*horresco referens!*) the sulphureous tunnels of our Metropolitan Railway, why, this cleanly, excellently-ventilated burrow is tame even to the confines of the commonplace.

We were for Chepstow this night, and when we had exchanged into the train waiting at the Junction, we found ourselves again in company of the vicar and the engineer. At Portskewett, the latter alighted for his pumping station, and for the intervening journey we were held in talk with the vicar alone. We knew nothing of Chepstow, and so the vicar charged himself with advising our wandering steps, in so far as the choice of an hotel lay. And so, in the High Street, he bade us good-night, we to one of the two hotels he favoured.

II.

IT had seemed to us that for this autumn exploration of the Marches of Wales, Chepstow was the most reasonable starting-point. Here was the most southerly of the greater strongholds that stretched from the sands o' Dee to within bowshot of the Severn estuary, over against the Gloucestershire shore; and but the matter of a few miles below the confluence of the Severn and the Wye were the New Passage and the Old, which for ages immemorial had been the highways into southern Wales or ever railway enterprise had rendered their short but intolerably tempestuous crossing obsolete.

Modern Chepstow is merely sordid. The lapse of ages and the changed conditions of life and travel have rendered its old-time chepe into a mere nothingness. If ever place lived upon romantic history, or existed by reason of its situation amid lovely scenery, Chepstow is that place *in excelsis*. Chepstow town and castle touch two extremes; the town is poor and shabby with that shabbiness that can never wear the interest of the delightfully ruinated castle, perched boldly upon its variegated cliff beside the Wye; while that roofless fortress is in its picturesque beauty in the first rank of the many deserted but impressive strongholds of our land.

The inhabitants of Chepstow live by selling to one another, and when the stranger comes within their gates, they, wearied with playing at shop, fall upon him and entreat him shamefully, even as the famished fleas of some long unoccupied bed, wearied of an unsatisfying cannibalism, despitefully use its long-awaited occupant. *We* were strangers, and the hotel people, using their prescriptive right in a place where strangers are rare, took us in, in a manner peculiarly unscriptural.

"You see," said one who condoled with us, later, "they reason thus: Hither come strangers to tour along the Wye. They stay a day or two; perhaps a week; possibly a fortnight, and then they go away, to return no more. Evidently the thing to do is to get as much out of them as possible, while they are yet here." This, of course, is logical enough, or would be, if those visitors had no friends, but there are few who lack of acquaintance so sorely that they have no one to whom to confide their wrongs, and certainly the overcharged Englishman is never slow to recount these mishaps of his touring; and still more certainly, the hotel-keepers along the valley of the Wye have earned so evil a repute in this connection that visitors have of late years been ever fewer and still more scarce.

We called upon the vicar, who overnight had promised to personally conduct us over the church, a fine fragment of Norman architecture with a delightfully quaint Baptistry. Close beside it is a worn ledger-stone that covers the remains of Henry Marten, the regicide, one of those who signed the death-warrant of Charles the First. He was a Republican of the most philosophical nature, and so independent that he quarrelled openly with Cromwell on account of his autocratic government; going even so far as to plot against the Lord Protector's life. Indeed it was only by an accident (happy or otherwise—whichever way your politics incline your thoughts) that Cromwell escaped shooting at the hands of his sometime friend.

Marten's share in the murder of his king met with an altogether inadequate retribution when the monarchy was restored and the second Charles enjoyed his own again. He was imprisoned for life in an angle-tower of Chepstow Castle, and the traveller is still shown in what is called Marten's Tower to this day, the window of his room which looks out upon one of the fairest views in England. Truly a most fortunate prisoner. Moreover, his imprisonment was of little or no rigour; "detention," and that of the mildest nature, seems to have been his lot. He had many friends in Chepstow and the neighbourhood, and—O! clemency—he was allowed to visit them on parole. Being also something of a wit, he dined out frequently and was everywhere an honoured guest, until he outraged propriety by asserting at the table of his friend Lewis, of Saint Pierre Park, that he would, if his life were to be lived over again, act once more as he had done at the trial of Charles the First.

He died September 9th, 1680, and was buried in the chancel of this church. In after years a vicar who could not endure that the bones of a regicide should be thus honoured, had them removed to this spot near the threshold of the building.

A portrait of Marten exists at Saint Pierre, near Chepstow, from which the accompanying illustration is taken, but whether or not this picture of a mild-faced, somewhat sad, gentleman is a correct presentment of the unrepentant rebel it is impossible to say. There seem to have been many sympathizers with Marten's views at Chepstow, for we find that even in this century there were churchwardens who had sufficient enthusiasm for his memory to give him a new tombstone when the old one had become decayed. His epitaph certainly is well worthy preservation, but simply for the sake of its anagram, composed by himself in what seems to have been a gratuitously querulous strain:—

BAPTISTRY, CHEPSTOW CHURCH.

HENRY MARTEN.

<pre>
                    Here
     September the 9th in the Year of our Lord
                    1680,
           was buried a true Englishman
          Who in Berkshire was well known
       To love his Country's freedom 'bove his own
         But living immur'd full twenty year
          Had time to write as doth appear
                  His Epitaph.
     H ere or elsewhere, all's one to you, to me
     E arth, air or water gripes my ghostless dust
     N one knows how soon to be by fire sett free.
     R eader, if you an oft-tryed rule will trust
     Y ou'll gladly do and suffer what you must.

     M y life was spent with serving you and you
     A nd death's my pay (it seems) and welcome too
     R evenge destroying but itself, while I
     T o birds of pray (sic) leave my old cage, and fly
     E xamples preach to th' eye ; care then, mine says
     N ot how you end but how you spend your days.
                    Aged 78 Year.
</pre>

N.B. The stone with the above original inscription being broken and the letters obliterated In order to perpetuate to Posterity, the memory of the burial of the above Henry Marten, who sat as one of the judges on King Charles and died in his imprisonment in the Castle of Chepstow, a new stone was laid down in the year 1812.

<pre>
           Geo⁰· Smith   ⎫
           William Smith ⎬ Churchwardens.
                          ⎭
</pre>

Was ever there a more whimpering malcontent than this, or ever such a pother over a mere surveillance exercised with a proper regard for the authority of the Crown?

His wife and daughters shared his residence with him; he was attended by servants, and the whole tower of four floors was at his disposal.

Southey, who should have been better informed, wrote of Marten:—

> "Often have these walls
> Echoed his footsteps, as with even tread
> He paced around his prison. Not to him
> Did Nature's fairest vanities exist:
> He never saw the sun's delightful beams
> Save when through yon high bars he poured a sad
> And broken splendour."

That is not particularly distinguished blank verse; the more, therefore, the pity that it is not true.

It is a singular thing that Marten should have risen to eminence in the councils of the Roundheads, who were not a playful and sprightly set of men; who, whatever they practised, certainly professed the most austere views. He was, to the contrary, a man of disreputable life, with the morals of an unregenerate Sultan, and a pack of creditors hanging persistently to his coat tails. Both Charles the First and Cromwell taunted him publicly with one of the most offensive of names, and a biographer who leans toward a favourable view of him says sweetly, "He was a great lover of pretty girls, to whom he was so liberal that he spent the greatest part of his estate on them." Such doings were never particularly difficult of accomplishment; but not thus should a Puritan expend his substance.

Eventually the notoriety of his life and his practical atheism caused his retirement from parliamentary scenes. The prejudice of the Briton in favour of morality in others caused the petition presented by the Puritan army to the Long Parliament, demanding "that such men, and such men only, might be preferred to the great power and trust of the Commonwealth as are approved at least for moral righteousness." The army had made the Commonwealth, and its petitions, that were such only in name, had to be hearkened to. Marten's political career then ended for a time.

His debts cost his father the (then) very considerable sum of 1000*l*. per annum, and some years later, during a short period when he was without a seat in parliament, we find him occupying the quiet seclusion of what was still, under the Commonwealth, called the King's Bench Prison, whither his extravagance had brought him. He was fetched away by a party from the House of Commons, who, to secure a quorum, procured his nomination and re-election to parliament for the county of Berks; and being again able to write M.P. after his name he could once more claim the privileges and immunities of a member of the House against arrest for debt. This was in 1659. A year later the Restoration was accomplished, and Marten gave himself up to the clemency of Charles the Second. His character is not pleasing. Ready always to sting with a bitter and witty tongue, he seems to

HENRY MARTEN,
THE REGICIDE.
[*From an old Print.*

have been lacking in personal courage, and the weak complainings that marked his end alienate whatever small sympathies we might have formed for him.

III.

FROM the parish church to the castle, the scene of Marten's imprisonment, is but a short step. It guards the passage of the Wye, which, tidal here and superlatively muddy, has a fall of between fifty and sixty feet, with a swift and dangerous current. Chepstow Castle stands on its limestone bluff, where the river bends abruptly, and looks over upon the fair landscape of Gloucestershire—toward England, as one might have said in other times. A severely utilitarian bridge of three arches crosses the river just below the castle, and lower still the railway bridge spans it in two spans of hideous ironwork, for which the younger Brunel, clever and daring engineer though he was, has deserved the bitterest reproaches; for it was nothing less than a crime, thus to mar the beauty of the Wye. But Chepstow people are extremely proud of it.

The founding of Chepstow Castle goes back to a very dim antiquity. Leland indeed, says that a tower in it, called Longine, was "erected by Longinus a Jew, father of the soldier whose spear pierced the side of Christ;" but, legends apart, it seems certain that the original stronghold was built by William FitzOsbern, one of Edward the Confessor's Norman mercenaries whose advice decided William of Normandy to invade England. After the Conquest, FitzOsbern was granted this lordship of Striguil, as Chepstow was then known, as the price of his treachery. His son Roger succeeded him and, rebelling against the king, forfeited his estates, which were granted to the De Clares. This powerful family took their name from Clare, in Suffolk, one of the hundred and sixty manors given to the founder of their house, Richard of Brionne, by his cousin-german the Conqueror. Walter, the third son of this Richard, received the Royal license to spoil and annex what lands he could from the Welsh, and the whole of what is now known as Monmouthshire became the reward of his enterprise. He it was who, to atone in some measure for the crimes committed and the blood spilt in his merciless forays, founded Tintern Abbey in 1139. Eight years after that act of tardy homage to Heaven, he died, childless, and his possessions fell to his nephew, Gilbert Fitz Gilbert, Earl of Pembroke, surnamed Strongbow. He, like his uncle, was buried at Tintern. Richard Strongbow, his son, the famous Earl of Pembroke who reduced Ireland, came next, and dying in 1176 left his vast properties to his heiress Isabel, who married William Mareschal. Mareschal succeeded to the earldom and fully maintained the reputation of his predecessors for untameable ferocity. His ways with the Irish and the Welsh were not more gentle than theirs; moreover, he was less amenable to the terrors of the Church, for having seized two manors belonging to the Bishop of Ferns, he died excommunicated and unabsolved rather than restore them.

The Bishop, either from the charity pertaining to his profession, unwilling that this fearless knight should remain in torment, or eager to recover his manors, paid a visit to the English Court, and accompanied by the king, Henry III., went to the Temple Church where the earl was buried, and where his cross-legged effigy may yet be seen. Standing before the tomb, he exhorted the spirit of the dead and graceless land-grabber:—" O, William, who liest here, an alien from salvation, if those lands which thou didst perniciously take from my church be plenarily restored, either by the king, who here listens, or by any of thy friends, I then absolve thee; otherwise I ratify thy sentence of eternal condemnation." Henry advised the earl's eldest son to restore the land, but he refused, whereupon the bishop excommunicated and cursed him also, with the prophecy that his name should be blotted out in one generation. And so it happened. His five sons died childless and his five daughters became his heiresses. Maud, the eldest, married Huge Bigod, Earl of Norfolk, whose grandson,

CHEPSTOW CASTLE

Roger, rebuilt Tintern Abbey in its present beautiful form.

The subsequent history of Chepstow Castle is the usual record of successions, forfeitures, and bestowals until 1643, when it was garrisoned for Charles I. by the Marquess of Worcester. Shortly afterwards, the garrison were surprised by the Parliamentarian, Major Throckmorton, in command of a party from Monmouth, but his party were in a few hours surprised in their turn. The Royalists then held it for two years, until Colonel Morgan, Governor of Gloucester, carried it by assault, after a four days' siege. Two years and seven months later, in May 1648, the Roundheads were betrayed overnight in the absence of the governor, and that well-remembered worthy, Sir Nicholas Kemys, a Monmouthshire gentleman, and a party took possession once more for the king. But these zealous Royalists were not long left in quiet enjoyment of their success. On the 10th of the same month Cromwell marched in person from Monmouth to Chepstow and laid siege to the castle. The garrison was summoned to surrender, but refused ; meanwhile Cromwell hurried to Pembroke to quell the rising there, and Colonel Ewer was left in charge of the investment. He went so vigorously to work that on the 21st of May a breach was made in the walls and the place was taken, the garrison fighting to the last. One hundred and twenty prisoners were taken and imprisoned in the Priory church; Sir Nicholas Kemys and forty others were barbarously murdered by the Roundheads.

Jeremy Taylor, the author of *Holy Living and Holy Dying*, was imprisoned in Chepstow Castle for some months during the Commonwealth notwithstanding his age and the acknowledged honesty of his opinions. The building remained in good repair until comparatively recent times. It was held in 1688 for the Prince of Orange, and held a small garrison well into the eighteenth century. Soon afterwards, the keep was used as a factory; but when the business failed the old timbers of its floors were allowed to fall into decay. It is now roofless and greatly mutilated. The castle is entered through a great gateway flanked by two drum towers. The strong oaken door still remains, and opens directly into the lower ward, where Marten's Tower stands, open to the sky, all its floors fallen in and rotted away. One may climb to the battlements by the stone staircase and gaze over the town out to the meeting of the Severn and the Wye, and may still notice the little private oratory within the tower, where, centuries ago, the knights and noble dames prayed. It surely was by one of life's most cynical ironies that Marten, who was a scoffer and an atheist, was imprisoned in this tower, with the free access to this little chapel.

Opposite to Marten's Tower stand the domestic offices of the castle, now occupied in part by the keeper. Here is seen a large vaulted cellar overhanging the river, with an arrangement for raising stores from the boats below.

Beyond the outer ward is the middle ward, where the great Norman keep stands. Beyond this again comes the upper ward, and, lastly, the barbican and western gate-house. The whole fortress occupies the long and narrow ridge of a cliff running parallel with the Wye, and falling abruptly on either side. The nucleus of the castle was the Norman keep from which the later wards spread out successively. Portions of the older walls have an intermixture of red tiles, somewhat like the Roman materials seen in buildings adapted from the relics of the Roman occupation of Britain; but it is extremely unlikely that anything of so great an age is to be found here now, or that these fragments of red tile are older than Saxon times.

IV.

THE walls and bastions of Chepstow town, still in great part entire, enclose ninety acres, and spread out far beyond the streets, and, pierced by the railway in one direction, run down to the river's edge upon the last piece of abruptly sloping land as you go toward the confluence of the Severn and the Wye. The riverside lands that now succeed between Chepstow and Caldicot are perfectly flat, the product of centuries of mud brought down from the Welsh uplands by these rivers, and of the silt cast up by the flood tides.

Boating on the Wye is not to be recommended to strangers, by reason of these roaring tides that come up swiftly from the Bristol Channel; but parties do occasionally venture down the river to an islet situated where the Wye and Severn join, and there they picnic by the meagre ruins of what, in more reverent and less democratic days, was called Saint Tecla's — now known by the eminently barbarous and sticky name of "Treacle"—Chapel. Saint Tecla, from whom, it seems, the place takes its name, was the daughter of a petty Welsh prince who, abandoning the pomps and vanities (such as they were) of the paternal court, retired to this remote spot, and, weary of earth, devoted herself to meditation and prayer. We moderns who are out of touch with the habits of the ninth century, might suppose that here was really another distraught Ophelia, but all that is left to us is mere surmise; we only know that the next pagan band of political pirates who chanced to sail up the Wye understood neither religion nor reclusion. They murdered the maiden, just to show their independence of the usages of chivalry, and went their ways. Since that day the isle has been holy. The pious people of the time raised a votive chapel to this British female protomartyr, and doubtless her relics—if the pirates left any relics —proved as miraculous in the hands of the clergy as such things always were in the keeping of the Church. But to-day there is nothing on Treacle Island in the shape of relics save mineral-water bottles and fragments of ham fat—and they work no miracles.

A place less frequented by picnic parties—entirely unspotted from the world and therefore worthy your very best regard—is Matherne, two miles below Chepstow, beside the high road that leads to Newport. There are interesting ruins at Matherne. Few people ever see them, because the majority of tourists are too lazy to turn aside from the highway, and others are ignorant of what awaits a little exploring enterprise. As for the residents in these parts, they don't care a crocket about anything of the kind.

Let me say at once that we only found the place by chance—and reckoned it a happy discovery. Here is the old-time Palace of the Bishops of Llandaff, now devoted to secular uses, and called the Palace Farm. It is nearly a hundred and ninety years since any of these bishops inhabited here, and the stately courtyard is now just the typical farmyard littered with straw in most picturesque confusion, and in wet weather afflicted with muddy sloughs of untold depths. Doves coo all day long in and about the beautiful old buildings, and the mullioned and traceried windows, suggestive of ecclesiastical uses, impart a piquant touch to the merely industrial doings of the farm.

Over across a broad meadow are the buildings of another old house—Moynes Court—built in the very earliest years of the seventeenth century by Godwin, Bishop of Llandaff, upon the site of an older house, at one time—so say the old deeds still extant—the property of the De Moignes. The place is, for a proper security, enclosed within a strong wall and defended by an outer gateway, flanked by two singular towers in the highest degree picturesque and original. The original oaken doorways yet remain, studded with great nails and strengthened with ornamental bands of iron, and above the archway of the gatehouse are still the arms of Godwin impaling those of his diocese.

Leland calls Matherne "a pretty pyle in Base Ventland," (as who should say Lower Gwent or South Wales) and his description still holds good. The church, with its great painted sundial on the southern wall of the tower, is most interesting architecturally, and historically from the fact that here was buried Tewdrig, or Theodoric, a Welsh Christian Prince of Gwent and Morganwg, who, mortally wounded in the hour of his great victory over the Pagan Saxons at Tintern, A.D. 600, was laid to rest, as he desired, on the spot where he died. Bishop Godwin has left it on record that the skeleton of Theodoric was discovered in his time within Matherne Church, the skull still in excellent preservation with a great fissure in it, showing where the Christian martyr, as he was accounted, received his death-wound.

For ourselves, we lingered here until twilight came and warned us that it was time we departed for Portskewett, where, fleeing from the inhumanities of the Chepstow hotel-keepers, we hoped to stay the night. We came again into the high road at the hamlet of Poolmerrick, and, in two miles and a half more, to Portskewett.

A small village, with scattered houses and roads, now shrouded in a Cimmerian darkness. As for village inn, why, there was none, since, as one of whom we inquired observed, "Them as owns the land here, d'ye see, is teetotalers, as ye might say." But the postmistress of Portskewett gave us a gleam of hope. "Perhaps," she said, "we might try the 'Black Rock.'" Yes, indeed, the Black Hole, if needs were; but where *was* the "Black Rock," and who was to ferry us over when we reached the waterside? "Over there," said the postmistress; and she pointed into the pitchy blackness of the night. "There is no ferry, the Black Rock Hotel stands on the shore." The name sounded ominous, and we sighed for the flesh-pots of Chepstow. But, it appeared, even the "Black Rock" was problematical, for it was an hostelry in a remote part of the village, and moreover, its licence had just expired. As a drink-shop it was impossible; as an hotel—? Well, we would try.

We did. Stumbling along stony lanes, we came at length upon a small group of lonely houses, looming darkly against the sky, with never a light to show if they were inhabited. A few steps more revealed a low cliff with a beach, and the sound of lapping waters, and the fitful gusts of wind made melancholy the already dreary sight of the lonely place. Away, out in the dark void of the night and the whispering waters, came suddenly the bright eye of a lighthouse that winked cheerfully at intervals, and heartened us again as we turned and knocked at the door of the Black Rock Hotel, standing in the porch under the wreck of the entrance lamp. We waited there, among the potsherds of what seemed to be a decayed civilization, and knocked again and again without response. At length, as we were deciding to go away, steps drew near from remote stone passages, heavy bolts were drawn back, and the door was opened by a winsome girl.

"Could we stay the night?" we queried.

Well, she didn't know; the landlord was away up at the village, but would return in about an hour. Would we wait and have supper in the meanwhile? We would, with all the pleasure in the world. We made our supper (so scanty was the provand and visitors so unlooked-for in these last days of the Black Rock) upon penitential bread-and-cheese and pickled cabbage; and the chairs upon which we sat and the table that bore the spread were ticketed with the little labels of the auctioneer. Outside the night was black, and when we looked forth of the curtained windows there came a dash of rain that blurred the bright ray of the winking lighthouse out beyond in mid-channel upon the reef that gives the place its name. In the loneliness of the great rambling building, pervaded only by one other person, a shuffling charwoman, we grew quite towardly, we three, as we sat in the cosy keeping-room and chatted over the sea-coal fire. And so we awaited the host's return, occupied with supper and in conversation with this Welsh girl, who was, in this absence of the landlord, host, as well as house-keeper and director-general of the household. She spoke English, this Cymric maiden, with all the precision of a foreigner talking in a strange tongue, and so charmed were we with this *séance* that when the landlord did return we somewhat regretted his advent. He decided that although his licence had expired that very day, there could be no objection to our staying in the house; so we were safely lodged for the night.

V.

This was Sunday morning, and we rose betimes and went forth to see what manner of place this might be in daylight. The house faced the Severn and a lawn, shaded with great trees, lay between. Early as we were, another was yet earlier, gathering late roses in the garden : our acquaintance of the last evening. She was our guide, philosopher and friend, and showed us all the features of Black Rock before breakfast, and primed our minds and enriched our note-books with the history of the place. Certainly she spoke our language in the manner of a foreigner, with an accent, and with a studied purity of pronunciation that we slurrers of a noble tongue—our own—never achieve. We mangle our spoken words, we clip and cut our syllables and ignore our vowels dreadfully, but vowels are so rare in the Welsh language that the Cymry treasure them and give them their full value in speech. For instance, we too often speak of Heref'd, *tout court;* but a Welshman will give you the "ford" in all its fulness.

We were the last guests at Black Rock. The landlord, it seems, had surrendered his lease and his licence (for a consideration) to the freeholders, who were bent upon leaving Portskewett without a licensed house. Those selfish fanatics had now succeeded, and it will go hard with tourists who are benighted there in future.

Black Rock impends over the Severn tide at New Passage. It is a hamlet outside the small village of Portskewett, and must at one time have been a bustling place—in the times before railways. When stage-coach passengers landed here, wet and miserable and buffeted with the rigours of that narrow but difficult passage of the Severn estuary, they were wont to rest at this inn that overlooked the water toward the English shore, and from it they resumed their journey into Wales, the greater number inwardly vowing rather to return by the circuitous route by way of Gloucester than again brave the winds and waves of this storm-tossed strait. Then Black Rock was in its prime. Consider. There was only one other way into South Wales unless one went round by Gloucester, and that was the Old Passage, nearer Chepstow, and only half the breadth of this three mile span, but notorious by reason of the many fatal accidents that had happened there to heavily-laden coaches. No wonder travellers disliked journeys into the Principality!

Then came railways, and they dropped their passengers, even as the coaches had done, on the brink of the water, which had to be crossed by boat. And although they were by this time steam-boats, yet the crossing was sufficiently uncomfortable, and the "Black Rock" inn, which now called itself Hotel, was as welcome a haven as ever.

And so it continued for many years. A spur line of railway ran from Portskewett station to the waterside, where the passengers landed or whence they embarked, and many more of them went straight through where old-time travellers stayed overnight, but the place flourished still. And then the Severn Tunnel grew from a project to an undertaking and progressed during fourteen years to its final completion in 1887. And then Black Rock, from being on the highway came to stand on a road that leads nowhere. The landing stage is gone, and the railway deserted. Weeds and nettles and wild flowers grow in its cuttings to-day; and now this Hotel, the Passage House, retires into private life as a country residence, and of the few houses—perhaps not more than five or six, all told—four or five are empty.

It is a wild, bleak place. No ferry-boats ply upon the water; traffic rumbles unseen below the river bed, in over three miles of burrow, and in mid-channel stands the reef that gives the place its name, with a little lighthouse that is only one degree more lonely than this out-of-the-world corner. The hotel, with its outbuildings and its singularly isolated position upon the verge of the water, wears a look that seems significant of some unacted drama whose fulfil-

MEN OF WRATH.

ment it seems passively to await, some moving tale that has yet to be told is hinted at in every stone and pebble of its beach, and a tragedy lurks in the look of the low cliffs lapped by the muddy water of the Severn. It is a look some few places wear that never yet have had a story, but there is one historic event connected with the ferry that is worth recounting in this place.

It was here in 1645 that Charles I. was pursued across the Severn by the Roundheads. Loyal ferrymen rowed him and his party to the Gloucestershire shore across these three miles, and presently came back, to be forced by a party of sixty of Cromwell's soldiers to take them over also. But the cunning of these sea-faring men was fully equal to their loyalty, so instead of landing the party on the other side they left them on a reef called the English Stones, which, it being then low tide, stood conspicuously out from the water. Here they left them, and the tide rising with that suddenness which characterizes the Severn, they were all drowned.

Beneath the very spot where these Men of Wrath met their death, runs to-day at a depth of one hundred and forty-five feet below the high water of spring tides that triumph of the modern civil engineer—the Severn Tunnel—and at Sudbrook, some few hundred yards outside Portskewett village, beside the water, stand the permanent pumping-houses which, day in and day out throughout the year, send a trail of smoke across the water. That inky smudge upon the sky is the outward and visible sign of a laborious and costly fight with Nature. The day when those tall chimneys show no sign of work, when the great pumping-engines cease to draw their diurnal quota of 30,000 gallons of water from below, the tunnel will become impassable from the rush of spring-water that has to be constantly kept in check.

During fourteen years of alternating success and failure the work of making the tunnel went forward. The works were from time to time drowned out by land-springs that issued in tremendous volume from fissures in the faulty rocks lying in broken strata beneath the Severn estuary, and high tides occasionally flooded the shafts from above. But pluck and science at last overcame, and a walk through the completed tunnel would be dark it is true, but thoroughly dry. It was not always so, even after the brickwork was completed, for on one grave occasion the water lay with a pressure of fifty-six pounds to the square inch on the thirty-six inches of bricks set in Portland cement, so that pieces of brick came flying out of the archway with the sound and force of pistol-shots, and the Severn water percolating through the fifty feet of rock between the river bed and the crown of the tunnel, came squirting between the joints in hundreds of separate rills, like discharges from a hose. Yet those bricks were the hardest kind that could be made: seventy-six and a half millions of them, set in about thirty-seven thousand tons of Portland cement.

The actual tunnel, exclusive of approaches, is 7664 yards in length, and descends from either side in a steep gradient until it reaches a level stretch in the middle. The impulse given to trains descending from one end carries them automatically a great way up towards the other, and in this manner no steam energy is wasted—an important consideration when it is seen that over forty trains travel through the tunnel every day. Seven minutes suffices for a passenger train to run through, goods trains are allowed twenty minutes. Since the opening for goods traffic on September 1st, 1886, and for passengers on July 1st, 1887, no interruption of the ordinary routine has taken place. The cost of the tunnel must have been immense, considering the years of work and the number of men employed upon it: at one time no less than 3628 men were on the weekly pay-sheets, and Sudbrook, from being a place with a name but no inhabitants became a thriving settlement, with a post and telegraph office especially erected, a mission hall, hospital, canteen, and other blessings of civilization.

These are all gone now that the industrial army has taken its departure, with pick and shovel, to other fields, and only the settlement of the Pumping Works remains.

The Severn Tunnel.

The interior of one of the pumping-houses is very well worth seeing, and, contrary to the expectation of nine out of ten visitors, the place is clean and tidy to a scrupulous degree of neatness. Each engine-house has two stories, reached by iron staircases. A platform runs round the four sides of each story, with the giant pumps working smoothly and quietly in the centre of the building, fenced off with a steel railing, bright as silver, like all the machinery that is visible. Other parts are daintily cased in polished wood. This installation of pumping machinery has a capacity of sixty-six millions of gallons a day; the average quantity pumped being less than half—about thirty millions.

All this water comes from an underground river confined within a tunnel of its own, unseen and unsuspected by the traveller, built underneath the tunnel through which the trains run. If the pumps stopped working for a day, this river would burst through its prison walls and undo the work of years, so the engineers, realizing the danger that would result from even a temporary accident to the pumps, have provided a duplicate set against all emergencies.

But, strange to say, not a drop of water is to be seen in the pumping works. Millions of gallons are continually being brought up and discharged into the Severn, but the pumps work in their houses, warm and oiled and well cared for, and not a speck of dirt or damp is visible anywhere. Marvellous triumph of science!

Even further steps are likely to be taken to turn the Severn Tunnel to public usefulness. Talk has been heard of utilizing the outflow of water, both as energy for the creation and storage of electricity and for supplying neighbouring towns that lack an adequate supply, with an abundance of water of the purest kind, drawn from this perennial source.

VI.

ACROSS the meadows from Sudbrook, at a distance of perhaps a mile from the Severn shore, stands the great baronial castle of Caldicot, set in a low-lying plain through which a sedgy rivulet winds towards the Bristol Channel. The old-time strength of Caldicot Castle lay in the marshy character of the surrounding land, which in times of rain and in the winter season became a wide-spreading lake, rendering approach difficult for the garrison and impossible to an enemy. Even until recent years these floods and heavy rain-storms isolated the castle as completely as ever, but since the Severn Tunnel works were commenced all the streams and marshes for five miles round have dried up, and winter no longer converts Caldicot into an island.

The origin of Caldicot takes us away back to the early part of the twelfth century, when Walter Fitz Roger, Constable of England, built a round tower here to protect his outlying lands from the Welsh. It was in 1122 that he built this keep, and but five years later he died as a monk in the seclusion of Llantony Priory. He was succeeded by his son, the great Milo Fitzwalter, created Earl of Hereford in 1141, who made some slight additions to this fortalice and died untimely in 1144, killed while hunting by the accidental discharge of an arrow. Indeed, this was a most unfortunate family, for of the five sons whom Milo Fitz Walter left, not one had issue, but succeeded one after the other to the title and estates and left them to be divided amongst their three sisters. The eldest son, Roger, married, but died childless as a monk in Gloucester Abbey, in 1154. Walter, the second son, died in the reign of Richard I. Henry, the third son, was killed some years later in combat with a Welshman who owned the barbarous name of Sytsyllt ap Dyfnwall; Mahel, the fourth, met his death by the fall of a stone from the tower of Bronllys Castle, in Brecon; and William, the youngest, suffered the same fate as his father,

CALDICOT CASTLE.

being slain accidentally by an arrow in the Forest of Dean. Of the three sisters, Margaret, the eldest, married Humphry de Bohun in 1170, who thus succeeded in right of his wife to the title of Earl of Hereford and the hereditary office of Lord High Constable of England. It was one of these Bohuns who refused to take a command against the French in one of the early Edwardian wars. "Sir Earl," said the English king in reply to this refusal, "you shall either go or be hanged;" to which the Earl rejoined, "Sir King, I will neither go nor be hanged:" and he kept his word.

The De Bohuns held Caldicot until 1372, when the Humphry of that time died and left two daughters, aged seven and three years respectively, in wardship of the Crown. Elinor, the eldest, was married to Thomas of Woodstock, Duke of Gloucester, sixth son of Edward III. The Christian names of himself and wife may yet be seen, carved in stone on the imposts of the postern-tower doorway, and thus give the date of its building *circa* 1380-88. In the latter year the Duke was mysteriously murdered in the prison of Calais.

From this time Caldicot Castle gradually fell into ruin. Its value as a border fortress had disappeared with the settlement of Wales, and it no longer met the more exacting requirements of the younger generation in the way of a residence; but before it was finally abandoned a great breach was made in the eastern wall, so that the building should be useless for defence. That breach remains to this day, but is now used as a carriage entrance by Mr. Cobb, a retired solicitor, who has purchased the castle from the Crown and fitted it up as a residence during the summer months.

In plan the castle is an irregular oblong, 320 feet long, by 250 feet wide. This space is enclosed by strong curtain-walls with the original keep at the north-west corner, and round towers at the south-east and south-west angles. The great enclosure thus formed was a courtyard, open to the sky, as now, and the garrison was housed in slight lean-to buildings on the inner face of the walls. These slight barracks have long since been swept away. There is no angle at the north-eastern part, the curtain-wall taking a

CARVED STONE, CALDICOT CASTLE.

wide curve instead, undefended by a tower. The original entrance was on the western face, between the keep and the south-western angle and is still marked by a tower of the twelfth century. The latest additions are seen in the great Gatehouse, built by Thomas of Woodstock at the same time as the Postern.

Mr. Cobb has held the Castle for six years. At one time he was a tenant under the Crown of Manorbeer Castle in Pembrokeshire, now, by the way, purchased by a London publisher, Mr. Elliot Stock. When he came to Caldicot, he found the whole buidling going rapidly to decay under the ancient ivy which

CARVED STONE, CALDICOT CASTLE.

shrouded the walls and tore the stones apart. He has now removed all this growth and cleared the moat from the accumulated rubbish of centuries; and after carefully restoring the Gatehouse and fixing a drawbridge on the pivot principle, which was found in the course of exploration to have been the type originally used, he took up his residence here.

The architecture of the Castle is largely conceived and executed in a masculine spirit: the masonry made up with immense blocks of stone, jointed, not with the exquisite, almost feminine, nicety of Raglan, but, though not rudely, with less care for grace than for strength. Heavy machicolated turrets flank the gatehouse, the machicolations supported on corbels carved with heads of Edward III. and his Queen, together with other portraits which are not now recognizable.

One beautiful window of Flamboyant character occurs in a range of three openings in the southern wall, and this, together with the hooded and richly canopied windows of the Gatehouse, gives a saving grace to the stern and rugged grandeur of Caldicot.

WINDOW, CALDICOT CASTLE.

The present owner has most carefully studied the architectural history of the fortress, and has designed and carried out, without the aid of an architect, many restorations of details; employing for this purpose masons who work directly under his own supervision.

Nothing has been added in the way of restoration for which there was no authority in the building itself; consequently such judicious work as this has rendered Caldicot Castle good enough to be an exemplar of old-time military architecture, and strong enough to last for centuries yet to come.

SAINT ARVANS.

We returned from Caldicot to Portskewett with the object of taking train thence to Chepstow and of walking from that place to Tintern; but things were ordered otherwise.

It was now twelve o'clock, midday, and the stationmaster's wife, who was the nearest approach to an official within sight at Portskewett, told us there would be no train until 4.30. The stationmaster's poultry were clucking and taking dust-baths among the cinders between the down rails; the stationmaster's house was redolent of hot Sunday dinner, his wife was floury from her kitchen, the signal box was empty, and all the station offices were fast locked. Clearly, they take life in easy fashion here.

There was evidently nothing for it but to retrace the road we had taken the day before. But it occurred to us that possibly there might be a short cut to Tintern without the necessity of going through Chepstow again, and so we inquired of the first person we met. He was vague in his information, but there came in the direction we were going one who carried a large-scale map which showed a useful lane leading to Tintern by way of Crossway Green and Saint Arvans. We fared together along the Chepstow road until this lane was reached, and chatted on matters literary and artistic. We talked of Thucydides and false quantities until our hearts burned within us, and at the parting of the ways we left him with regret.

VII.

AND so we came, at the tea-tide hour, into Tintern on this mellow Sunday, and upon the instant of our seeing this lovely place on the hill-side and along the level pasture lands beside the Wye, we decided, if it were possible, to make it our head-quarters for a week.

The Beaufort Arms, gay with scarlet geraniums, stood opposite the grey Abbey; on the lawns were guests taking their tea, and the stables and the trim gravel drives were smart with traps and dog-carts. But we passed by, in full view of all these things, and sought cottage lodgings for our sojourn. And presently we discovered such a cottage as Cockneys dream about but do not find; where rusticity sits embowered amid roses and jasmine and honeysuckle, all in their proper seasons; where orchards occupy one moiety of the cottager's land, and a strange medley of flower and kitchen-garden is in luxuriant and prodigal possession of the other, while towering and picturesque ruins close the upland view, and a rapid river gleams beyond and between apple-trees on the lowlands.

One happy week we stayed here, as mellow autumn crept on, while the countryside reeked with the sweet smell of pomace, and cider-making went forward in all the fruitful orchards round about. Before almost every cottage door were barrels and hogsheads, kilderkins and puncheons, filled or being filled with fresh cider, and each village church was preparing for its harvest-thanksgiving with gorgeous heaps of rich red apples, golden-russet pears, Brobdignagian kitchen-garden produce, and miniature shocks of wheat. Spinsters, youthful and middle-aged, comely or plain, were everywhere busy with the holy and gratifying duty of helping bachelor curates decorate ecclesiastical interiors; deriving much spiritual consolation from approving themselves such useful handmaidens of the Church. Meanwhile impious farmers leaned over field-gates and peered into barns and lofts bursting with abundance of harvest, and cursed heartily because the kindly fruits of the earth were so plentiful—and therefore so cheap. It would be a novel sort of Providence that should satisfy a farmer.

In this rustic retirement the busy world of London receded into a very dim and misty perspective. Was it possible, one thought, that the office was a reality; that the machines still raced of afternoons in the basement, and that newsboys yet continued to riot up the narrow street, vociferous with the latest news? Did the banging and shuffling in the composing-room, with the thumping of formes and the rattle of type, continue as aforetime above the ceilings of the editorial offices, and make miserable as ever them that cudgelled their weary brains therein? And how fared the men whom one habitually greeted in Fleet Street? Had Gavroche of the *Silhouette* at last exhausted the sweepings of the Paris studios in his ill-drawn crowds of Pierrots, Pierrettes, and nameless feminines? Yes, indeed, and no; all these things were subsequently found

TINTERN ABBEY.

ASTOR, LENOX
TILDEN FOUNDATIONS

as of old, and, alas! Gavroche is more prolific than ever.

Days were mellow but nights grew cold and even, occasionally, eager with a hint of frost. The harvest moon rose gloriously in the evening sky, and touched to an unearthly beauty the grey ruins of the Abbey, standing dark and half hid in mists from the water-meadows, while cottages grouped near gave forth a yellow and hospitable light that spoke of chimney corners and cosy nooks. Few were the wayfarers after sundown, and a deep stillness fell when day was done, broken near at hand by the half-human cough of sheep, and the noise of neighbouring pigs, snoring most melodiously in their styes. As night wore on, owls would hoot and scream romantically in the ruins, disturbing the jackdaws, who replied with peevish notes; while in the woods that clothed the surrounding hills of Tintern the foxes barked shrilly. Those woods that seemed in daytime so quiet and lonely, became filled with all manner of noises that proceeded from things that crept and ran and flew in nocturnal liveliness. The fauna of these hillside growths arose when mankind yawned and thought of bed.

And Tintern was, night by night, soon asleep, villagers and visitors alike, for what joy was there in keeping a needless solitary vigil when all this little world had gone to rest? So we to our eyrie generally at ten o'clock, when London was beginning to settle down to its evening's entertainment. To reach our night's quarters, it was necessary to put our hats on, walk round to the side of the cottage, and ascend a stone staircase into our bedroom in the gable, where old-fashioned four-post bedsteads and a grandfather clock sent us back to the atmosphere of the last century, and where two windows, one of ordinary proportions, the other perhaps about the area of a pocket-handkerchief, commanded views of the Abbey on one side and of the Wye on the other.

On the latter side ran a little lane, down which came the rural postman, early in the morning; on the side of the

Abbey rose the sloping garden, whence came the fragrant scent of earth and dewy flowers through the leaded casement. Beneath was the cottage kitchen, and through the flooring came whiffs of coffee and the hissing of breakfast bacon as potent inducements to early rising.

No breakfasts so delightful as those at Tintern: the cottage door thrown open, the window wide, so that the morning air, and the chatter of the jackdaws in the ruins, the grumblings of the pigs in the orchard, and the clucking of the fowls might enter and give an earnest of the country while we read our letters and absorbed the latest news from town. We had company, too, at breakfast, and company of the most sedate and wellbred kind. Sarah, whom familiar folks called "Sally," sat beside us, a cat of demoniac, yet judicial aspect; her fur protrusive in tangled tags that seemed to hint at a recent bath, a proposition which is absurd, as Euclid, that ancient of knotty problems, would say. No cat so ladylike in manner, though so severe of look; and as for Bingo—excellent dog—who took the other side with trustful gaze, why, he was a polished gentleman, and received our favours with a combined gentleness and self-respect beyond all comment. Another pensioner of the household was Jack, the white cat with pink eyes, a haughty and insufferable Albino, exclusive and unfriendly, and—in the phrasing

"A CAT OF DEMONIAC ASPECT."

of our hostess—"as deaf as a beetle." Breakfast done, Bingo would take his ease on the sun-warmed flagstones without, while "Sally," with a sporting instinct that I must confess does not become her sex, would go a-poaching, and, in the most compromising manner, bring home rabbits not far short of her own size. I am afraid Sally will come to a bad end.

A wonderful garden, this at Tintern, growing luxuriantly over the site of the Abbey refectory, whose pillars and pointed arches are buried deep under pigsties, cabbage-beds and flower patches. Rosemary and lemon-thyme grew there, and its borders were rich with "monks'-money," which, gathered and disposed in vases, made the cottage sitting-room mantelpiece silvery and crackly with its dried petals. "Fare-thee-well-summers"—otherwise Michaelmas daisies—with their violet petals and orange centres, gave a regretful autumnal tinge to places, and "Job's tears" spangled all the walks, while, amid the shrubs, peeped fragments of carved and moulded stone, capitals of Gothic shafts, and fragments of ancient tiles. In the loft, too, where the apples were stored in odorous heaps, were fragments of the monks' hospitium; and to see these, and the view of the Abbey gables from the garden, were brought many strangers, chiefly Americans. Indeed, Tintern is so world-famed that throughout the year, but

"TRUSTFUL GAZE—GOOD BINGO."

chiefly in summer and in early autumn, excursionists of every sort and condition come hither and gladden their hearts with a contemplation of its beauties, and rejoice the country folk with much pecuniary profit. But there is one class—that of the day-tripper from Birmingham and the Black Country—which Tintern folks do not welcome. Rather do they bide at home on the evil days when those grimy artisans descend upon the place in their hundreds. Then do cottagers lock those doors and garden-gates that of other days are left so trustfully open, for, indeed, this species of excursionist is apt to sprawl promiscuously, and, moreover, his honesty does not begin to vie with the simple morals of the villagers. We always locked the garden-gate and the doors of our rooms on these inauspicious occasions, after having once discovered a number of hulking fellows in the Eyrie, turning over our belongings in search of what both Mr. Kipling and themselves might call "bloomin' loot."

"O MOON, LOOK GENTLY ON THIS WICKED WORLD!"

Nor do these folk add greatly to the gains of those who provide for the excursionist of the day trip, for mostly they would appear to bring their provender with them, both meat and drink. These be known unfavourably to the licensed victuallers as "nosebag trippers." Yet, when night has

PIOUS FOUNDERS. 41

come and they stagger toward the station, many of them would seem to have drunken more deeply than their pocket-bottles would warrant, and so, doubtless, the licensed victualling interests of Tintern profit in degree. But not thus should one return from a day in the country. O moon, look gently on this wicked world!

VIII.

TINTERN ABBEY was a monastery belonging to the Cistercians, or White Monks, an offshoot from the Benedictine Order. Of the first building, erected in 1131 on the site of the lovely ruins that now stand beside the Wye, no vestige remains. It stood for exactly one hundred and thirty-eight years and then gave place to the present stately building which was begun in 1269 and completed in 1288.

The successive lords of Chepstow were never wearied of granting lands and lavishing gifts upon the Abbey of Tintern, moved thereto not so much from a love of the Church as from a wish both to stand well with the powerful ecclesiastics who overawed the temporal power in the Middle Ages, and from a desire, before they went to their place, to compound for their sins on earth in the eyes of heaven.

The evil consciences and superstitious fears of these ruthless mediæval knights enriched the Catholic Church throughout what must, for want of a readier term, be called the civilized world. It was not merely the workings of an academic piety that led them to endow chapels and oratories, that induced their immediate posterity to erect monuments and brasses covered with the most fervent and frequently reiterated supplications to the Blessed Virgin Mary and the Son of God. " Mary, help," " Jesu, mercy," and similar invocations were not lukewarm and conventional prayers then, whatever they may be now. The conscience-stricken assassins, pillagers, violators of sanctuaries, and liars, miscalled the "flower of chivalry," felt that they needed all the supernatural aid that restitutions and gifts might buy. Their conception of an avenging power was that of a deity on a par with their sordid selves, to be appeased, like a rapacious baron, by grants of land and riches.

Let us congratulate ourselves that we live in times when dispossession by force, at least, is not possible; but though we can penetrate the poetic glamour of the age of chivalry and know it for merely a period of barbarism, yet let us be thankful for the villainous careers of these nobles and warriors, for they, like the villain of the Transpontine drama and he of the romantic novel, are picturesque and interesting, while the even course of the good is no man's entertainment.

But with the advent of the Lollards in the early years of the fifteenth century came the first signs of religious reform, and in little over a hundred years from their persecution at the hands of Church and State, the monasteries, great and small, and the religious colleges and chantry chapels, were abolished. Superstition, indeed, waxed greater, but the power of the Church over the minds of men had waned, and no longer did the abbeys and priories receive fat manors as peace-offerings to the Most High. Indeed, conditions were entirely reversed, and spoliation took the place of endowment. The march of events deprived the religious houses of their lands and revenues, and cynically rendered all the bestowals of centuries but a series of ruinous loans of which the interest consisted in the added value of the meads and pastures wrought out of savage wildernesses by the unremitting toil of generations of monkish communities. And to complete the grim humour of fate, the possessions of which the monasteries were despoiled were reconveyed by royal grants to the very class from whom they had been obtained. Thus it was that to Henry, Earl of Worcester, fell Tintern in the reign of Henry VIII., and from him it has descended to the Dukes of Beaufort.

The architecture of Tintern Abbey is of that period when

the Early English style was merging into Decorated; perhaps the most interesting phase of Gothic art. The lancet windows of the earlier period have here given place to mullioned lights, and the first beginnings of the gorgeous tracery that was to come are to be observed in the simple quatrefoils of the clerestory that remain still, for the most part, in admirable preservation. The walls of the Abbey, although roofless, are almost entire, the greater ruin being wreaked upon the chapter-house and the domestic offices. Even the pillars and the pointed arches of the nave are tolerably perfect, and sufficient remains of the great east and west windows for their design to be readily noted. The ground within the building has been levelled and made into a beautiful lawn, and throughout its great length of 228 feet the sunlight comes in summer with most romantic effect, touching with glory the few moss-grown tombs of Clares and Bigods, abbots and priors, whose masses, to be said "in perpetuity" for the repose of their souls, have been silent and discontinued these three hundred and thirty years and more.

But how to render the true inwardness, the *vraies vérités*, of Tintern? Surely not by disquisitions on monastic life, and still less surely by an architectural history of the Abbey.

Let us first look at Tintern with the eyes of a long-dead tourist who described his holiday on the Wye more than a hundred years ago.

IX.

THE eighteenth century sent its quota of travellers to the Wye and the Welsh borders, and some of their published accounts are truly wonderful. Of these "picturesque travellers," as they loved to describe themselves, I think the Reverend "William Gilpin, M.A., Prebendary of Salisbury and Vicar of Boldre, near Lymington," as his title-page sets forth, the most commanding figure. He wrote more picturesquely than he knew when he suggested the use of a mallet upon Tintern, wherewith to improve the appearance of that fine ruin; but, even so, the lengthy interludes in which he enlarges upon foregrounds and compositions are wearisome. Observe, now, the perspicacity of this remark: "Castles and abbeys have different situations agreeable to their respective uses. The castle, meant for defence, stands boldly on the hill; the abbey, intended for meditation, is hid in the sequestered vale." Prodigious! Again, Mr. Gilpin found that Tintern Abbey had been "an elegant Gothic pile," but it did not come up to his expectations. "Though parts are beautiful, the whole is ill-shaped. No ruins of the tower are left, which might give form and contrast to the buttresses and walls. Instead of this, a number of gable-ends hurt the eye with their regularity, and disgust it by the vulgarity of their shape. A mallet judiciously used (but who durst use it?) might be of service in fracturing some of them, particularly those of the cross-isles, which are both disagreeable in themselves and confound the perspective." Alas! 'tis generally the artists who "confound the perspective," both interjectionally and in execution. But no matter, *revenons à notre Gilpin!*

It was in 1770 that our author made his tour, and, although the aspect of the ruined Abbey remains the same now as then, Tintern must needs have changed wonderfully in the space of one hundred and twenty-three years—and time enough, too; or is it that we see with different eyes from those of the greatly-daring tourists of that time? For "picturesque" travellers, as they might call themselves, yet it remains for this age to see beauty where our forbears "discovered," as they have put it, "terrour and desolation" only. Doctor Johnson, even though certainly *he* never called himself a picturesque tourist, discovered no fine frenzy of admiration for Hebridean scenery, for instance, although 'tis impressive indeed. As for Scotland, we know right well that he regarded the road that led into England as the finest prospect in Caledonia. The truth is, the discomforts of old-time travel jaundiced folks' eyes, and, sicklied

OLD-TIMED TINTERN.

o'er with the pale cast   ness, they damned these wilds for deserts, and so a   d, cursing. Not that the Reverend Mr. Gilpin was so e phatic. I am thinking he was an amiable *dilettante* with a nice fat prebend, any amount of leisure, and a passion for scribbling; and I can imagine him landing from his boat at Tintern, walking up the lane to the Abbey, and poking his delightful prebendal nose into the cottages, thereafter departing with delicacy and caution; his black hose and silver-buckled shoes, his black, silver-headed walking stick, and his clerical cambric neckcloth the admired cynosure of all eyes. But to let him give his own testimony:—

"But were the building ever so beautiful, encompassed as it is with shabby houses, it could make no appearance from the river. From a stand near the road it is seen to more advantage. Among other things in this scene of desolation, the poverty and wretchedness of the inhabitants were remarkable. They occupy little huts raised among the ruins of the monastery, and seem to have no employment but begging; as if a place once devoted to indolence could never again become the seat of industry. As we left the Abbey, we found the whole hamlet at the gate, either openly soliciting alms, or covertly, under the pretence of carrying us to some part of the ruins, which each could show, and which was far superior to anything which could be shown by any one else. The most lucrative occasion could not have excited more jealousy and contention. One poor woman we followed, who had engaged to show us the monks' library. She could scarcely crawl, shuffling along her palsied lambs (*sic*) and meagre, contracted body by the help of two sticks. She led us through an old gate into a place overspread with nettles and briars, and, pointing to the remnant of a shattered cloister, told us that was the place. It was her own mansion. All indeed she meant to tell us was the story of her own wretchedness, and all she had to show us was her own miserable habitation. We did not expect to be interested as we were. I never saw so loathsome a human dwelling. It was a cavern loftily vaulted between two ruined walls, which streamed with various coloured stains of unwholesome dews. The floor was earth, yielding, through moisture, to the tread. Not the merest utensil or furniture of any kind appeared, but a wretched bedstead, spread with a few rags and drawn into the middle of the cell to prevent its receiving the damp which trickled down the walls. At one end was an aperture, which served just to let in light enough to discover the wretchedness within. When we stood in the midst of this cell of misery and felt the chilling damps which struck us in every direction, we were rather surprised that the wretched inhabitant was still alive, than that she had only lost the use of her limbs."

A hundred and twenty years and more have passed since this description of Tintern was written. The gables of the Abbey, which so offended the Reverend Mr. Gilpin's eye, are standing, as firmly now as ever, but there are no signs at this day of abject beggars or loathsome hovels. Perhaps that thrilling account was more picturesque than accurate. Let us hope so. To-day Tintern is a lengthy place. There is, perhaps, a distance of a mile and a half from one end to another, with frequent intervals between its cottages and many windings of its one long street that follows the course of the Wye; but the place is prosperous to a degree.

The two Tintern parishes, Chapel Hill and Tintern Parva (this last now more frequently Englished as Little Tintern), are conjoined nowadays for ecclesiastical purposes; that is to say, there is a church at either parish, but they are both served by one parson, who conducts morning service in one and evensong in the other. Now it must needs chance, doubtless, by some contrivance of the Devil, that the one parish is of High Church sympathies, if not indeed of Ritualistic tendencies, while the other is violently Low Church. I have no distinct recollection of which is Low and which High, but I have no doubts that if both are earnestly bent upon winning to that Haven where we would all be, it will not be a matter of great significance Up There.

High Church and Low. 47

But here recollections of Mr. Andrew Lang's delightful essay upon the *Wrong Paradise* crowd upon my mind, and give me to think that if there be not separate domains

CHAPEL HILL CHURCH, TINTERN.

up beyond in the Gardens of the Blest for these contending factions, the apostolic blows and knocks that characterize their meeting here below might be most disastrously renewed.

Indeed, it goes hard here with the parson who, if he be not a Janus, must take sides and show his preferences; and surely no Christian priest can allow himself thus to deteriorate into so paltry a simulacrum of a Pagan god! But Tintern lacks nothing in places of worship. On Sunday evenings the church and the chapels—Baptist, Wesleyan, and what not—are in full blast; their lights shining brilliantly, and the organs and the harmoniums, the chanting and the singing, fill the lanes with a resonant weekly piety, most musical, long-drawn, and melancholy.

Thus it is that a Tintern Sunday is not a joyous day for the Londoner. Week-days show it in most pleasant aspect. On Chapel Hill, that overlooks the village, there stands an old church, or rather an old foundation; the present building is modern. Around it is a churchyard with an astonishing number of curious tombstones, and from it one can have the most delightful of views over the Wye and the surrounding amphitheatre of hills; Barbados Hill, between whose base and the river runs the high-road between Chepstow and Monmouth, with the whitewashed cottages shining so dazzlingly in the sun; the distant Wyndcliff; the rocks of the Devil's Pulpit on the Gloucestershire side of the Wye, over against the Abbey; and, down in the valley beneath you, the village, with the white roads winding among the meadows and the orchards like ribbons.

From Tintern chimneys the blue smoke begins to rise on summer afternoons at four o'clock. Tea is making, and households all foregather for its due celebration. On those afternoons when we were not too far afield, we made a point of taking tea with our host and hostess, and thus became in receipt of much edifying local gossip and not less amusing local speech. The warring elements of Welsh and English made a curious hotch-potch dialect not readily to be forgotten.

E

X.

One needs not to be an Old Mortality to be interested in the rude literature, and appreciative of the primitive art, of tombstones. The contemplation of them need render no one melancholy; for none have force of imagination sufficient to picture themselves the occupants of a space so narrow as the last resting-place of their mortal frame. And it is a truism that every one considers all mankind mortal but himself. This is the reason why we can laugh and joke and crack ribaldries amid the clustered graves of some swelling country churchyard, where the level of the enclosure has been raised with the interments of countless generations, whose decay has enriched the ground, until there is no place so fertile nor any spot where the lush grass and clover, the buttercup and the marguerite, grow so lustily.

If we could picture ourselves the occupants of these grass-covered mounds, fellows with the worm and habitations of corruption, we should turn away from God's Acre with disgust, and shun the neighbourhood of every church. But our imaginations are not so vivid: we do not even feel the necessity for pitying the quiet population of the place, but think that here is rest and sweet oblivion from all the toils and trials, the vexations, injustices, and ever-deferred hopes of this wicked world.

They are the quaint and grotesque among tombstones which keep one's name and memory green more surely than the costlier memorials of suave and instructed design; and an eccentric epitaph confers upon its subject a more certain immortality than great achievements in arms, in love, in literature, or in song. This is philosophy—of a sort: all philosophy is of sorts and inconclusive; but you may test the truth of this philosophy in observing how surely every tourist worthy his salt copies all the strange and ludicrous epitaphs he encounters upon his way; and how certainly he recites their absurdities to his gaping circle when his touring shall have been done and the winter's evenings are come again. Look to it, ye notoriety-seekers who pencil your undistinguished names upon the walls of historic houses and carve them deeply in the hoary trunks of ancient trees; who desecrate with your plebeian patronymics the carven altar-tombs, the priceless panellings that loving hands fashioned, centuries before the sun of your little day had risen.

TOMBSTONE: SAINT ARVANS.

Consider carefully—and see that your executors be mindful also—that you will infallibly, by becoming the subject of some artfully-worded epitaph, be thus insured of a deathless, if somewhat adventitious and graceless, fame, where now the memory of you is shortlived, and your attempts at recognition fleeting. For, surely enough, the walls you disfigure with your autographic scribbles become at last filled, and then ensues the man with the whitewash-brush.

"The Mouldy Mansions of the Dead." 53

The Man with the Whitewash brush carries a moral with him, besides his brush and pail. He typifies several things, too numerous to be mentioned here, and he spells Oblivion, with a big O. He is hereby offered as a homely simile to all preachers who are of a colloquial turn in the pulpit.

But now to come to a due consideration of the pictorial examples here set forth. It is in the more remote parts of the country that "uncouth rhymes and shapeless sculpture" most do raise the traveller's smile, and especially here, in the neighbourhood of Tintern, do weird cherubs and peculiar

EPITAPH : TINTERN PARVA.

tombstone devices abound. In fact, the country round about seems to have at one time possessed quite a local school of mortuary art.

Here is an example from Saint Arvans, by Chepstow, that is peculiarly naïve. Its inscription is undistinguished for either elegance or singularity, and so is omitted, but its round-mouthed cherub gazes upon the narrow limits of the little graveyard with an ineffable glance that wears the highest expression of innocence and other-worldliness.

Monmouth is an English county, but within its borders

the Welsh Celt inhabits still in large numbers, and the churchyards hold generations of Pritchards and Morgans and Richards's and Williams's. The living representatives of these Cymric clans are in constant evidence, and their tongues bewray them for Welshmen; for although most of them "have the Sassenach"—*i.e.* speak English—they pronounce it with the just and well-considered accent of the foreigner who has acquired the tongue without the utter

> IN
> Memory of phiLip
> Stead Who died des.
> ember The 13th
> 1736 Aged 67
>
> Life is Unsartain
> And deth is so shuer
> Sin is The wound
> & Christ is the Cuer

EPITAPH: MITCHEL TROY.

familiarity that mangles its syllables. Thus it could only have been an Anglo-Saxon who carved this epitaph from Tintern Parva, for what Welshman would pronounce "Richards" with this deletion of the second "R"? The spelling here unmistakably proclaims the nationality of the monumental mason who carved it; he spelled phonetically, and he was not a Taffy.

Hereabouts, no less than in other parts, epitaphs are largely admonitory, and the records of the departed insist with almost indecent iteration that "as they bee so shall wee." Witness this excruciating headstone from Mitchel Troy; but, alas! the moral lesson is apt to be lost in the unconscious humour that sets it forth. But we can well afford to dispense with moralizing. The prig is rampant in the land, and humour, conscious or unconscious, is scarce enough. See here, then, a wasted opportunity of pointing a moral whose loss we need not regret, since it makes us chuckle and congratulate ourselves in finding cause for laughter amongst the mouldy mansions of the dead. Observe this would-be terrific tableau, carved with intent to

"TRANSPONTINE DRAMA."

make us tremble and mend our ways; but we laugh instead, and depart less repentant than ever. And to think that it might have been otherwise had the designer approved himself less of a caricaturist!

A near neighbour to this, which looks like a scene from a Transpontine drama, is this curious affair of cords and tassels, done in stone and presided over by a smirking, self-satisfied angel with a snub nose. This exhausts the curios of Chapel Hill churchyard, but some three miles along the road beside the Wye lies Llandogo, and there, in the hillside field of graves that slopes towards the river, are yet more singularities. There lies "E. M.," and we learn that

"She was a Maid
  That ever lov'd ye truth.
Always delighting in it
  From her youth.
And her last Legacy was
  That her Friends
Should———"

TOMBSTONE : CHAPEL HILL.

But what that legacy was remains unknown, for the concluding words are sunken in the earth. It does not, however,

WILLIAM ELLES
MORE DECEASED
The 22 DAY OF
SEPTEMBER 1690
God to Keme hence
As he thought Best
from sorrow sett
me free my souls

EPITAPH : LLANDOGO.

require any great amount of perspicacity to discover that this legacy was a homily, and nothing on which probate duty was payable.

Close by the Truthful Maid—sweet girl!—lies William Ellesmore, and his memorial may well stand forth without comment. His epitaph is eloquent of misery indeed, and *bonâ fides;* unlike those witty (but apocryphal) lines upon a certain, or uncertain, solicitor named Strange:—

> "Here lies an honest lawyer,
> That is Strange,"

but, most certainly, not true. *There* lies Ben Trovato, not physically recumbent but mentally oblique!

XI.

WE had not been tourists worthy our salt if we had left Tintern without first seeing Raglan Castle, the last place that held out for King Charles in the Civil War, and now in the foremost rank of our romantic and historic ruins.

But a long day at Raglan is not readily achieved by those who do not live in Raglan village. A branch railway runs from Monmouth Troy station to Usk, and there is a station for Raglan at the distance of about a mile from the village; but the first train reaches it about midday, and the last leaves for Monmouth at the absurdly early hour of a quarter to three in the afternoon. There was, then, nothing for it but to walk the ten miles or so from Tintern early in the morning, and return by the afternoon train.

We set out early one day when clouds and sunshine and occasional rain-showers gave the ten-mile walk something of an exciting nature. The way across country from Chapel Hill to Raglan lies by way of Old Furnace, an almost entirely deserted hamlet that was once a busy settlement of wire-drawers and tin-plate workers. The road winds up the hill-side, with oozy moors and dark pine coppices on either hand, and a mountain stream splashes picturesquely among the great, lichen-covered rocks that crop up here and there from above the spongy turf, spangled with wild flowers and the nodding stems of tall foxglove. Here and there one comes upon ruinated engine-houses and dilapidated ovens, overgrown and green with waving ferns, and banked-up reservoirs of water, choked with duckweed and populous with all manner of amphibious creatures. 'Tis many a long year since the water-power of Old Furnace was in request, and the hatches of the mill-leets are rotting away with neglect. The very cinder-heaps are beautiful with the verdure that so quickly springs up in this moist and sheltered spot, and the gardens of the deserted cottages are all run wild with the curiously unkempt and debased descendants of their sometime well-ordered patches of vegetables and flowers. The cottages themselves are, many of them, roofless and ruined, and those that have still a decent roof-tree are turned to account as store-rooms for the apples, of which there is generally so great an abundance in these parts. But four or five cottages of this decayed hamlet are yet occupied, and we sheltered from a passing rain-squall in the porch of one that stood beside the road. An old man sat there in his shirt-sleeves, peeling potatoes for dinner, an ancient so old that the flush of life had fled his cheeks and left them of that grey pallor that resembles nothing so much as dough; an aspect only to be noted in the faces of the very aged. As he looked up and gave us good-day, his light, china-blue eyes were positively startling, set in that bloodless skin, and on their pupils was that *signum senilis*, the white ring. But this was no sign of impending dissolution, for by his talk and the manner of him, here sat one who bids fair to become a centenarian, and more. He was eighty-eight years of age, he told us; had been a wire-drawer, and recollected when all these ruined houses were occupied and the furnaces in full work. His son-in-law worked in the tin-plate works at Chapel Hill down yonder. Yes, the men were locked out now. It was the coal-strike that had compelled the masters to close the works. The men earned good wages, yes; from £2 to £4 a week, but they worked hard for it. The lock-out would mean great distress for Tintern. No, the men had not saved anything, as you might say. They lived from hand to mouth. Was it true that the workmen, as a class, were continually in debt at the Abbey stores? Yes, they were, but they could always get credit. It was not an unusual thing for a tin-plate worker to run an account of £30 or £40 for groceries and provisions. "But some save money and keep out of debt, surely?" we asked. Yes, some did, but they were exceptional.

Preparations for dinner were going forward in the stone-flagged cottage at the hands of a middle-aged woman of robust aspect. She came to the doorway with a little, delicate-looking girl of eight or nine years of age, and joined in the conversation. Yes, this was her little girl. "Grandfather's pet," said the old man, stroking her curls. No, not her eldest. Her eldest boy was in London, training for the ministry. What denomination? Congregationalist. Expected him to be ordained soon. Would go then to London, to hear him preach.

The rain had now cleared off and we resumed our way to Raglan, passing the hamlet of Trelleck Grange, where we asked our way at a tiny cottage perched above the road. A tattered and melancholy woman gave us our direction. "'Tis a mile before you do come to Star Pitch," said she. "When you do come to the other side of it, you will take the right-hand road." "Star Pitch," it seemed, on explanation, was merely "Star Hill," and we found subsequently that "pitch" is the usual term for "hill" throughout Monmouthshire.

Who accounts himself happy? The tin-plate workers of Chapel Hill, doubtless, would not acknowledge that theirs was a particularly enviable lot, yet this woman—her husband was an agricultural labourer, she told us—looked upon them as thrice-blessed with princely wages, with only themselves to thank for their continual comparative poverty. She only wished her husband had the same chances as they enjoyed. Farming was in a terrible way, and wages were very low.

We passed Star Pitch and came upon the edge of a high table-land that formed the water-shed between the valleys of the Wye and the Usk. Below lay a profound valley that stretched for miles on the map, dotted with many villages and intersected with countless rills; but we saw little of it from where we stood, for the mists still steamed and wavered in the cauldron of this deep hollow, set round about with tumbled hills. The eye could not plumb its depth, so filled was it with the rolling fogs that even this sunny day could not disperse; but above the topmost shreds of tattered vapours peaked, blue with its distance, the sharp cone of the Sugarloaf, and minor eminences raised in every direction their less significant crests.

Here the road forked in many inconsequent and meandering ways, and we rejoiced consequently at seeing a cart stopped in the road, its occupant talking with much pantomimic action to a cottager. We made so bold as to interrupt their colloquy one moment, to ask the way, but the gesticulating occupant of the cart, with much stammering, referred us to the other party to that dialogue, and drove away. We received our direction, but asked the reason of the driver's singular conduct. "Oh," said our informant, "that's Mr. Pritchard. He doesn't understand English."

We were indeed upon the borders of Gwalia!

"THE PICTURESQUE."

As we went down the hillside road to Llanfihangel-tor-y-Mynydd there came slowly, so slowly, with grunts and groans and faltering steps, his figure bowed and bent and contorted painfully with rheumatism, an old man. It seemed to us that in his gnarled person the Æschylean tragedy, the continual warfare between Man and Nature, had found a neutral object, for he wore, with a little imagination, more the appearance of an ambulant tree-trunk than aught else. To speak with more sobriety, he was the complement of the scenery—the incarnated convention that obtains in "picturesque" sketches. The artists put such figures as his into their scenery, and here, at last, was their convention justified.

This village, one amongst the twenty-three Llanfihangels of Monmouthshire, was small to insignificance, with a restored little church (*every* church is restored nowadays) of Early English character and the bell-turret type, in no wise remarkable. Then followed Llansoy, within another two miles, and, finally, four miles farther, Raglan.

XII.

RAGLAN village calls for little remark. It seems to be fairly prosperous, is clean swept and altogether well ordered, and certainly is not remarkable in any way for its appearance. The church is the only old building in Raglan: a building that formerly contained many and magnificent monuments of Herberts and Somersets, and that consequently fell upon evil times when the fury of the Puritans swept over the country. To-day there remain but a few mutilated fragments of their effigies, and they are stowed away in a dark and dusty corner behind the organ.

The Castle stands quite apart from the village, in midst of level meads, and surrounded by tall forest trees. It was built about the time of Henry VI. by Sir William ap Thomas and his son William, Earl of Pembroke, the same unfortunate nobleman who was beheaded at Banbury.

This Earl of Pembroke had been Sir William Herbert of Raglan before his elevation to the peerage in 1468, and was "the first man," according to Fenton, the historian of Pembrokeshire, "by name, birth, and descent a Briton, who, since the Norman Conquest, was advanced to a title of honour." This nobleman was a zealous Yorkist and had earned his patent of nobility by the pursuit of Jasper Tudor and his companion Lancastrians, and by the capture of Harlech Castle, which had long held out against the king. In 1469 he was sent with a considerable army to quell the Lancastrian revolt in the north, with Stafford, Earl of Devon, to assist him. The rival armies met at Edgecote in Oxfordshire, and the leaders of the Yorkist troops were lodged at Banbury the night before the battle, "and there," says Hall, "the Earle of Pembroke putte the Lorde Stafford out of an inne, wherein he delighted muche to be for the love of a damosell that dwelled in the house." This "damosell" caused many "crakes" and quarrels between the earls, and so heated did they become about her that Stafford deserted, with the whole of his contingent of six thousand archers. In consequence of this withdrawal the Earl of Pembroke lost the fight on the morrow and was dragged from Banbury Church at the instigation of "John Clapham, Esquire, servant to the Earl of Warwick," and beheaded, together with his brother, in the porch.

Very little remains of the Castle which this father and son erected here, and it seems, from the general style of the architecture, that an almost complete rebuilding took place when the Somersets came into possession of the property by marriage. They soon acquired titles in addition to riches, and were raised to the peerage with the style of Earls of Worcester. Sir Henry Somerset, the fifth earl, was advanced to the rank of marquis by Charles I., and to that nobleman's time belongs the greater part of the present building.

The Castle buildings occupy a space of over four acres, and the general effect is, even now that its walls are ruined and roofless, one of great splendour. Raglan, though so

RAGLAN CASTLE.

strong a place, was built with that large regard for comfort and beauty which characterized domestic-military architecture of this late period. It remains a matter for astonishment how so extensive and stately a building of stone as this could have been erected in a part of the country where no building-stone is to be found, and in a district so far removed from the waterways which are almost always found in close proximity to the larger buildings of olden times. Water transit formed a ready means of transport in days when roads were ridiculously inadequate even for ordinary wayfaring purposes, and but very rarely do we find large stone buildings of any great age on sites far removed from sea or river. But whence came the stone of which Raglan Castle was built? It is a fine-grained, light-grey material which cannot nowadays be matched anywhere, and the destruction of all the books and accounts within the library at Raglan has rendered it impossible to discover anything relating to the building of this lordly pleasure-house. That the very best of materials and workmanship were lavished upon this magnificent seat of the Somersets, the sharp, fresh-looking mouldings and devices of its outward walls still prove. The blocks of stone that go toward rearing the frowning machicolations are cut and laid in cement with the utmost delicacy, and the shields and badges of that ancient family remain, despite violence and neglect and the lapse of centuries, as clearly defined as when the carvers first lay down their mallets and chisels. A singular variation of the well-known portcullis device of

BADGE, RAGLAN CASTLE.

the Somersets may be seen represented in stone beneath the battlements, and may be compared with the eighteenth-century cast-iron fire-back, exhibiting the more usual form of that badge, which is to be found in one of the empty rooms in the Gatehouse towers.

The Marquis of Raglan was, at the time when the Civil War broke out between King and Parliament, one of the wealthiest nobles in the kingdom. He lived here in great magnificence in a castle-palace at once a fortress and a residence of the most luxurious ease. The sumptuous appointments of the Great Hall, with its carved oaken roof, its marble fireplaces, and rich windows, are dwelt upon with great gusto by writers who saw them in times before civil strife broke out in the land and caused the ruin of this and many another princely abode; and the vast cellars still remain that were at one time filled with wines of the rarest, and prove that good fare accompanied magnificent display. Yet with all this profusion of art and good living, with all the splendour of a seventeenth-century nobleman's life, who counted himself among the very richest of the wealthy peers of his day, luxury had not brought degeneracy. The nobles, equally with the peasants of the time, were a strong, able-bodied, and lusty race, with evident vices, it is true, but also with the virtues of early rising and simple faith which seem, somehow, to have grown unfashionable in later years.

FIREBACK, RAGLAN CASTLE.

HENRY SOMERSET,
FIRST MARQUIS OF
WORCESTER.

Life in the Seventeenth Century. 69

Our forefathers were no slug-a-beds. Early rising was the order of the day, even in the comparatively modern times of Charles the First; and even those of whom we are accustomed to think as the leisured classes of the seventeenth century had left their bedrooms and were breakfasting at seven o'clock. The nobility of that time breakfasted at seven o'clock in the morning, dined at ten, supped at four o'clock in the afternoon, partook of "livery" between eight and nine in the evening, and soon afterwards went to bed, and doubtless slept soundly, because "nerves" had not yet become the terror of life and the fruitful cause of sleepless nights.

You will see presently why our ancestors had no nerve-troubles.

The usual breakfast-table of a nobleman of the Marquis of Worcester's rank would be spread on fast days with a loaf of bread in a trencher, two manchets (a small loaf of the finest bread, weighing six ounces), a quart of beer, a quart of wine, two pieces of salt fish, six baconed herrings, and four white herrings or a dish of sprats. All this for two people. The breakfast-table of the marquis and marchioness on flesh days was furnished forth with one loaf, two manchets, one quart of beer, one quart of wine, half a chine of mutton, or a chine of beef, boiled.

Dinner was served in great state. At eleven o'clock in the forenoon the castle gates were closed and the tables laid for the household: "two tables in the dining-room, three in the hall, one in Mrs. Watson's apartment where the chaplains sat (Sir Toby Mathews being the first), and two in the housekeeper's room for the ladies' women.

"The marquis entered the dining-room, attended by his gentlemen. As soon as he was seated the steward of the house, Sir Ralph Blackstone, retired. The comptroller, Mr. Holland, attended with his staff, as did also Mr. Blackburne, the server. The daily waiters, Mr. Clough, Mr. Selby, Mr. Scudamore, and many gentlemen's sons with estates of from two to seven hundred pounds a year, who were bred up in the castle. My lady's gentlemen of the chamber, Mr. Morgan and Mr. Fox."

At the first table sat the nobleman's family and such of the nobles who were visiting at the castle. At the second table sat the knights and the honourable gentlemen, attended by footmen. The steward took the head of the first table in the hall, the comptroller, the secretary, the master of the horse, the master of the fish ponds, Lord Herbert's tutor, and gentlemen under the degree of a knight, attended by footmen, and plentifully served with wine.

At the second table in the hall sat the server, with the gentlemen waiters and pages, twenty-four in number, who partook of the food left from the marquis's table. At the third table in the hall sat the clerk of the kitchen with the yeomen officers of the house, two grooms of the chambers, etc., etc.

Other officers of the household were: chief auditor, clerk of the accounts, purveyor of the castle, two ushers of the hall, closet keeper, gentleman of the chapel, keeper of the records, master of the wardrobe, master of the armoury, twelve master-grooms of the stables, master of the hounds, master falconer, porter and his man, two butchers, two keepers of the Home Park, two keepers of the Red Deer Park, footmen, grooms, and other menial servants to the number of one hundred and fifty.

The out-officers were the steward of Raglan, governor of Chepstow Castle (Sir Nicholas Kemys), the housekeeper of Worcester House, London, thirteen bailiffs, two counsel for the bailiffs to have recourse to, solicitor, etc.

XIII.

It was here that Charles I. sought and obtained refuge after Naseby in 1645, and here he remained until September 15th, when the news of the surrender of Bristol to the rebels had made Raglan too uncertain a retreat for distressed royalty.

Early in the spring of the following year the neighbouring garrisons having been reduced, a portion of the Parliamentary forces appeared before this, the last and most formidable of all the strong places in Monmouthshire that remained loyal to Charles, and summoned the garrison to surrender the castle to the Parliament. This demand was received with indignation, and rejected with contumely, but the hostile detachment lay around Raglan until they were reinforced in June by the redoubtable Colonel Morgan, who approached with a considerable body of troops from Worcester. Several sallies were made from the castle at this time, and a few skirmishes resulted unfavourably to the Roundheads, but the surrender of Oxford to the Parliament detached a large number of troops and caused a reinforcement of Morgan's command. He was now in a stronger position, and immediately sent the Marquis of Worcester a formal summons to deliver up Raglan Castle, which ran as follows:—

"My Lord,—By his Excellency's command, this is my second summons, whereby you are required forthwith to deliver to me, for the uses of both Houses of Parliament, the Castle of Raglan, with all ordnance, arms, ammunition, and provisions, and all other necessaries that belong to war, that are now in it; which if you will be pleased to do, you may haply find mercy, as other garrisons have had; and if you do refuse, expect but the ruin of yourself, your family, and this poor distressed country. For I must acquaint your lordship that his Excellency, Sir Tho.

Fairfax, having now finished his work over the kingdom except this Castle, hath been pleased to spare his forces for this work, which are now upon their march this way with all materials fit for it; though I make no doubt that I have of mine own strength sufficient to effect it. If your lordship will deny to submit to this summons, and that more blood must be spilt, your lordship may be confident that you shall receive no favour from both Houses of Parliament. So, expecting your answer this night, by nine of the clock, I rest your lordship's servant,

"THO. MORGAN.

"From the Leagur before Raglan,

"June 28, 1646."

With this letter was enclosed a copy of a proclamation purporting to come from the king, authorizing the outstanding Royalist garrisons to submit to the Parliament; but the Marquis of Worcester in his reply casts some doubt upon the genuineness of the document, holding, as many others had done, that Charles was under arrest and that, even if the proclamation was *bona fide*, it had been extorted from him by force. The Marquis replied to Colonel Morgan:

"SIR,—I have received this day two advertisements from you; the first I read, containing, as you would have me believe, a true copy of his Majesty's warrant to several garrisons upon honourable terms to quit. But, truly, sir, it is not in the power of man to make me think so unworthily of his Majesty, that to one, in the opinion of the world, that hath given, himself and family, soe great a demonstrance and testimony of his and their faith and fidelitie towards him, that he would not please so much as name his name, or Raglan. I entreat you, give me leave to suspend my belief.

"And for your second summons, it makes it too evident that it is desired that I would die under a hedge like a

king, beggar, having no house left to put my head into, nor means left to find me bread. Wherefore, to give you answer, I make choice (if it soe please God) rather to dye nobly, than to live with infamy. Which answer, if it be not pleasing to you, I shall not think you worthy to be styled by me your loving friend,
"H. WORCESTER.

"From my House of Raglan,
"June 28, 1646."

Other letters passed between besiegers and besieged, until Sir Thomas Fairfax arrived in August, from Bath. The earthworks thrown up by the colonel's sappers had by that time progressed very greatly and were brought within seventy yards of the castle walls. Sir Thomas wrote to the Marquis, on the 7th of August:

"MY LORD,—Being come into these parts with such a strength as I may not doubt but, with the same good hand of Providence that hath hitherto blessed us, in short time to reduce the garrison of Raglan to the obedience of the Parliament, I have, in order thereto, thought good to send your lordship this summons, hereby requiring you to deliver up to me, for the Parliament's use, the said garrison and Castle of Raglan; which, as it only obstructs the kingdom's universal peace, the rendition may beget such terms, as by delay or vain hopes cannot hereafter be expected.

"I remain, my lord, your lordship's most humble servant,
"THO. FAIRFAX.

"Your lordship's speedy answer to this summons is desired."

To this the Marquis rejoined:

"SIR,—Although my infirmities might justly claim privilege in so sudden an answer, yet, because you desire it, and I am not willing to delay your time, to your letter of summons to deliver up my house, and the only house now in my possession to cover my head in, these are to let you know, that if you did understand the condition I am in, I daresay out of your judgment, you will not think it a reasonable demand. I am loth to be the author of mine own ruin on both sides; and therefore desire leave to send to his Majesty to know his pleasure what he will have done with his garrison. As for my house, I presume he will command nothing; neither am I knowing how, either by law or by conscience, I should be forced out of it. To these I desire your return, and rest your Excellency's humble servant,

"H. WORCESTER.

"From my poor cottage at Raglan,
  "Aug. 7, 1646."

Fairfax replied on the following day:

"MY LORD,—Touching your sending to his Majesty, it is that which hath been denied to the most considerable garrisons of England, further than an account to his Majesty of the thing done upon the surrender; which I do else freely grant to your lordship. And for that distinction which your lordship is pleased to make, that *it is your house*; if it had not been formed into a *garrison*, I should not have troubled your lordship with a summons; and were it disgarrisoned, neither you nor your house should receive any disquiet from me, or any that belong unto me.

"This I thought good to return to yours, and thereby to discharge myself, before God and the world, of all extremities and sad consequences that will ensue upon the refusal of the rendition of your garrison upon my summons.

"I remain yours,
  "THO. FAIRFAX."

Other letters passed on both sides, but without further effect, until the 15th of August; when, the garrison becoming short of provender, even to the point of starvation, the Marquis of Worcester opened negotiations with

General Fairfax for an honourable capitulation. On the 17th, the capitulation was agreed to, and the articles signed.

Article the first. The garrison, ammunition, and artillery of Raglan, to be surrendered to General Fairfax on the third day after the ratification of the treaty, namely, at ten o'clock on the morning of the Wednesday following, being the nineteenth day of August.

Article the second agreed that all the officers, soldiers, and gentlemen of the garrison should march out with horses and arms; colours flying, drums beating; trumpets sounding: matches lighted at both ends; bullets in their mouths; and every soldier with twelve charges of powder and ball; with permission to select any place, within ten miles of the castle, for the purpose of delivering up their arms to the General in command; after which the soldiers were to be disbanded and set at liberty.

Article the third engaged the General's safe-conduct and protection to all the gentlemen and others who had sought refuge within the walls of Raglan Castle, to their respective homes.

Article the fourth was an enlargement of the preceding article, by which three months' protection was guaranteed to certain other gentlemen, until they should either have made their peace with the Parliament, or departed the realm.

Article the fifth guaranteed the protection and care of the sick and wounded left in the castle.

Article the sixth contained an indemnity for all words and acts of the garrison during the siege.

Agreeably to these provisions, Raglan Castle was surrendered to General Sir Thomas Fairfax on Wednesday, 19th August, 1646. The garrison of eight hundred men had been reduced to about half that number by wounds and the privations of the siege. The horses, too, were in the last stage of starvation, and had even eaten their halters in their hunger. Only three barrels of powder were left in the whole range of the castle.

Twenty pieces of ordnance were captured when the rebel troops took possession, and there marched out, under the provisions of the treaty, four colonels, eighty-two captains, sixteen lieutenants, six cornets, four ensigns, four quarter-masters, and fifty esquires and gentlemen; with the aged Marquis of Worcester, in his eighty-fourth year; Lord Charles Herbert, his sixth son; the Countess of Glamorgan, wife of his eldest son; Lady Jones; Sir Philip Jones of Treowen; Dr. Bailey, the chaplain; and Commissary Gwyllym; a distinguished company.

XIV.

"THE garrison had no sooner marched out," says one who witnessed these things, "than Fairfax entered the castle, took a view of it, had some conversation with the Marquis, and then, quitting the scene of his last operation in the way of siege, proceeded to Chepstow, where he was received in triumph by the committee, and, after a brief halt at that castle, returned to his headquarters at Bath."

Fairfax approved himself one of the most fairly-minded and honourable soldiers of either side of this contest between King and Parliament. For his part and on the part of his command, he was exact in the observation of the conditions upon which Raglan had been delivered up. He was a brave man, courageous to recklessness, a scholar and a man of great good taste, and it is owing to his placing a guard over the Bodleian Library at Oxford, upon the surrender of that town to him, that that splendid collection of books escaped the pillage which usually was the lot of valuables in places surrendered to the Puritans—those whining humbugs who formed the greater part of the hosts called by some writers of the time the Army of God.

When Fairfax received Raglan Castle at the hands of the aged Marquis of Worcester, he allowed no violence towards the vanquished, nor, indeed, any taunts or expressions of triumph. He had himself experienced reverses and knew the

SPOILS OF RAGLAN.   77

bitterness of defeat, and chivalrously protected his late foes from insult. But upon his departure, the rage of these sour-minded zealots of the Parliament broke forth, and in the result, all the priceless ancient manuscripts with which the library of the castle was filled, were either stolen, or thrown upon the bonfires lighted and fed with the splendid fittings of this beautiful residence. The great keep was undermined and set on fire, so that a great lump of the massive masonry, which defied the artillery and the picks of these furies, fell when the floors and timbers were burnt, and the rest stands to this day, a monument of the hateful passions of civil war, and the bigotry of the Roundheads.

For the Marquis of Worcester was a Roman Catholic, and it was not to be expected that the rabble would let this opportunity pass without showing their dislike of that ancient faith. Indeed, one of the disturbing signs of the times had been shown here as early as the beginning of the Long Parliament, when some emissaries of the House had appeared before the gates of Raglan to demand from the Marquis of Worcester, as a Popish recusant, all the arms and warlike materials stored in the building. Had this search-party been composed of well-considered officials, rather than of the lowest type of pursuivants that could be got together for this odious errand, the stores of Raglan might well have been confiscated before ever the Civil War broke out; but, as it was, the ignorant fellows who formed this posse were easily foiled by the marquis, and frightened almost out of their wits by the roaring of Lord Herbert's waterworks in the keep, which they foolishly mistook for escaped wild beasts, and so ran, hot foot, out of the castle precincts.

The spoils of the castle were sold by order of the Parliamentary Commissioners, together with the estates of the Marquis of Worcester, valued at £20,000 per annum. Cromwell had a portion of the proceeds settled upon himself, and the greedy adventurers who hung on to the skirts of the pseudo-religious revolution gorged themselves with the rest. The lead stripped from off the roofs of Raglan

Castle alone fetched £6000, and the timber felled in the parks brought many thousands more.

The total loss to the Somerset family was calculated at over a million pounds, and the old marquis, true to his honourable motto—*Mutare vel timere sperno*—through all his misfortunes, died at last of grief and weariness in the Tower, whither he had been sent by those men whose hearts were harder than the nether mill-stone—the leaders of this civil strife. He was committed to the care of Black Rod, but died in the December of the year that witnessed his stand for his king and the sacredness of his hearth and home.

Ever since that time, Raglan has been left to solitude and decay. When Charles II. came back to the throne of his forefathers, some recompense was made to the son of the old nobleman, but he died, not many years after the Restoration, in a philosophic retirement, busied only with his scientific researches and the publication of his *Century of Inventions*. Henry, his only son, succeeded as third marquis and seventh Earl of Worcester. In his person this loyal family received the honours that were their due. He was installed as a Knight of the Garter and created Duke of Beaufort in 1682, and was the builder of that great mansion of Badminton, near Chippenham, which has taken the place of Raglan as chief seat of the Somersets. He died in the seventieth year of his age, in 1699; a Papist, like his forbears, and a supporter of James II. to the very last.

But Raglan enshrines all the romance of this steadfast family, and at this time these ruins are among the most romantic in England. The moat is still partly filled with water, and a little sally-port leads down to it in a way the most suggestive of conspiracies, midnight assignments and escapades. Peacocks strut proudly about the lawns, and squirrels abound in the lofty trees. Tourists come and peer with delightfully horrid creeps and romantic shiverings into the great dark cellars which they are pleased to think dungeons, and when the custodian of the ruins tells them how prosaic a purpose those cellars served, they go away feeling injured and sceptical of everything else. Amateur photographers come hither only to be confronted with a notice displayed at the gate, by which it appears that the Duke of Beaufort charges a guinea to professionals and half-a-crown to amateurs photographing in the castle. These charges go towards the cost of maintaining the ruins in good order and keeping them from decay. And in this connection it must be said that lovers of ruined castles owe many thanks to the duke for the care with which he has maintained Raglan and furnished wooden stairways and platforms by which access to every part is rendered possible.

We left Raglan with wishes, rather than hopes for a speedy return to its charming rurality, and caught that all too early train for Monmouth and Tintern.

XV.

THE unfortunate traveller who proposes to journey by train between Tintern and Raglan has an opportunity offered him of exercising his patience in the long wait he has to endure at Monmouth Troy station, either going or returning. An hour is wasted in this way on both journeys, and the only solace one gets is in a languid observation of one's fellow-martyrs, grouped despondingly upon the platforms, studying the week-old contents bills of the London daily papers,—a form of historical reading that soon palls—or else diligently tracing on the time-tables the routes and hours of trains they have no thought of travelling in. Some, bolder and more shameless than the rest, while away the time by turning over and reading, in pretence of purchasing, the books and magazines that Messrs. Smith and Son display so confidingly upon their bookstalls: a debilitating form of reading disastrous at once to the moral fibres and the literary sense.

"Yes," said the bookstall clerk when we spoke to him, "some people, I should fancy, have an idea that we keep a free library here. They'll take up a book or a paper and read it till their train comes in, and then they'll put it down and go off without a thank you. P'raps they'll buy a penny paper to keep themselves in countenance; but, as for consciences, they haven't got any. Look here," he showed us a row of "yellow backs," soiled, and offered at half-price; "these, you can see by their titles, are good saleable books, but they have got so soiled and fingered by the old women and the clergymen that we can't offer them as new any longer."

"Old women and clergymen, you say, are the worst offenders?"

"Yes; old ladies and clergymen, I should have said, because the farmers' wives and others wouldn't have the cheek, as you might say. We can't very well tell 'em to put the books down; besides, it would be such an unpleasant thing to do, it would make *me* as uncomfortable as it ought to make *them*. Do I 'specially mean clergymen? Yes, I do. they've got less conscience than anybody; you believe me, there's a lot done under a white choker, and that's a fact."

There are two railway stations at Monmouth. This one of Monmouth Troy is a mile or more outside the town, and derives its second name from the Duke of Beaufort's place, Troy House, that stands in a park overlooking the railway. The house, in its turn, is named, like the adjacent village of Mitchel Troy, from the little river Trothy that flows into the Wye below Monmouth. At the time of the destruction of Raglan Castle, Troy House was the residence of Sir Charles Somerset, brother of the Marquis of Worcester; now it belongs to the Duke of Beaufort, the descendant and representative of both. The house is supposed to have been built by Inigo Jones; it contains, besides a number of historical portraits, a cradle that is said to have held the infant who was afterwards to become Henry V.

An End to All Things.

"Ay, he was porn at Monmouth," as Shakespeare makes Fluellen tell Captain Gower.

But everything comes at last to an end: even the wait at Monmouth Troy station and the Cromwell Road, in London, are not really interminable, although they are both un-

"OWLS."

conscionably lengthy. The Wye Valley train came crawling into the station and we boarded it, coming at length to a late dinner in our cottage beneath the Abbey ruins as the sickle moon glorified all the water in Wye, and the whispering woods on the hilltops echoed again to the "to-whoo" of the owls.

XVI.

Wyeside,
Tintern,
Sept. 10.

MY DEAR M.,—I have not, you see, left Tintern yet. I fancy I hear you ask, " What possesses him to stay there ? a place that has been done to death." I'll tell you what : The beauty of the landscape, the charm of the ruined abbey, the quietude of the place, and the idyllic simplicity of my quarters ; four reasons, and others ready to " show cause " if required. Tintern, I know (none better), has been described and illustrated again and again ; but none of these pictures or descriptions have shown me the true Tintern ; the thing's impossible to be done . . .

I am waked in the morning by the jackdaws (many hundreds of them) who fly from the trees where they roost all night, back to the holes in the abbey walls, where they chatter all day long ; the seagulls too, that adventure occasionally up from the Bristol Channel, keep up a continual piping. There's country life for you !

Last Sunday we had a look round at a little village on the Gloucestershire bank of the Wye, a mile or so from here. Quite a tiny place, directly on the river-side, very pretty, called Brockweir. We gossiped with an old man who was sunning himself beside the river, afflicted with erysipelas and a painful family romance. How readily these country folk open their hearts to strangers ! His son—" as good a boy as ever lived ; a teetotaler and careful of his money "—conceived a sudden passion for the sea. One day he packed up a few things in a bundle and went ostensibly to Chepstow to see an aunt who lived there. Three days passed and yet his parents heard nothing of him. A week later came a letter from Dublin. He had reached there in a sailing vessel from Cardiff, and was coming home in her. Later came a second letter saying that he was apprenticed on another vessel just starting on a coasting trip up the Channel as far as Southampton. He hoped to be home within a month. That was twenty years ago; he has not returned, and they have never heard from him again.

Another " ower true tale " for you. The cottage where we are staying belongs to the Duke of Beaufort, like seven-eighths of the land on the Welsh side of the Wye. Twenty years ago it was freehold and belonged to the sea-faring man who lived in it after many years spent on the wave. But the reek of the sea came up from the Channel and claimed him again. He sold his little freehold to the Duke for £150 and purchased a small sailing-vessel with the proceeds. He christened her the *Providence*, and sailed away to make a fortune in the coasting trade, but was wrecked on his first voyage and lost everything but his life. The Duke gave him a little plot of land and a cottage on Chapel Hill, and there he lived the remainder of his days.

Brockweir, unlike the rest of this district, is held in little pieces by many freeholders. I had an offer of a freehold cottage in the heart of the village for £35 and could have rented a rambling old house overhanging the Wye (and likely enough to be washed away by the next floods) for £12 per annum. It was all creaks, mice, draughts, and damp; valuable enough as *mise en scène* for a Christmas blood-curdler, but altogether too speculative for me. Fancy abiding by the chance of being carried away suddenly by floods, and your household being distributed in a fragmentary state among the rocks and reaches of the Wye! For my part, I had rather it were fancy.

This desirable property belongs to a Dibdin. There are an extraordinary number of Dibdins living at Brockweir, all related to one another in some degree. An old man told us that the great Charles, author of *Wapping Old Stairs*, was born there and that his parents were farm-hands in the village. That statement, you can see at once, is untrue, but our informant was one of the Mormon settlement in Brockweir; one can't expect accuracy of a Mormon. Oh! by the way, I should have said "Moravian"—or "Malthusian" is it?—no, Moravian is correct.

The country folk say that apples are not going to keep this year; I don't know why, neither do they, apparently; their wisdom, if it is wisdom, is of the deductive kind, as thus—stored apples, the crops of other exceptionally dry years, have not kept well; *ergo*, the apples of this droughty year will not. Nevertheless I have flown in the face of all warnings and purchased two bushels (!) of table-apples—" Phil. Rossas " and " Cisseys " they call them here—at half-a-crown a bushel.

ROADSIDE STOCKS, PORTSKEWETT.

I picked them myself from the Abbey orchard; they go from Tintern station to Paddington to-day.

Cider making is now the occupation of all this neighbourhood. We saw them making it by hand-mill at Coedithel Farm, near here, and the farmer gave us each a glass of the newly-pressed juice. There was a large admixture of pears with the apples and the drink was delicious. We told the farmer it was nectar fit for the gods, and suggested what a pity it was that it could not be kept in this condition. He seemed rather inclined to think us somewhat blasphemous,

SUNDIALS. 85

but said that to the countryman's idea fresh cider was not drinkable. Now, this time next year it would be in prime condition, and if we were in the neighbourhood then, we should have a glass. Do you know, I am so charmed with Tintern that methinks I shall be here at this time next year, to take him at his word.

Are you interested in stocks? Not the gambling counters of the Stock Exchange nor the "hardy annuals;" (or biennials are they? forgive this botanical incertitude) but the byegone instruments of village justice. Here are some, designed for the accommodation, or incommoding, of three persons, by which the pensive peripatetic artist gathers that at Portskewett — whence this sketch—there were in olden days either Puritans of an unusual strictness or else petty delinquents in plenty, beyond the size of the village.

It is a far cry, my friend, from stocks to sundials; a flight in fact, from the disgraces to the graces of life, for the possession of a dial proves a care for the winging of time,

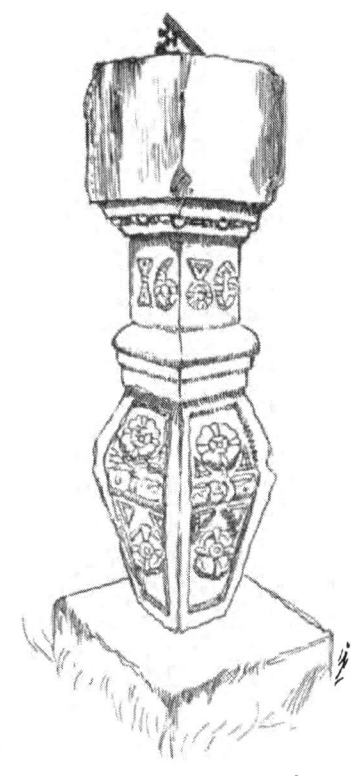

AN OLD SUNDIAL, ST. ANN'S.

and them that note his flight do not, nor ever did, spend the hours in such vile durance as the wayside stocks implied. You are something of a *connoisseur* in dials, and so I will not venture upon any raptures respecting this minor example from the lawn in front of Saint Ann's at Tintern. It is a pleasing seventeenth-century piece of stone carving, but without inscription, either upon pedestal or gnomon, saving the date and the initials I.W. But I rejoiced when, the other day, exploring in the Monmouthshire *hinterland*, we came, all unwittingly, upon the finest dial that I, at any rate, have ever seen. Take a fairly large map and look up Trelleck in this county. You will find it some five miles north-west from Tintern.

A word or two first as to Trelleck, a decayed town placed in a position where it is utterly impossible that any town should thrive under present conditions. It stands away from waterway or highway and no one ever goes there but energetic and inquisitive pedestrians like ourselves. They have their reward, for town—so to call it—and neighbourhood are filled with hoary traditions of Roman, Briton, Saxon and Norman; and Druidical remains delight the antiquary equally with the cinder-heaps of Roman blast-furnaces. "Trelleck," they say, derives from *tri llech*, the three stones, and true enough, three granite monoliths supposed to be commemorative of a great victory gained by Harold over the Welsh, are still to be seen in a field near the church. In another field close by are the Virtuous Wells, not so called from any moral quality attaching to them, but from the medicinal character which their waters are said to possess. The chiefest of these springs stands surrounded with pasture, and is approached by rough stone steps. The water bubbles over a rude basin set in an alcove where ferns and mosses grow luxuriantly, and the red rust stains which it has left show its ferruginous character. Love-lorn maids were used, in byegone times, to come and drink the waters of the Virtuous Wells, as, in some sort, a love-philtre; they are wiser now.

Another curiosity of Trelleck is a great grassy mound, now grown over with trees, that stands near the Three Stones. Tradition has it that here were buried the Welsh who fell at Harold's victory, but the antiquaries deny this picturesque legend and say that it simply represents the site of a small castle held in ancient days by the Clares.

And now for the sundial. It is about eight feet in height

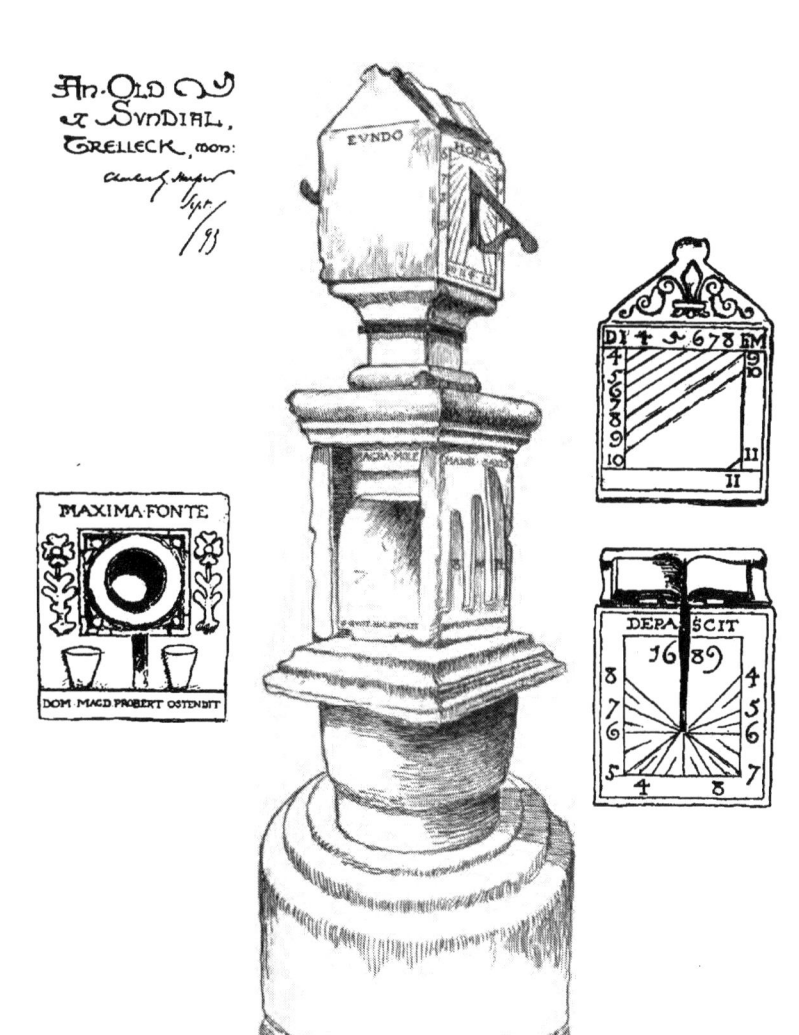

LADY PROBERT'S
SUNDIAL.

THE
PUBLIC LIBRARY

ASTOR, LENOX
LILDEN FOUNDATIONS

LADY PROBERT'S SUNDIAL. 89

and stands at this time upon an ancient font brought from the church at a previous restoration. This drawing shows it and the design of the dial. Unfortunately the stone of which the latter is made is decaying, the inscriptions thus becoming almost illegible.

They commence at the top with: "*Eundo hora diem depascit*=as it goes so the hour consumes the day"; while beneath, on three of the four sides of the pedestal, are representations of the three things for which Trelleck is notable, with the legends:—
"*Magna mole; o, quot hic sepulti; major saxis; hic fuit victor haraldus; maxima fonte*": that is to say "Great in its mound, O! how many are buried here; greater in its stones; here Harold was victor; greatest in its springs." Finally there is the inscription which shows to whom we are indebted for this curious work of art—"*Dom: Magd: Probert ostendit.*" "Good lady, I drink to you from the waters which you have commemorated."

AN OLD DOORWAY, TRELLECK.

This Lady Maud Probert, it seems, was the widow of a Sir George Probert who died in 1676,—which gives us, approximately, the date at which the dial was erected. It is strange to learn from the history of this now extinct family how the name of Probert came into existence.

It seems that the Proberts claimed descent from the Welsh princes in the same way that almost every Irishman of our acquaintance owes his origin to the Milesian Kings; but that, as Mr. Kipling might say, is another story. At any rate, an ancestor of the Proberts in the time of Henry VI. was a sort of forest-guard here and held certain privileges from the Mortimers. He possessed the (very evidently Welsh) name of John ap Howel ap Jenkin, which his son, in the peculiar fashion of Welsh patronymics, changed to Robert ap John. His son, again, was, in deference to this

CHURCHYARD CROSS, TRELLECK.

national custom, Thomas ap Robert, and his immediate descendants, becoming Anglicized, gave some sort of finality to this puzzling fashion by changing the name to Probert, for which, to be sure, our best thanks are due to him.

In this way you can trace the nationality of the Prices, the Powells, the Upjohns, and the Pritchards of the London Directory; even the terrible name of Prodgers can thus be resolved into something less awesome.

So much for Trelleck and the subjects in connection with it, and no more on any other matter. I must close this letter now, for my host calls me to see the pigs—a treat for which I hope to be duly thankful.

XVII.

AT length the time came when we were to leave Tintern, and we left it, with regret, for Monmouth; exchanging our cottage lodging for the more sophisticated shelter of an hotel owing allegiance to the Duke of Beaufort.

The Dukes of Beaufort seem paramount wherever the traveller goes in South Wales. The "Beaufort Arms" is the inevitable sign of the chief inn or hotel of every town or village, and the portcullis, the Beaufort cognizance, appears on every possible thing. This ubiquitous device swinging at the entrance to the country hostelry assures entertainment (generally of the most expensive kind) to the tourist, and hotel-keepers beneath its aristocratic guard never unbend before anything less impressive in the way of luggage than a Saratoga trunk.

When we marched up to Agincourt Square at Monmouth and entered the Beaufort Arms Hotel, we handed our knapsacks to the "boots," who, naturally, received them with the utmost contempt. "Luggage?" queried the landlord. We pointed to the "boots'" burden, and lo! we no longer commanded the respect of "mine host." But we bore this contumely as well as we might, and assumed as lordly an air as the possession of but two knapsacks would permit.

The hotel stands in the very centre of the town, over against the Castle yard, and next to the Town Hall in Agincourt Square. Of Harry of Monmouth's birthplace but a few fragments of red wall and one traceried window remain.

Says Gilpin:—"The transmutations of time are often ludicrous. Monmouth Castle was formerly the palace of a king and birth-place of a mighty prince; it is now converted into a yard for fatting ducks."

The ducks are gone now, and a broad parade-ground has taken their place, whereon the Tommy Atkins of Queen Victoria's reign goes through his drills : the unromantic successor of the bowmen, the men-at-arms, and the arquebusiers of previous centuries.

Monmouth stands where two streams, the Monnow and the Wye, join. " If you look in the maps of the 'orld," as Fluellen says, " I warrant you shall find in the comparisons between Macedon and Monmouth, that the situations, look you, is both alike. There is a river at Macedon; and there is also moreover a river at Monmouth; it is called Wye at Monmouth, but it is out of my prains, what is the name of the other river : but 'tis all one, 'tis so like as my fingers is to my fingers, and there is salmons in both." Truly, there are salmons in both the Wye and the Monnow, to this day; though as for the Euphrates, it were well to be silent.

One enters Monmouth town from the Monmouth Troy station, through the suburb of Over-Monnow that stood in olden times without the walls of the town. It was in this part that the Monmouth caps, at one time the peculiar manufacture of the place, were chiefly made. The town walls are now but a dim memory, and the sole remaining hint of fortification is seen in the ancient gateway that spans and guards the Monnow Bridge; a gateway ancient beyond all knowledge, and exceedingly picturesque, grimy and rugged.

This is the capital town of Monmouthshire, geographically and ethnologically a Welsh county, but politically included in England. Yet, in the usual haphazard and erratic ordinances of the legislature, Monmouth is for some purposes English and for others Welsh. Judicially, it comes within an English assize circuit, but is included in the scope of the Welsh Intermediate Education Act; yet it is excluded from the operation of the Act for Sunday Closing in Wales. The county is thoroughly Welsh in religious sentiment and political feeling, and in many districts of it the Welsh language is still spoken.

MONNOW GATE,
MONMOUTH.

JONES OF MONMOUTH.

It was here that Henry V. was born in 1388. "I can tell you, there is goot men porn at Monmouth," said Fluellen at Agincourt; and none better than Harry of Monmouth, who was proud indeed of his Welsh blood and his descent from Cadwallader. "I am Welsh, you know, good countryman," says he to the choleric knight, who replies characteristically enough, "All the water in Wye cannot wash your Majesty's Welsh plood out of your pody, I can tell you that: Got pless and preserve it, as long as it pleases His grace, and his Majesty too."

But that aspiration was not to be granted, for, seven years later, the king died, in his thirty-fifth year, to the grief of a nation that loved him for his bravery and his recklessness alike. It must be confessed that the portraits of Henry V. do not satisfy our ideal of that warlike prince, the Scourge of France, the idol of his army. They all show him as a long-visaged, close-cropped, small-chinned, and somewhat cockneyfied looking youth; rather dull than dashing in appearance, and not at all like the valiant commander our fancies picture him; but the wretched-looking statue of him, set up in front of the Town Hall in Agincourt Square in 1794, is beyond all probability. It should be destroyed forthwith, and so relieve the town of Monmouth from the reproach of caricaturing its hero.

Another of Monmouth's worthies was William Jones, the founder of the free schools established in the reign of James I. This benefactor was a successful merchant in London, whither he had been sent in boyhood. His people were country gentlefolks, but the absurd local legend runs that he was a poor lad, a native of the neighbouring village of Newland, in Gloucestershire, who, according to a preposterous writer of guide-books to Monmouth who flourished in the beginning of the present century, "was born of poor parents who derived their subsistence from their daily labour, and thus their son was compelled, at an early age, to procure a livelihood by the same means. His first place of service," says this prodigal phrase-maker, "is reported to have been at an inn at Monmouth, where he was employed in the menial offices of the house, such as cleaning knives, shoes, and work of that nature." That is to say, in plainer English, he was supposed to have been Boots.

According to the pleasing fiction generally credited at Monmouth, this poor boy walked up to London and obtained a situation as errand-boy to a city haberdasher, whom he served so sagaciously that his master advanced him to the post of clerk, and thence by stages to buyer, manager, and partner. At last, when the merchant died, he left his business to the quondam Boots, who thereupon—O bliss!—married his benefactor's widow. But, perhaps, as that widow must by that time have become a very venerable piece of antiquity, we cannot really congratulate the *nouveau riche* upon this latest triumph.

The next exploit, so runs the tale, of Mr. William Jones, was to appear at Newland, clad in the ragged duds of a pauper, and there to seek charity of folks who had known his parents and himself in the days of his youth. This has been the time-honoured legend and theatrical expedient of so very many romances, novels and plays that we at once know the result. Of course the virtuous villagers sent him away with contumely and naught else, and equally of course, he was received with kindness at Monmouth, and his supposed wants supplied. He is represented as going to an old shoemaker, in whose debt he left the town years before. "Did you know one Will Jones?" says he, "a rapscallion who left Monmouth in your debt for a pair of shoes lang syne." "Ay," replied the unsuspecting shoemaker, "I knew a boy of that name, sure enough, but 'twas an honest lad, and if he could have paid me, he would have, never fear." "Ah," rejoined the tramp, "'tis well to have confidence," and then departed.

He left the town without disclosing his identity, and returned to London, presently to re-visit Monmouth in gorgeous raiment, and with plans for benefactions in his pockets. The Corporation received him with the consideration due to so fortunate a fellow-townsman, and he declared his identity with the pauper whom they had relieved so short a time

HENRY V.

before, adding that, in recognition of his reception and the compassionate nature of the Town Council, he was prepared to endow and build a free school for Monmouth children, and to provide almshouses for a certain number of poor folks. Having done this, and having conferred upon the trustful shoemaker an annuity of ten pounds, he left the place in a blaze of glory, and Monmouth knew him no more.

"There is goot men porn at Monmouth." Geoffrey of Monmouth was another of these men, but one of a much earlier period, living, indeed, in the remote times of the twelfth century. He was a monk of the Benedictine Priory whose fragments are now included in a modern schoolhouse in the midst of the town. Here Geoffrey wrote his Latin version of the *Brut y Breninodd*, or Chronicles of the British Kings, a romantic work more valuable as a literary production than a history. His work has, however, from the literary and legendary standpoints, the very great distinction of affording the basis whence Malory's *Morte d'Arthur* and all the beautiful romances of the Round Table have sprung. Geoffrey died in 1154. A room with a beautiful oriel window is shown as "Geoffrey's Study"; but the style of its architecture belongs to a period at least two hundred years later than his day.

For the rest, Monmouth is rather a modernized town, and of a poor aspect. An extraordinary number of tramps and vagabonds, both English *and* foreigners, make this town a halting-place on their route from England into Wales. There is a Union workhouse and a casual ward here, and the tramps make the latter a convenient stage on their road to Abergavenny, where the next casual ward is situated. The suburb of Over Monnow and the little yards and alleys of Monnow Street are frowzy—" and a word modern etiquette never allows ye," as Ingoldsby says, in another connection— with the fourpenny lodgings of the more moneyed class of tramps—the pedlars and their like. But Monmouth is situated delightfully amid lofty green hills that look down upon it on every side. The Kymin Hill is the loftiest of these, and was in 1801 enriched with a kind of summer-house or belvidere called grandiloquently the Naval Temple, in honour of Nelson, who inaugurated it on the occasion of his visit to Monmouth. At this time the leading bookseller of the town was publishing a description of the neighbourhood and was fortunate enough to secure Nelson as a customer. He never forgot the honour of that morning visit of the distinguished Admiral, and took very great care that no one else should go ignorant of it; so in his book the name of Nelson, and eulogies of him occur on almost every page, together with what the author said to Nelson and what Nelson replied to

SIGN OF THE
WHITE SWAN.

him, and one wanders through those dreary pages of Nelson-and-water with vain hopes of discovering any light upon Monmouth except that Nelson said it was a nice place; which, indeed, anyone can discover for himself.

We saw everything that was to be seen and heard all that was to be heard, and departed one fine morning for the valley of the Monnow, noting ere we left Monmouth the strange sign of the White Swan Hotel, which exhibited an angry bird with defiant beak and flapping wings, restrained by a calm and stony cupid.

XVIII.

FOUR miles from Monmouth we came to Welsh Newton, a little road-side village notable as the burial-place of John Kemble, a Roman Catholic martyr who suffered late in the seventeenth century.

When the average Protestant comes unawares upon the memorial of a Roman Catholic martyr he thinks he has lighted upon something that, if not unique, is at least of the rarest, so great is the fame of *Foxe's* (Protestant) *Martyrs*, and so forgotten the sufferings of the adherents to the older faith. But the Roman Catholic priests of Charles the Second's time were among those who reaped an awful aftermath of torture and death, and of their number was John Kemble, of Welsh Newton, by Monmouth town. He was a missionary priest who had been educated at Douay, where he had sung his first Mass on the 2nd of March, 1625; and he was eighty years of age when the rumours of Popish plots and the sensational accusations of Titus Oates directed suspicions against the Roman Catholics. Before he was taken into custody at Pembridge Castle by Captain Scudamore of Kentchurch, there were some who advised him to fly; but when he was apprised of the coming of the party to arrest him he replied that according to the course of nature, he had but a few years to live, and that to die for his religion would be an advantage to him; therefore he would not abscond. He was committed to Hereford Gaol, ordered to London, and re-committed to Hereford to take his trial, being brought back, tied upon a horse on the whole of that weary journey. Arraigned and condemned, he was brought to Widemarsh, Hereford, already half-dead, and there he was turned off on August 22nd, 1679. But before the rope was adjusted he begged (that ardent devotee of tobacco) for a last pipe between the gaol and the scaffold, and his last request was granted. Coming to the place of execution, he was asked if he had anything to say before he died. "It will be expected," he said, "that I should say something; but as I am an old man, it cannot be much; not having any concern in the plot, neither indeed believing there is any. Oates and Bedloe not being able to charge me with anything when I was brought up to London, though they were with me, makes it evident that I die for professing the old Roman Catholic religion, which was the religion that first made this kingdom Christians; and whoever intends to be saved must die in that religion. I beg of all whom I have offended, either by thought, word, or deed, to forgive me; for I do heartily forgive all those that have been instrumental or desirous of my death."

Then he drew his cap over his eyes, prayed, and commended his soul to God. The cart in which he had been standing was drawn away, and he hanged at least half an hour before he died, "yet," said the spectators, "we have never seen anyone die so like a gentleman and a Christian."

His body was handed over to his nephew, Captain Richard Kemble, and he lies by the churchyard-cross at Welsh Newton. Immediately afterwards, his grave began to be a place for pilgrimage, and miracles were reported to have been worked by prayers offered beside it. Mrs. Catherine Scudamore was instantly cured there of an obstinate attack of deafness, and other cases of healing by faith are recorded. The rope by which he was hanged was reported to have much virtue, and Captain Scudamore's daughter was supposed to have been cured of a serious sore throat by an application of it; but one need not pay much attention to that as a serious testimony. The graveside long remained a resort of the afflicted and is even now the goal of an annual pilgrimage. The churchyard-cross by which Kemble lies has been restored and the inscription on his gravestone re-cut with pious care, but his memory is kept green in the country side, not so much by the story of his sufferings as by the singularity of his last request, and it remains in Herefordshire and Monmouth to the present time the most usual thing to say

PEMBRIDGE CASTLE. 103

to a parting guest, " Wait awhile, and have a Kemble's pipe before you go."

It is said that the Kemble family of actors was descended from this martyr.

JOHN KEMBLE'S GRAVE.

Pembridge Castle, that now succeeded to Welsh Newton on our route, stands beside the road in an open position amid gently undulating fields and pastures where no one would suspect a castle of standing. It is now a farmhouse and has that delightfully picturesque aspect usually found in such mixtures of domestic and military architecture. It would not appear that the lords of Pembridge were ever of great importance, for theirs was a castle of small dimensions and weak position. Sheltered as it was behind the advanced trilateral border defences of Skenfrith, Grosmont, and White Castles, there was the less need of great strength while yet a fortification of some sort was necessary. It seems likely that the masters of Pembridge Castle were landowners who, to hold their own, found it necessary to build a fortified residence in readiness for any possible attacks on the part of the Welsh from whom they had filched their acres.

The site of the castle is on the crest of a gently sloping hill or down, that overlooks the beautiful vale of Pencoyd. The buildings are surrounded with a deep ditch, the outer bank forming, even now, a steep turfy glacis. The gateway faced the east. The plan was square, with circular angle-towers and a round keep at the north-west angle. None of these towers remain complete. The north face of the castle is entirely gone; there are fragments of the keep and of the western curtain wall. The south wall is in good preservation, and the south-east and south-west towers still rise to three parts of their original height, but the whole of this southern aspect has been confused with the purely domestic, but not unpicturesque, architecture of the eighteenth-century farmhouse. The south-eastern tower seen in the illustration with the quaint but modern conical slate roof is now used as a beer cellar. The gateway and the guard-rooms are in ruins. Around three sides of the castle are the barns and outhouses and the litter of the farmhouse, but to the southward the best view is obtained. Great graceful ash-trees grow on the grassy bank of the moat and all around are the mountainous Welsh hills—Cwmcarfan and Craig Screethin; Garway Hill and the Sugarloaf, blue and beautiful.

The road to Skenfrith lay through the valley past the hamlet of Broadoak, a place that takes its name from an immense oak-tree standing where four roads meet and branch severally to Ross, Monmouth, Abergavenny, and Pontrilas. This road-side settlement is not of ancient date, but

PEMBRIDGE CASTLE.

already it has outlived whatever prosperous days conjured it up from the lonely cross-roads, and is woebegone in the extreme and almost entirely deserted. The oak, now polled and shorn of something of its old-time majesty, remains, and beside it stands a lonely beerhouse. The empty cottages round about are all in different stages of decay; roofs sagging, or entirely fallen in, gardens long since grown wild, and windows smashed with the missiles of every passing urchin for years gone by. Even that old highway, the Abergavenny road, that passed through the hamlet is shrunken. Originally of great breadth, it is now contracted between little lawns that have been allowed to grow from the hedgerows on each side, and only the crown of the highway is now in use.

The road now dipped suddenly and wound deeply among watercourses and high banks on either side for a mile or more, when presently it again lay, flat and in a long straight perspective, along a narrow strip of level land between wooded hills. The first sign of Skenfrith was the ruinated keep-tower of its castle, ivy-covered and ragged with bushy shrubs that peeped problematically over the distant hedges. Then came the bridge and the Monnow, swiftly running in a deep stony bed between abruptly scarped banks. The Bell Inn, a comfortable-looking village hostelry, white-faced and quaintly gabled, the resort of anglers, faced the bridge; but fishermen filled the house to overflowing, and it was only in a humble cottage by the church that we were able to stay the night.

XIX.

SKENFRITH village was called into being only as a dependency of the castle, and ever since that fortress by the ford was deserted and dismantled hundreds of years ago, in times beyond the memory of man and before itinerants took to scribbling, the place has dragged on a decrepit existence in this unhealthy sink between the hills, saturated with the showers and melting snows of spring, scarcely dried by the heats of summer, inundated with the rains of autumn, and by the spates of the river; so that rheumatism and bronchitis, diphtheria, whooping-cough and agues are the commonest ailments of its unfortunate inhabitants. The Monnow sends up clinging mists at night and in early morning, and not before the sun has performed half his

THE MONNOW BELOW SKENFRITH.

daily round of a summer's day is the air clear and distant objects visible.

The village is merely one short, but broad and straggling, street, traversed by strips and selvedges of grass, grown where the scanty traffic rarely comes. It is a delight to the eye, haphazard and unconventional, frankly poor in general effect, but striving and utilitarian in detail, as where modern cottages, pigsties, and a hideous modern flour mill are built on to and over against the castle ruins. The cottages come well within the picture, but the flour mill, gaunt and uncompromising, standing beside the bridge, has had to be dodged in sketching. In this view of Skenfrith you see all the village except the mill, the Bell Inn, and the vicarage, hid behind the distant trees. There is the ancient, ramshackle New Inn, with its creaking sign, and, peering over the churchyard trees, is the curious belfry, like a dovecote, of the parish church, contrived in a most remarkable fashion, of open timber work.

The castle, built chiefly of red sandstone, is somewhat larger than that of Pembridge, but of very similar plan. Its north side runs almost parallel with the Monnow; the north-east angle rising directly from the stream. The walls still rise to a considerable height, covered thickly with ivy toward the top: the lower parts have been stripped of their facing for building material. Of architectural detail there is none. The circular keep stands toward the centre of the empty shell; the space within the curtain walls is now an apple orchard. The castle was never a residence but an early and remarkable type of Border stronghold, garrisoned in time of warfare and tumult to hold and protect the passage of the Monnow where the road runs from Abergavenny to Monmouth—a most important strategic position. A stone bridge of three arches now spans the fishful stream, but there is little doubt that when Skenfrith Castle was maintained, there was only a ford, and certainly in those times the ford must always have been difficult of passage, and sometimes impassable.

In times of flood Skenfrith Castle must have been impregnable, for then it would have been an island, and in those early days projectiles of any considerable flight were not yet known. A remarkable feature of the castle is that no doorway on a level with the ground was included in the original plan of the keep. An opening in the first floor gave access by a removable plank or gangway which would be drawn up on the outer walls being stormed and the garrison hard pressed.

Even in the days of Elizabeth these walls were ruinous and the occasion of some superstitious dread, for, as a petitioner of the queen's ministers wrote, "The voyce of the county goeth, there is a dyvell and his dame, one sitts upon a hogshed of gold, the other upon a hogshed of silver." The writer of this startling legend was, at the time, a prisoner in the Tower of London. He proposed that he should be set at liberty to find this treasure for the queen's majesty, probably thinking that even an encounter with devils would be preferable to durance. It is not known, however, if Gloriana's advisers rose to this bait.

XX.

WE walked quietly into Grosmont by way of a deserted estate called Part-y-Seal, a derelict demesne with a modern lodge beside the road, empty and shattered with neglect and damp. Within the rusty and broken gates, at a considerable distance, stood a large mansion in a similar condition, and Nature was resuming her dominion over all the lawns, pastures, and arable lands round about. The hedges were growing into the fields, the brambles pushing their long runners farther and farther from their allotted space, sour weeds and lusty nettles lorded it over the sweet grass where the cows fed aforetime; the carriage-drive was thickly grown with moss and grass and seedling oak-trees; the very doorstep of the mansion cracked and parti-coloured with lichens. This was an estate purchased when the price of land was high, some years ago, and afterwards sold for less than a fourth part of its cost to a horse-dealer as a grazing farm.

Grosmont presently appeared at some distance ahead, seated, as its Norman-French name would imply, on a high hill. Higher hills are grouped around. That on which the town and castle stand is a spur hill, practically inaccessible on its northern side, from its steepness and the waters of the river Monnow below. On the south-west side runs another stream, flowing to join the Monnow to the eastward.

SKENFRITH.

THE NEW YORK
PUBLIC LIBRARY

ASTOR, LENOX
TILDEN FOUNDATIONS

GROSMONT CASTLE.

Roads of the most steep and fatiguing character lead upwards from the south and east, taking their rise immediately after fords (now bridged) are passed. Here stand what are now farm-buildings of a massive character, doubtless at one time fortified outbuildings for the proper guarding of the fords, and at the southern farmhouse a small pointed observation window, commanding the road, may yet be seen, high up in the wall. To the westward, Grosmont Hill seems quite unprotected by any natural features until, in rather more than half-a-mile, the road dips suddenly at Cupid's Hill, where one house, the Cupid's Hill Inn, stands. At the foot of this hill ensues a plain, through whose red loam the Monnow and tributary streams have eaten deep and winding beds. Here a bridge carries the highway into Herefordshire.

Grosmont, it will thus be seen, had many natural advantages for defence, and the crest of the hill seems to have been, from the earliest times, occupied as a retreat from pursuing foes. The ruins of an extensive castle remain, but in so shattered a condition that but few

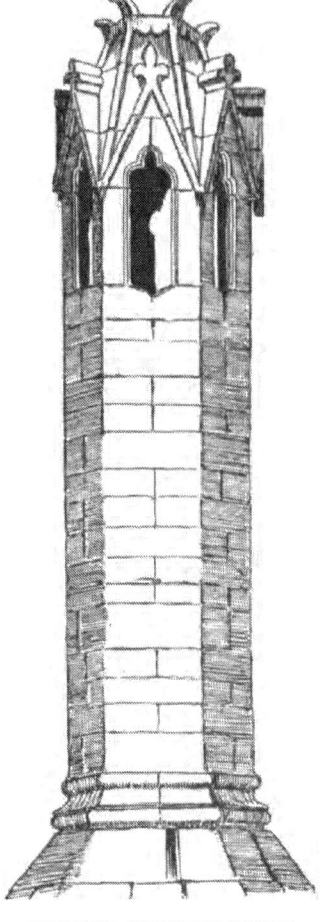

CHIMNEY, GROSMONT CASTLE.

architectural features can be recognized, save a singularly beautiful chimney-shaft in stone, surmounted by a carved coronet, standing high and isolated amid the crumbling walls —a subject for curious speculation on the traveller's part, as he approaches. It is a relic, probably, of the earls and dukes of Lancaster, with whom the castle was a favourite residence, particularly of Henry, Duke of Lancaster, the grandson of Edmund Crouchback, surnamed Grismont, from his having been born here.

Grosmont has had its stirring times. Llewellyn laid siege to it, but on the arrival of Henry III. with a large force, the Welshmen " saved their lives by their legges," as an old chronicler has it; a tribute at once to their prudence

GROSMONT.

and their agility. At a later period (March 11th, 1405) was fought the battle of Grosmont. Owen Glendower had made a sudden attack on the castle with some eight thousand Welshmen. Prince Henry, afterwards Henry V., thereupon marched from Hereford with a small army, and, falling upon the Welsh, defeated them with great slaughter.

This is the last event of importance connected with Grosmont, for with the fallen fortunes of the House of Lancaster came the dismantling of the castle, in common

GROSMONT CASTLE, EVENING.

THE NEW YORK

with others in Monmouthshire, at the command of the Yorkist king, Edward IV.

Probably the town of Grosmont dates its decline from the same period. Once it was a place of considerable extent, as the numerous causeways radiating from it show to this day. Certainly it possessed a mayor and corporation until very recent times, and it has, even now, a market; but it is now shrunken to the estate of a small village occupying the plateau of the hill. Even its inhabitants call it " the village," so a small place it must be ; and from the little market-hall, seen in the foreground of the sketch, one can see all Grosmont and a great deal more besides. .

Here, also, the land belongs to the Dukes of Beaufort, and the village gives to them the title of Viscount Grosmont. Grosmont Church shows, by its size and beauty, how important a town this once was. It is Early English, cruciform in plan, with a peculiarly handsome octangular tower and spire at the intersection of the transepts. The extensive nave has been disused for many years and is now, apparently, a receptacle for coals and miscellaneous rubbish. The roof is intact but the interior is dilapidated to extremity: its paving-stones smashed to minute fragments, its piers and arches green with damp. But even this is preferable, from the archæologist's point of view, to the shamefully poor restoration of the choir by Seddon, an altogether clumsy and abominable travesty of what must have been an exquisite example of the First Pointed style. In the nave are a curiously carved slab to a former mayor of Grosmont and an unfinished recumbent effigy of gigantic proportions, supposed to represent Edmund Crouchback, Earl of Lancaster. In the churchyard are the remains of a churchyard cross and a plain flat stone, popularly supposed to mark the grave of John à Kent.

XXI.

GROSMONT folks seem to have but few troubles and infrequent calls upon their time. It was in one of our walks about the castle that we made acquaintance with the shopkeeper—emphatically *the* shopkeeper, because there is only one—of the place; and he had followed us there for the rare pleasure of feasting his eyes upon strangers. He was the postmaster also, and wore an aspect of becoming gravity, as who would say, "I am a Government official; respect the cares of State with which I am intrusted."

He was a good soul, this shopkeeper-postmaster of Grosmont. We had several talks with him in that little shop, and in the parlour beyond. It was one afternoon when we happened in at this compendious place that we found him talking over the counter to a lowering fellow who sat atop of an upturned sugar-barrel, nursing a gurgling baby.

A large and genial smile spread over the postmaster's features as we entered.

"This," said he, indicating with a glance the fellow on the barrel, "is the constable, in case you should have any occasion—"

"Ah!" said I, in the same jocular spirit, "that's worth knowing."

But this village exponent of authority was not to be joked with, even though he was not in uniform. He cocked his eye at us with a sour suspicion and mopped the baby's brimming mouth in sulky silence.

And then we went home to tea at the "Angel," there to experience another rencounter. As we passed through the parlour, we noticed two farmer-like men in the corner settle by the window, two mugs of ale on the table before them, from which they sipped in the manner of men to whom time was no object. One called a "Good afternoon" to the hindmost of us.

"Good afternoon to you," said I, this laggard.

"You're a stranger, here, I suppose," said he, "what d'ye think o' Grosmont?"

"Nay," said I, "I'll offer no opinion; what do *you* think of it?"

He was a fat man and easily amused, and he shook with chuckles like a table jelly.

"D'ye ever hear tell, look you, o' such?" said he to his companion. "Well, ye see, look you," he resumed, "'tis a public place, this, and, d'ye know, I mightn't like to say all I thought, look ye, about it."

"What," said I, "is Grosmont as bad as that?"

"Well, there are things, d'ye see, and folks' tongues will wag," and therewith he wagged his podgy head like the adipose elderly Bacchanal he was. "But what part might ye have come from—Hereford?"

"No, London."

"Ay, London, surely. I've got a daughter in London, an' she's always on at me to go up and see her; but I says, look you, 'No, my girl, I'd get lost there, sure enough.'" Here he took a final pull at his beer, and putting down the empty mug, said, "And so ye came to Pontrilas?"

"No," said I, "we walked from Chepstow."

"Ye walked from Chepstow! That's more than I could do now, but when I was of your age (and I think a stronger man), I've walked from here to Hereford and back."

"Well, there's nothing wonderful in that," I replied, somewhat nettled at this physical comparison at the hands of a stranger. "The distance is only twelve miles each way, and we have often done our thirty miles, sometimes more."

"Ah!" said he, waiving argument; "what d'ye drink?"

"Nothing, as a rule."

"What! no beer, no whiskey?"

"No."

"Then you wouldn't p'r'aps stand us a glass of ale, eh?"

"Why, yes," I said, "if you want one," and I had his mug refilled for him. "And now," I said, "you'll excuse me, I want my tea."

"No," said the farmer, "I want to know, look you, what you *do* drink. D'ye drink milk?"

"Sometimes."

"Well, then, if you come to my farm, d'ye see, you shall have as fine a glass o' milk as ever man drank. I can't say no fairer than that, can I?"

120　THE MARCHES OF WALES.

"No, certainly you could not; but I don't know where your farm is."

"Why, if ye just ask for Kingswood Farm, anyone'll tell ye. 'Tis past the housen at top o' th' hill, whatever, and then acrost two meadows on the right hand."

And then, with his forefinger dipped in the ale he proceeded to trace a beery plan on the mahogany table.

"Mind," I said, at last retreating, "I shall be calling for that glass of milk."

But the "best glass o' milk" waited some days yet before we could find time to go over to Kingswood Farm. We had work to do at Grosmont Castle, where, by the way, we found, pinned to one of the trees, the manuscript announcement reproduced in reduced *fac simile* below. We stole it for its eventual appearance in these pages, where it may puzzle some readers and amuse others; but no prize is offered for its solution.

Notice　　　　　 1 october 1892.

*THERE HIS GOING TO
BE TEA PARTY ON OCTOBER 15
KITES BE LONG GRECY POLE
AND EVERY THINK ELSE HERE
BY J Rowberry.*

ANNOUNCEMENT OF A LOCAL TEA-FIGHT.

XXII.

WE stayed at Grosmont as a convenient base from which to explore the celebrated ruins of White Castle, to which this was the nearest village, and the postmaster became our guide, philosopher and friend during our stay.

THE VILLAGE POST-OFFICE.

Consider how beneficent an institution is the village post-office, the friend of man, equally with that "noble animal" of the copy-books, the horse. When summer comes, and you hie to the least frequented hamlets of the countryside, you will find the village post-office your first necessity; for at each stage of your journey there await you at these outposts of civilization certain letters and papers that keep the pedestrian *au courant* of affairs and well informed of how the world wags in his retirement from the haunts of men. Yet though the village post-office performs such kindly and important functions, it is commonly but a humble place, where miscellaneous and such mutually antagonistic goods as butter and note-paper may be purchased at the price of good money and fair words. That is to say, more succinctly, the village post-office is also the general shop, behind whose heaped-up counter the postmaster or postmistress stands entrenched, amid a multitude of tins and boxes, the letters of the lieges guarded by a substantial screen from promiscuous handling; the screen itself hung profusely with printed bills emanating from Saint Martin's-le-Grand, setting forth the various times and methods of posting to all manner of impossible places whose very names make the rustics gasp with astonishment.

These outward signs of officialdom make the postmaster an object of a dumb admiration and endue him with an official halo. He is tacitly credited with a profound knowledge of seas and lands, of continents and countries; and really, it is astonishing how readily a reputation for postal omniscience may be achieved by the rural postmaster with the aid of the current "Postal Guide" and a due exhibition of official, or postmasterial, infallibility.

But for good companionship, commend me to the rural postman who tramps his daily round of country lanes in storm and shine, in weather wet or dry, with his well-filled wallet and his stout oaken walking-stick. He has frequently a fund of quiet humour and a goodly store of curious local information that is worth your while to extract at the cost of a walk with him upon his rounds and the price of a glass of "something to keep the chills out," quite irrespective of the temperature. He knows all the scandal of the neighbourhood, and propagates more for your edification, and not a happening upon his beat, but he knows everything that is to be known about it. But question him only with an eagerness tempered largely with discretion, for be well assured that he also is an official. Cause him but the least suspicion that you are " pumping" him, and, like an oyster, he closes with a snap, and the pearls are beyond your grasp.

We had the good fortune to walk the greater part of the distance to White Castle one morning with the rural postman of Grosmont, and saw how eagerly his coming was awaited at the hamlets, farmhouses, and roadside cottages on the way. He was a good gossip, and told local stories that may not be divulged in this place. Also he was something of a philosopher, as a rural postman certainly should be, and not being "a native of these parts," was filled with a quiet humour at the expense of Monmouthshire and Herefordshire folks.

RURAL POSTMAN.

"To hear them Herefordshire people talk," said he, " 'tis enough to make ye die a-laffing. They call everything ' he ' except a tom-cat, and that they call ' she.' Herefordshire white-faces we do call 'em 'bout here, and Monmouthshire folks is ' blacklegs.' Why ? Because, d'ye see, Monmouth people is colliers, mostly ; and Hereford folks is called ' white-faces ' from their white-faced breed of cattle."

We left our humorous friend at a short distance from

WHITE CASTLE.

the Abergavenny road, which leads toward White Castle, and then toiled upwards, through deep lanes and hillside orchards to where the old stronghold stands, overlooking the broad valley.

XXIII.

WHITE CASTLE, called originally by the Welsh Castell Gwyn, and by the Norman knights and chroniclers Castell Blaunch, and Album Castrum, stands in an unfrequented part of the country, very difficult of approach. It is situated on the summit of a lofty down in the parish of Llandeilocressenny, but remote from the village, the neighbour of only two or three small farmhouses.

The history of the castle is bound up chiefly with its neighbours of Grosmont and Skenfrith. It occupied the apex of a trilateral disposition of strongholds against the Welsh, and the three positions were usually held by one lord. It first belonged to Brian Fitz Count, Earl of Hereford, then to the Cantilupes for a time. William de Braose, Lord of Abergavenny, was seized of it in the reign of Henry II. until he was banished; when the Welsh retook it, to be won again by de Braose's son, Reginald. The haughty but unfortunate Hubert de Burgh was for a time the owner of White Castle, and the Welsh princes, as yet unconquered, frequently raided it during these kaleidoscopic changes of ownership. It was finally annexed to the Duchy of Lancaster, and its ruin probably commences from Edward the First's conquest of the Welsh, when, being no longer needed from a strategic point of view, and utterly unsuitable for a residence, its massive walls were allowed to fall gradually to decay.

The poet Churchyard wrote of the famous Monmouthshire Trilateral:—

> " Three castles fayre are in a goodly ground,
> Grosmont is one, on hill it builded was;
> Skenfrith the next, in valley it is found,
> The soyle about for pleasure there doth pass,
> Whit Castle is the third, of worthie fame,
> The country round doth bear Whit Castle's name;
> A statelie seat, a lofty princelie place,
> Whose beauty gives the simple soyle some grace.'

The poet exercised the usual license of his kind, for White Castle was even then much dilapidated, as may be gathered from an inquiry in the reign of James I., when it was spoken of as "ruinous and in decay time out of mind."

It stood at that time in probably very much the same condition as we find it now, ages having but little effect on such cyclopean masonry and stupendous earthworks, and, being so far removed from the busy world, its deserted precincts have been left to moulder, untouched by the hand of man.

The building is of about the time of King John. Its position on a broad hill that overlooks so wide an expanse of country gave its defenders a great advantage in being able to descry an advancing force at a distance of some miles, but this was counterbalanced by disadvantages equally obvious. The ascent, for instance, is not so abrupt as at Grosmont, nor made additionally secure by the neighbourhood of any considerable streams. Thus, it was necessary that the artificial defences of this advanced post should be of a greater magnitude than commonly seen. The plateau is of great breadth, and is covered far beyond the castle building and ditch with spur earthworks, which were probably constructed to contain, within the wide enclosure thus formed, the goods and cattle which would be driven into the neighbourhood of the castle for protection during the Welsh raids. This great enclosure is an early form of the third or outermost ward which is so frequently seen to be the feature of later fortresses, as at Ludlow and Chepstow, and doubtless, had the castle been occupied after the early years of the first Edward's reign, it also would have been modernized, and provided with curtain walls and towers of solid masonry. But the functions of White Castle ended practically with the subjugation of the Welsh, and developments never came, for, as we have seen, its position rendered it entirely unsuited for residence.

The outer works of ditch and mound, therefore, remained of earth, and were most likely provided with a strong defence of wooden palisades.

WHITE CASTLE.

THE NEW YORK
PUBLIC LIBRARY

This repository for herds and flocks leads to the great barbican, defended by a shallow ditch and a curtain wall, and four towers, whose scanty fragments still remain, show this part of the castle to have been particularly strong. These walls are much shattered, yet their plan and the plans of the towers are readily discovered, but, save a few loop-holes for arrows, no architectural features have come down to our times. From the barbican the citadel was entered by a drawbridge across the dry ditch, which here is nearly one hundred feet in breadth and forty feet deep. This central ward rises grandly above the surrounding works, placed on the very summit of the hill and raised further by an artificial mound. Its plan is an irregular hexagonal, with curtain walls ten feet thick at their base, and thirty feet in height. Four towers, besides the two massive gatehouse towers, defend the angles, and these rise to a height of more than sixty feet, with walls thirteen feet thick and a boldly splayed foundation going down into the rock. The space enclosed within their ward is unusually large, and must have been planned to hold a very numerous garrison. A small gateway, in which the remains of a portcullis may be traced, is wedged in between the boldly-projecting gatehouse tower, and would have been the most difficult of access to an enemy, even in the event of the outworks being carried. But it is the final lot of castles to be taken and of theatres to be burnt, and the history of White Castle shows it to have been taken not once but several times. We have no account of the manner in which it was surrendered, but the strength of its position, the excellence of the military engineering that characterizes its every detail, point to capitulation through hunger rather than to capture by assault.

Inside the central ward grow great trees, and rank nettles, and shapeless heaps of stones lie about everywhere. Some of the original plaster-work is left even now upon the walls, and this and the holes where beams were once inserted show the defenders of the place to have been lodged in buildings of a somewhat meagre nature within the strong shell of the fortress; indeed, they would appear to have been largely of a temporary nature, with slight walls and lean-to roofs.

Our work at Grosmont was now finished, and that evening on returning from White Castle we planned a start for the morrow, selecting Peterchurch as the end of the next day's walk.

XXIV.

WE left Grosmont this morning and passed into Herefordshire over Cupid's Hill and two tributaries of the Monnow in the succeeding valley. Here appeared the modern castellated entrance to Kentchurch Court, the residence of a Scudamore, whose family has been settled here over five hundred years. It was a Sir John Scudamore who married a daughter of the rebel Welsh chieftain, Owen Glendower, who, robbed and insulted by that filibuster of the Marches, Lord Grey of Ruthin, revolted against Henry IV., and carried on a harassing border warfare for years until, the endurance of his people becoming exhausted, he subsided into obscurity. The end of his career is uncertain, but he is thought to have died at Monnington, near Hereford, in 1415. In 1680, there was discovered in Monnington churchyard a grave supposed to be his last resting place. The body was found then "whole and entire, and of goodly stature."

Glendower was a man of considerable learning and address. He had gained both in London in the reign of Richard II., in the Temple and at the Court of Westminster. His superior knowledge, however, gained him, among his own people and on the Borders, the reputation of a wizard, and he is supposed to be identical with the mysterious sorcerer remembered in Grosmont and the country-side as John à Kent, perhaps more accurately "Gwent." There is a reputed portrait of him in Kentchurch Court, representing a grim-visaged, monk-like man with the tonsure, a rosary and monastic robes. He holds an open book in his hand, and scowls horribly out of the picture. In the background is apparently a ruined castle on a hill, with a castellated house approached by a bridge in front, possibly meant for Grosmont Castle and Kentchurch Court.

It is difficult to reconcile the supposed finding of Glendower's body at Monnington with the grave ascribed to John à Kent at Grosmont, and other traditions assert John à Kent to have been a monk who, holding with the Lollards, was

JOHN À KENT.
(*From an old painting.*)

compelled to seek refuge at Kentchurch, then an extremely remote place. The Church is supposed to have denounced him as being in league with the Devil, a heretic and a practitioner of sorcery, and it seems likely that this accusation is the fountain-head of all the wild and picturesque legends of which Grosmont is so full that even to this day the threat of " Johnny Kent is coming " is sufficient to bring refractory children to order. The most striking legends of this wizard, are that he caused his familiars to build the bridge over the Monnow, between Cupid's Hill and Kentchurch in one night; and that he was cunning enough to baulk the Devil of his soul. He had made the usual compact with the Enemy for supernatural powers during his lifetime, the consideration being his body and soul after death, whether buried within or without the church, but when at last, full of years and magic, he died, he directed that his body should be buried in the wall of Grosmont church, thus evading the contract. The proper reflection here seems to be that the Devil should have employed a lawyer.

XXV.

Now the distant whistling of railway trains could be heard, and we came, along a flat stretch of road, to Pontrilas. "Pontrilas," we had sufficient Welsh to know, meant "the Bridge of Three Streams," and, true enough, the name was admirably descriptive, for there was a bridge where the roads met, under which flowed three brooks, the Dulas (Black Stream), the Dore (Dwr=water), and a nameless rill; all three parting company at the bridge and flowing their several ways.

Pontrilas is an insignificant place; a dreary junction, surrounded by some few tarred warehouses, and populous with coal trucks marshalled in the sidings, but otherwise "remote, unfriended, melancholy, slow."

SOME LIFE AT PONTRILAS.

But stay, there was some life at Pontrilas. A train came in from the south, and a portly man carrying a bulky portmanteau dashed up the road. He was bundled into a carriage, the train departed, and Pontrilas dozed again.

Anglers frequent the neighbourhood of Pontrilas and the

Golden Valley. Pontrilas Court, a fine Elizabethan manor-house, standing near the junction, is now a kind of hotel, kept exclusively for the benefit of angling parties, and rod and line are in evidence everywhere, through the next village of Ewyas Harold, on to Abbeydore and Peterchurch.

Ewyas Harold was the site of yet another castle, of which all that now remains are a formless heap of stones and some half-obliterated earthworks on a mound near the church. Says Leland:—" The fame is that it was builded by Harold

CARVEN HEAD, EWYAS HAROLD.

before he was kynge, and when he overcame the Welschmen, Harold gave this castell to his bastard."

The name "Ewyas" is considered to derive from the British *Yw-ys*, the Yew-place, and this theory is borne out by the abundance of yew-trees still to be seen throughout the district.

The church of Ewyas Harold, of Early English date, is small and has been restored, but a fine and massive tower of the same period, still exists in an untouched and interesting state. In the chancel remains a recumbent female effigy in a recess in the north wall, under a handsome Early English canopy. The figure is supposed to represent the Lady Clarisa Tregoz. She holds her heart clasped in her hands. The tomb is daintily carved and in tolerably good preservation; and a carefully rendered little head with quaint head-dress carved on the label-stop of the canopy is quite charming.

XXVI.

As the traveller crosses the wild and hilly common from Ewyas Harold and gains its farther end, he sees the Golden Valley stretched out below him as in a map, and the Abbey church of Dore immediately beneath, rising grey and massive from the level lands, immediately skirting the river Dòre. It is quite a little stream, this so-called river, but it has made fertile all this lengthy valley that runs for ten miles from Dorstone to this spot. As the "Golden Valley" it has been known for many centuries, whether from its fertility or from a curious perversion of a Welsh name, it cannot with certainty be said, but certain it is that the Welsh "Dwr," meaning 'water,' was the original name of the Dore stream, and it has been assumed, with great show of probability, that when the Normans penetrated to what is now Herefordshire they heard this name—phonetically so similar to D'or—pronounced, and adapted it to a novel orthography and a new meaning. The Abbey of Val d'Or, too, was the official title of the monastery, and from this Norman-French to the English "Golden Valley," was an obvious step.

The situation of Dore Abbey is exactly similar to that of Tintern. It stands amid level meads, abundantly watered, and secluded from the outside world by surrounding hills. These hills are not so immediately impending as at Tintern, neither are they by any means so bold and lofty; but the essential requirements of these Cistercians were well satisfied: retirement, fertility, and water were all here.

The ruinated abbey is now used as the parish church of the insignificant and scattered village of Abbeydore, and

Dore Abbey.

the site of its long-destroyed nave is occupied by a populous churchyard. Here and there, among the tombstones, can yet be seen the bases of pillars, and one or two slender shafts of the nave arcade remain to show how grand a foundation this had been before the Reformation.

The monastery was founded by Robert, youngest son of Harold, Lord of Ewyas, in King Stephen's time, and it remained, from 1147 to 1534, one of the most stately religious houses in the Marches and the favourite burial-place of wealthy nobles of the district. It fell with the lesser monasteries and for one hundred years became the quarry to which the farmers and yeomen of the neighbourhood resorted when they lacked building materials. In this way went the nave, cloisters, and out-buildings, and it was not until 1634 that John, Viscount Scudamore, a descendant of the Scudamore to whom Henry VIII. granted the abbey lands, restored the remaining portion to religious uses by re-roofing the roofless choir.

Shorn of all save its lovely choir, transepts of two bays, north and south choir aisles, and striking ambulatory, in which last the peculiar arrangement of these White Monks in the matter of screens can be observed, the wreck remains an exemplar of Early English architecture of the most beautiful type. The four great arches of the crossing remain, but chapter-house, scriptorium, domestic offices, all are gone, and the massive tower, built into the south-east corner of the south transept, is of seventeenth-century date.

The abbey mill still remains in active usefulness, reduced now, 'tis true, to grinding secular corn, but near by comes modernity in the shape of a railway station to emphasize the gulf between the days of the monks and this era of steam and prosaic commerce.

Not that the weed-grown and mouldy platforms of that auriferously-miscalled line, the Golden Valley Railway, wear much the aspect of a modern railway station. The line is poor in the extreme, the prey of the Midland and Great Western companies and the luckless victim of their jealousies. Time was when the Golden Valley Railway ran a distance of only some thirteen miles from the Great Western junction of Pontrilas to Dorstone. It was first built and equipped as a speculation by local squires and capitalists, and for a time it thrived and prospered, and, marvellous to relate, paid dividends. Then, in an evil hour, it was decided to effect a junction with the Midland Railway at Hay. From that date commence all the misfortunes of this little line. The two great companies have been fighting over its body ever since, and their mutual enmities deprive it of that goods traffic which it formerly enjoyed, which the ill-judged extension was calculated to augment.

So the hurry and bustle of traffic but rarely disturb the abbey lands and the forgotten graves of the generations of monks whose Order has long since passed away.

XXVII.

I LIKE to think of the old monks and lay brothers who built the abbeys and other religious houses and tilled the fruitful meadows beside their fishful streams in these remote valleys, but I cannot conceive of their holding many of the views ascribed to them by gushing writers on their architectural remains. They were neither the sentimentalists that these folks would have us believe, nor were they, generally speaking, the gross gourmands that so many painters have painted them.

The painters have all fallen into an absurd habit of thought and practice by which one might be led to believe that the whole duty of monks—Benedictines, Carthusians, Dominicans, Franciscans, what order you will—was to eat and drink, drink and eat, both day and night. It never occurs to these cumbrous humorists in paint that a friar might conceivably have limits to his appetite, or that there were occasions when it would be his duty to perform the offices of his church; while to imagine a lean abbot would be a feat quite beyond them. Yet there must occasionally have been priors and abbots and monks who scaled something under sixteen stone, who were not for ever caressing portly paunches that wagged repulsively under greasy cassocks, or eating fat oysters with an infinite and loathsome gusto; and the bibulous creatures hob-nobbing incoherently in well-stocked cellars were not, one likes to think, so usual a religious type as the German oleographs would suggest. The Benedictines were probably the faint prototypes of this lax and jovial crew. That Order in early times fell away from the strict discipline and the austere rules on which it was founded, and to their retrogression is due the formation of the Cistercian Order, enthusiasts for all the primary severities that characterized monastic life in its beginnings.

The Cistercians were not a cultured or a learned body. Their settlements are found throughout England in the most lonely and sequestered places, where they tilled the soil in valleys far removed from the highways along which travelled peer and peasant, rich and poor, whose claims for hospitality and alms occupied so greatly the time of abbots and priors whose communities lay amid the haunts of men. They were not, to the same extent, the missal painters, the writers of chronicles, or the prodigal dispensers of largesse that the older Order became. They were originally farmers who farmed for a subsistence in their rapt and ecstatic retirement from the world, and to their efforts we owe whatever softly beautiful features their silent haunts now possess. The vales of Dore, Tintern, and Fountains, the fertile neighbourhoods of Waverley and Jervaulx, are the results of their patient tillage.

The Cistercian monk was enjoined to continual silence. His diet was of the coarsest and scantiest, without meat and with very seldom any fish, and from Easter to September he had only one meal a day. His discipline was rigid; the slightest departure from the rules of the monastery, even an untied shoe-string, entailing confession and penance. He was filthy in his personal habits, revelling (for piety's sake and for the mortification of the flesh) in dirt and vermin, for the adage, "Cleanliness is next to godliness," had not then attained to the status of proverbial philosophy.

Therefore it was perhaps just as well that the canons of his Order kept him in seclusion from a more cleanly and less religious world. These austerities extended to the banning of shirts or boots, and were further aggravated by his confinement to the cloisters except on very rare and exceptional occasions. A brother monk preached to him on the sins of gluttony and luxury as he took his bread and water with his fellows in the refectory, the windows of which were perpetually open in order that to the other mortifications of the stubborn flesh might be added the pains of ague and rheumatism, and he was only in the most Arctic weather allowed to warm his shivering body in the calefactory, a special room in which a fire was kept when the temperature fell toward zero. He was always taking part in the services of the abbey, which took place at frequent intervals throughout the day and night; and he was not even allowed to sleep in peace, for to attend these holy offices he was called from his miserable pallet when less godly persons were fast asleep. Altogether, the life of a modern convicted malefactor would be far preferable to the existence of an early Cistercian monk.

The abbot led a happier life. It may, indeed, be said that he lived while his rank-and-file merely existed. In the early days of the Cistercians his quarters were in the abbey, but, in later times, he was sumptuously housed in a building in the precincts, known as the Abbot's Lodge. Here he resided in state, receiving distinguished visitors, and setting forth every now and again on important ecclesiastical business, or the affairs of state upon which distinguished clerics were frequently employed. Always he journeyed with a large retinue and with much pomp and circumstance.

The lay brothers, at the other extreme of monastic life, had a no less happy time. They were, it is true, merely the servants of the monks, literally hewers of wood and drawers of water and performers of all the menial offices of the establishment. But as they were drawn from the poorest, the lowest, and even occasionally from the criminal classes, the lay brothers probably reckoned themselves happy in a certain livelihood, decent lodging, and the protection of the Church. They worked upon the farms, in the workshops and gardens, and—happiest immunity—were exempt from most of the fatiguing religious services.

XXVIII.

WE shall ever remember Abbeydore, chiefly for the rainy afternoon that rendered our walk thence to Peterchurch as penitential a pilgrimage as ever holy friar made or mediæval evil-doer vowed as a salve for grievous sins. We would have taken train but that three hours was a long while to wait, so we walked along the railway track instead between Abbeydore and Vowchurch; and all these weary five miles it rained with a deadly and most dreadful persistence. There was but one consolation in misfortune—that the railway went in a direct line, while the country roads wound circuitously past the hills of the Golden Valley.

We quitted the railway at Vowchurch Station, just to visit the little village church which stood so invitingly on the hillside—so impervious to rain is archæological enthusiasm—and though the rain had searched the thickest portion of our clothing, and the chills of this autumn day were like to make our teeth rattle with cold, we were glad to stay awhile and examine as singular a little building as can well be found. The country people, who have noticed the uncommon name of this village and of another called Turnastone, its near neighbour, give their origin in a legend of two sisters, who, entering into pious rivalry, commenced at the same time to build these two churches. "I vow I will build my church before you turn a stone of yours!" one is supposed to have told the other; and she did it. But this seems rather an obvious play upon words, an ingenious invention made to fit, than a convincing derivation.

The little church of Vowchurch consists of chancel and nave, without aisles. The most striking peculiarity of it is seen in the supports of the roof, which are not rested upon the walls or corbelled out from them in the usual manner, but are upheld by twelve massive oak pillars, six on either side of the nave, placed against the walls of the church, so that those walls are not constructional but only placed from necessity of keeping out cold and damp. The roof would stand, thanks to the oaken pillars, equally well without support from the walls.

At Peterchurch, known favourably to anglers as the

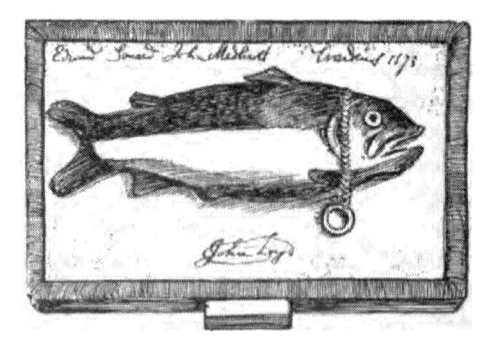

THE GOLDEN VALLEY TROUT.

Metropolis of the Golden Valley, we found a refuge from the weather in the cosy Boughton Arms and so what ill shall be said of this prosperous but commonplace village, beyond that passing innuendo just conveyed? The village and church have been alike renovated in a manner the most thorough and pitiless; the great clumsy early Norman church with its tomb-like interior scraped and plastered and scoured until not a stain nor any of the mellow tints with which Time had beautified it are left. A singular stone tablet, bearing the carved and painted effigy of a trout gorged with a golden chain, is still to be seen on the wall of the south aisle, and this is at once the most interesting and inexplicable thing in the place. It is traditionally supposed to represent a fish caught in the Dore river, close by, which had a golden chain fixed round its neck in the manner shown. Hence, say some local pundits, the name of the Golden Valley. But we know better. For the rest, Peterchurch has two notable objects in its churchyard—an ancient monolith of great age and unknown origin or purpose, and a fine yew tree, of all yew trees the largest and most patriarchal of aspect.

On the morning after our arrival at Peterchurch we set out for Urishay Castle, a farmhouse that in the still unsettled days of Elizabeth was built in a strongly defensible position upon the hillside on the western shoulder of the Golden Valley. The motto of its sixteenth century builder was identical with that of the volunteers of this nineteenth century: "Defence not defiance." He thought, not of raiding his neighbours, but of the troublous times that had gone before, and, believing all things possible to the impecunious Welshmen, took care that forays should not find him unprepared. Hence the loopholes and the high-placed windows of this farm-house fortalice.

Urishay Castle stands at a distance of one-and-a-half miles from Peterchurch, on a lofty hill scarred and seamed in every direction with the remains of ancient British encampments. It occupies the highest point and stands on a bank within a still partly-filled moat of great depth, now occupying the extremely prosaic but undeniably useful position of duck-pond to the farmhouse which is the present representative of former strongholds. The building that now bears the honourable name of Castle is a fortified residence of Elizabethan date, built of rag-stone and red brick, the greater part of it spoiled to the eye from having been painted (or tarred) black. The Tudor windows have been all modernized, so that, were it not for its size and bold outline; the fine pargetted ceiling that is still to be seen in one of the farmer's rooms; and the desecrated chapel standing beside the moat, there would be little to detain the tourist. As it is, the place wears just the appearance of the moated grange of the Christmas numbers and the Mariana legend. It has no records that deserve the name of history; its successive owners, from the original Urry of the Hay (or enclosure) to the later De la Hays, were happy in their small estate and lack of ambition.

It is two miles of ancient lanes and trackways from Urishay to the next link in this chain of castles. These roads cross and re-cross one another so frequently and are so numerous beyond the needs of the population of the present time as to bespeak an ancient and long dead civilization, probably Roman, perhaps even earlier. They are all hollow roads, and of a great depth, eight and in some places even twelve feet below the level of the fields, and traces of stone causeways are frequently to be discerned. They hid all the view from us as we walked, and it was not until we came within a stone's throw of Snodhill Castle that we saw it at all.

Snodhill Castle was, according to Domesday Book, in the possession of a Norman some few years after the Conquest; one of William's followers, Hugh l'Asne by name, literally "Hugh the Donkey," a surname bestowed whether in derision of asinine obstinacy or in recognition of some ass-like patient faithful service, it cannot be said. Instances of this singular custom of bestowing names derived from the animal world may be noted in the patronymics of the Della Vaches and the family of Lupus, of whom the present Duke of Westminster is the representative.

From the successors of Hugh the Donkey, Snodhill Castle descended to Richard Neville, Earl of Warwick—the famous "King-maker,"—and from him to the Duchy of Lancaster. Elizabeth granted the manor to Robert Dudley, Earl of Leicester, and after other changes it finally fell into private hands. Its history has been in no way remarkable, and the ultimate fate of the castle was ignominious, it being destroyed to provide materials for the building of Snodhill Court, a mansion now itself of a respectable age, that stands beneath the castle hill.

The ruins stand on a steep hill, surrounded by an amphi-

URISHAY CASTLE.

theatre of grander eminences. It could never have been a large fortress, and the keep, it seems, was diminutive. But few fragments of it are in their original position, and from them it may be gathered that this was merely a superior manner of frontier peel-tower.

From Snodhill one comes presently to Dorstone, a wind-swept village beneath Meerbach Hill. Dorstone church has been so thoroughly "restored" — as that maliciously humorous expression goes—that there remains absolutely nothing of interest in it. Yet this late Norman building was at one time of the keenest interest to archæologists and historians. It was an *ex voto* foundation by Richard de Brito in 1178 as an expiation, in some sort, of his part in the murder of Thomas à Becket, and during a restoration previous to one that has taken place recently, a stone was found inscribed with that explicit dedication. It was not preserved, but was most likely broken up for road metal. To do the most modern restorers justice, however, it may be acknowledged that they would not be guilty of so grave an error of judgment: an ancient paten discovered in a coffin during the recent renovation, and now preserved within a niche in the chancel, proves that, rather than lose sight of an interesting piece of old work, they would readily rob the dead.

Dorstone, the etymologists say, derives from the Saxon pagans' "Thor Stein," by which the cromlech called nowadays "Arthur's Stone," is indicated. It stands on the summit of Meerbach Hill that overlooks the winding reaches of the Wye, which comes down from the uplands by Hay and Glasbury in resistless force and eats away the meadow lands in times of flood.

XXIX.

THE Wye ran swift and broad and muddy with recent rains at Clock Mill Ferry. We were excellently well pleased to reach the opposite bank and to jump out of the tiny punt, leaky as a riddle and unseaworthy to a degree, that bore us over.

These were level lands upon which we had now come, and featureless in themselves, but redeemed from utter insignificance by "devious Vaga" and the towering buttresses of the hills towards Dorstone. This was the country of tumps and timber-framed houses, where wood was plenty and stone is rare; where every heap or hill or eminence of any sort was a tump, whether it were mountain or molehill. Rain still impended as we crossed the many meadows between the hither side of the ferry and the high road. Surely passengers were few here, for the ribbon-like footpath that went zig-zagging through the grass was now and again scarcely discernible, and on some of the stiles barbed wire was disposed, regardless of consequences to passers-by. My companion scratched the palm of his hand with one of the barbs, and, for myself, I was so unfortunate as to sustain a triangular rip in an obvious portion of my clothing. But consolation (of a sort) came with the recollection of that saying by some forgotten philosophic humorist, "a tatter may be the accident of a day, but a patch is premeditated poverty."

And so, with tattered duds, scratched hands, and tired feet, we came at eventide to Eardisley, through the little roadside villages of Winforton and Willersley, mildly interesting with their framed houses and timbered churches, earnest of Herefordshire architecture. A bare and lonely old toll-house commanding three roads came first, then the railway-station with a tramp cobbling his boots on the bridge, and behind him the setting sun. We were at one with the tramp, in respect of foot-gear at least, and were properly subdued by leaky soles and muddy roads to a fellow feeling with the vagabond. Indeed, so destructive had been the Golden Valley roads and the weather in villainous alliance with them that, saving perhaps that we carried more coin, there would have been little to choose between us tramps *en amateur* and that professional wayfarer.

Beyond the railway came the church, the crowded church-

HARPERS OF QUEBB. 145

yard entered from the road by a new and imposing lych-gate. The church itself, a handsome building in the Decorated and Perpendicular phases of Gothic architecture, of noble proportions. Within, lofty aisles and slender pillars, and delicately-carven label-stops to the mouldings of the arches; evidences, these, of the headgear of the fourteenth century. Monuments, epitaphs, ledger-stones everywhere to Harpers of Quebb—their only relics. Here, in the aisle, Henry

CARVEN HEAD, EARDISLEY.

Harper of Quebb, 1687, sleeps "in a comfortable hope of a Joyfull Resurrection;" his wife, too, "the pious and Eminently Knowne charitable to the poore, Elizabeth Harper." In the chancel-aisle lies "the truely Vertuous Alice, the Beloved Wife of Thomas Harper of Quebb, in this Parish, Gent., 1680"; and in the churchyard without, many more. But the gem of the church is, without doubt, the elaborate Barnesley cenotaph, which I need not ask your pardon for transcribing *in extenso* :—

> *Bubbles Broken*
> *But* Death's *the* Gate *to* Life.
> UNDERNEATH
> are deposited (in hopes of a Joyful Resurrection)
> ·the Remains of
> *William Barnesley* of Eardisley Park *Esqr*
> who departed this life 23rd Jany. 1760
> Aged 57
> ALSO
> of *Elizabeth*, his Wife
> Daughter of *Walter Price* of Kaevenblane *Esqr*
> who died 8th April 1773 Aged 63
> From the Death of his Father.
> they were involved in tedious Law suits
> for Thirty Five Years
> to the Great prejudice of their health
> and Estates ;
> at length they overcame, and died
> Conquerors.
> " *Blessed are the Dead that die in the Lord.*"

What more amusing blend of pity with the fierce joy of the victorious litigant would you have than this?

Then, by the churchyard gate lies a blacksmith with the singular epitath :—

> " My Sledge and Hammer lie declin'd
> My Bellows have quite lost their Wind,
> My Fire's extinct, my Forge decay'd,
> My Vices in the Dust all lay'd ;
> My Coal is Spent, my Iron gone,
> My Nails are drove, my Work is done.
> My fire-dry'd Corps lies here at Rest.
> My soul, Smoak-like, is soaring to be blest "
> Here lieth the Body of Thomas Bevan of the Woodseves in this parish, Blacksmith,
> whose Skill and Industry gained him ye Custom, and whose Good Nature and upright
> Dealing procured him ye love of his neighbours and ye Character of an Honest man."

But away, away ! The shadows deepen : let us to our inn.

XXX.

A GLORIOUS morning. Sunshine and dried roads in place of pelting showers and deep mud ; gossips leaning over garden gates down the village street. Took an early stroll through the village and met a condoling stranger. " Hope your brother is better," said he. "He is not," said I. "I saw him last night—" "I think not," I replied, "for he has been dead these thirty years and more." "Bless me, you're not—" "No; my càrd, sir." Apologies. *Exeunt* severally. Back to our inn, disgusted at resembling anyone else.

Breakfast in a weary, bare-floored room (say) 60 by 30 feet. Little table in midst of vast expanse of flooring; one hundred and fifty Windsor chairs, more or less, ranged round the walls—a depressing spectacle: surprised oneself every now and again expecting an audience to fill those chairs, but ourselves remained the only occupants of the room.

We paid a visit, after breakfast, to the village cobbler, and had our boots half-soled while waiting. This was by no means a wasted morning, for in this way we discovered—think of it!—a bootmaker who was neither a Radical, a Unitarian, or an Atheist; who was, in fact, as staunch a Conservative as ever gave the toast of "the Queen, the Church of England, and Old Port for Ever." A *rara avis* indeed! He held that "Muster Gladstone was ruining the country." He had watched the course of Parliamentary life these fifty years, and he felt that it was vanity, and greed of office, and obstinacy that characterized the Liberal party and its leader. Had he not seen the disastrous effects of unneeded legislation upon the country? "Look here," said he, and he held up a boot with heel and toe worn down, "the Conservative party may be compared for the moment to a bootmaker who consults his customer's best interests by toeing and heeling that boot. The Liberal party,"—here he tapped the boot significantly with his awl—"is the bootmaker who unnecessarily re-soles that boot, either because he wants a bigger job, or else because he doesn't know his trade any better. That's the way I look at it." Oh! most sapient cobbler of Eardisley.

We passed the remainder of the day in some desultory exploration of the mile-long village, at one time the seat of a gloving industry, but now solely agricultural. Many old timber-framed houses, with absurdly massive chimneys, line its one long street, and a gigantic oak-tree, the largest in Herefordshire, stands on the common. Eardisley Castle, of which nothing now remains but its triple moat, was held by the Baskervilles, a long line of warlike knights, from the early years of the thirteenth century until 1684—from an early Sir Ralph, to Benhail, the last of the Baskervilles, who was living here in comparative poverty in 1670. Their ruin dates from their espousal of the king's cause in the war between Charles I. and the Parliament, when their castle was burnt to the ground, only one of the gatehouses being left. In this poor remnant of his father's lordly stronghold died the last Baskerville. The remaining property was purchased in 1684 by William Barnesley, a Bencher of the Inner Temple, whose son, having offended his father by his marriage with a portionless London girl, was disinherited, either in fact or intention.

The estate became the subject of long and tedious litigation, embittered by the fact of William Barnesley, junior, being weak both in mind and body. His wife fought his battles for him, and the result has been seen in the triumphant epitaph quoted above. His son was a lunatic, and thus the property again changed hands, since which time the history of Eardisley, so far as remarkable events are concerned, ceases.

Returning to our quarters at the New Inn, a building, to judge from appearances, of a greater age than any other of the Eardisley houses, we experienced the musical capabilities of the Herefordshire farm-labourers. When ale has done its work, and moves the countryman to song, the result is not pretty, and drink, it may fearlessly be said, though productive of noise, is never conducive to melody. Certainly, when sentiment reaches the beery villager, it becomes simply excruciating. So this night, when the pot-house songsters of the Red Lion sounded the deepest depths of maudlin melancholy, life seemed scarce worth the living. As we came up the village street we heard a mournful, loud yet husky, wailing, long-drawn and dismal. The bar-parlour of the Red Lion was brightly lit, and upon

POT-HOUSE SONGSTERS.

its white blinds were projected the shadows of several rustics. One was standing up with difficulty, as we gathered from a swaying silhouette that topped the rest, and from the opening and shutting of this shadow's great mouth, we judged that this was he who was brutally tugging at the heart-strings of his audience with his doleful ballad. And this was the burden of his song :—

> "You nevver miss a muvver till she's gawn
> That was the chair she sat upon
> An' I fancy I sees 'er to-day
> A-sittin' in the old awm-chair-r-r
> You nevver miss a muvver till she's gawn."

This repeated several times had brought the audience of the parlour very low indeed, for when we peered in at this little assemblage of half-seas-over agricultural labourers, one was weeping copiously into his pint-pot and several were wiping their moist noses in the familiar and pleasing manner of the British working-man : that is to say, with the backs of their hands. We held a convivial evening in self-defence.

Ah! good-night, good-night, ye maudlin clod-hoppers: send you less raucous voices and more jovial chants!

XXXI.

WE bade adieu to Eardisley the next morning and pursued a five-mile long road with scarcely any remarkable feature along its course until Lyonshall came in sight. Lyonshall was a name that promised well, and certainly that earnest of interest was not altogether misleading, for although the leonine appellation resolved itself into the comparatively insignificant derivatives of Lynhales, Lenehall, and Levenshall (whose origin I shall not attempt to unravel) yet there are relics of a byegone importance there that bid the traveller stay. Lyonshall is now a small village, standing where Offa's Dyke crosses the roadway. It has, beside its church, the ruins of a castle that belonged in times past successively to the Devereux, Touchet, and De Vere families. Dyke, church and castle stand grouped together, the latter built upon a mound. It seems to have consisted of a circular keep with outworks of an octagonal form, and an encircling moat. It ceased to be occupied after the beginning of the fifteenth century and has for many years been in utter ruin. The moat, still filled with water, is, as it should be, romantically black and sullen, and the fir-crowned mound, with the wind soughing through the tall stems, and the resinous smell of the fir-cones pervading the place, makes a very proper setting for this border fort.

When Lyonshall was passed, the Clee Hills became visible, miles away; Titterstone showing plainly, with his characteristic red quarry scar, the dominating feature of the landscape, which here was flat and uninteresting.

The only person we met on the road between this and Pembridge was a drover in charge of an unruly flock of sheep. I think he was the foulest-mouthed of all that particularly foul-mouthed profession I have ever met, which is saying a good deal. He asked us for a match, and it was thus we had an unsought opportunity of testing his quality. Before we could hand him a light he was rushing up the road after a sheep who was making off in the directon of Pembridge. He came back, panting. "You adjectived noun, you," said he, and he planted a well-directed kick on that unfortunate truant. His hair was of a brilliantly ruddy hue—call it auburn, in all charity. He wore the filthiest linen smock, and out of his mouth proceeded language to match. What devil is there in sheep to produce such a vocabulary? He lit up a short clay, black and pungent, and kept our matches. "Yes," said he, "I'm a poor, sanguinary drover, I am. I've come from Leominster an' I'm goin' to Yardsley with these here—ah! yer would, would yer?"—and he laid about him amongst the restless sheep with his big cudgel. "Does I mean Eardisley? Don't know nothen about that. Ain't never heerd it called nothen but Yardsley, I ain't. Does I like droving? No, I don't, blame me if I do; it's hot work an' tiring and poor wages paid for 't. Yes, I'm married, wuss luck. Does I regret it? yes, I does regret it, if so be that means as I wish I warn't. I works for Squire Powell. Don't know him, don't ye? Well, that ain't your loss, I reckon; damned old peg-leg skinflint. What's meanin' o' peg-leg? Well, you *are* a greenhorn, you are; no offence, I hope. He's got a wooden leg, he has; that's the meanin' o' peg-leg. I gets fifteen shillun a week. And a cottage? Yes, *and* cider. No, I dunno as I does well on that; no, I ain't saved nothen. What's the use o' savin' anything? parish's bound to help ye; bound to keep ye when ye're past work an' 'bliged to bury ye when ye're dead. They can't help theirselves. Why not? Well, they dussent leave yer carpse lyin' about, dare they? *Come* up, will ye?" A shower of blows descended upon the nearest sheep, and the drover and his flock departed up the road; animals all, with never a soul between them.

The road now gradually dipped toward Pembridge which presently came in view in a long perspective of timbered houses built in one interminable draggled street: the footpaths paved with portentous cobbles and the roadway furrowed and ridged with the rains and snows of years byegone. Pembridge is built on a bank above and parallel with the swift river Arrow, and was at one time a flourishing market town, but now ekes out a decrepit old age without trade or any kind of commerce. It is actually too far gone in listlessness to die away altogether and so have done with its worn-out existence. When a house gets far advanced in decay it is not repaired but abandoned, and so an end of it, and its ruins rot away and slowly return once more to their elements. Thus it is that Pembridge is a depressing place; quaint, it is true, but untidy and given over to memories of the fat times that were but shall never come again.

The great church of Pembridge is eloquent of byegone prosperity; for such a building as this was not meant for a mere village. It would serve a town of some five thousand inhabitants admirably, but now is absurdly roomy for this place. The most striking feature of it is the detached belfry that stands upon its north side—an octagonal building of timber, based upon a foundation of stone, and dating from the fourteenth century. Its interior has all the appearance of a barn; consisting of several entire tree-trunks, carrying the roof, with an interlacing maze of timbers overhead that support a heavy peal of bells. Fortunately it has been left untouched and still remains among the most interesting of the very few detached belfrys in England. The reasons that induced the old builders to occasionally depart from the usual practice of designing their belfrys as integral parts of their churches have never been satisfactorily explained, but

PEMBRIDGE BELFRY.

have usually been set down to a difficulty, in some instances, of obtaining a satisfactory foundation to withstand the vibration caused by the ringing of the heavy bells. A belfry-tower attached in the usual way to a church would cause death and destruction if it fell upon the rest of the building, but a detached tower would in falling injure only itself, and possibly the ringers.

The Pembridge belfry-tower may, considering the nature

SHOBDON. 153

of the ground, have been planned in this unusual way for that reason, but other examples in different parts of the country do not help the supposition, for, as in the oases of Gunwalloe and Talland churches in Cornwall, the foundations of the towers go right down into the rock.

XXXII.

FIELD-PATHS led from Pembridge to Shobdon, a scattered village situated on a gentle hill, and called originally by the Anglo-Saxons *sceope-dun*, literally Sheep's hill. It is notable only for the neighbourhood of Shobdon Court, a red-brick and stone mansion of great size, built during the last century by Viscount Bateman. The entrance to the lovely wooded park is untidy, and the great range of stables melancholy with broken windows. Everything around is unkempt and dishevelled and the court wears the appearance of a superannuated workhouse.

Directly adjoining the Court is the church, re-built some years ago in the singular style to which that of the Pavilion at Brighton bears the nearest resemblance. The few remains of the old Norman church are set up to serve as picturesque ruins in the park. Three arches are left, and they are as characteristic of their period as any examples still in existence. The larger arch seems to have divided the nave from the chancel, the two smaller ones were probably doorways. All are sculptured most richly and elaborately with representations of birds, beasts, and foliage in the grotesque and blood-curdling convention of the period. Dragons and other mythical chimeræ, strange creeping and flying things, that surely never flew or crept upon this earth, hideous knights and repulsive angels are carved, together with the characteristic Norman scroll—and knot work; and there is not a pin to choose on the score of good or evil looks between the angels and the demons, the dragons and the valiant knights, who cover all the available surface of these carven stones; they are all equally dreadful. Yet though the Norman was incapable of making his saints and celestial beings appreciably less horrid of aspect than the fearful fauna with which his imagination peopled the infernal regions, and though, if he had any sense of facial beauty or sweetness of expression, he could not put those graces into his work, we must none the less admire both the strength of his imagination and the technical excellence, the rich appearance, of his stone carving. A testimony to the high appreciation in which the Shobdon carvings are held is seen in their having been selected as the most suitable examples of Norman work to be reproduced in casts for the architectural court of the Crystal Palace. One is only astonished at the want of anything like a just taste that permitted the destruction of Shobdon church, and the abandoning of these foremost examples of twelfth-century decoration to the rigours of all weathers.

To the sylvan beauty of the hilly park at Shobdon succeeds a wide stretch of flat lands, known at one time as Shobdon Marshes. They have long since been drained, but the oozy nature of the ground remains, and the numerous springs which feed the Arrow and the Lugg render all these surrounding pasture-lands among the most fertile of the fruitful county of Herefordshire. Here is Mortimer's Cross, those fatal cross-roads that gave a name to the battle fought beside them, four hundred and thirty years ago. The traveller stands at the Cross in these pastures beneath the gentle eminence of Shobdon, and sees the peaceful country stretching away on either hand, with the Mortimer's Cross Inn and a cottage or two dotting the wayside. Here on the level plain, through which wanders the winding course of the river Lugg, was fought on Candlemas Eve, the 2nd of February, 1461, the battle of Mortimer's Cross, so called from the proximity of the cross-roads where, centuries before, the piety of the Mortimers had erected a wayside shrine. On this fatal field, fought under the shadow of Edward's castle of Wigmore, and within a few miles of Leominster and Ludlow, fell over four thousand of the Welsh and Irish men-at-arms who, led by the Lancastrian, Jasper Tudor,

Earl of Pembroke, had advanced with the hope of for ever crushing the Yorkists. Before the battle commenced, three suns were seen to rise in the sky above the rival armies and presently were joined in one. The Earl of March was sufficiently astute to seize at once upon this extraordinary manifestation as an omen favourable to himself, and exhorted his men to a desperate courage by pointing out how the heavens themselves presaged a victory for his House. The Roman generals, who from the flights of birds and other accidental circumstances, enlisted the gods upon their side, could have done no more: Prince Napoleon in our own times, in his descent upon Boulogne, with that historic (and histrionic) tame eagle, did no less.

All day long the battle of Mortimer's Cross raged, and not until sunset could the Yorkists claim a victory. But when that victory was won, the neighbouring villages of Kingsland, Eardisland, and Shobdon were spattered with the blood of the fugitives flying from the fatal field to which they had been led in a certain hope of extinguishing the White Rose for ever. They were strangers in the very heart of the Yorkist country, and as they straggled one by one into the surrounding villages, which owned the Earl of March as feudal lord, his vassals cut them down and stabbed them mercilessly to death with the pikes and bills that at the time formed the usual weapons of the peasantry. Edward, after this victory, adopted the "sun in splendour" as his cognizance. Marching to Hereford, he caused all prisoners of rank to be immediately beheaded, and, as soon as that deed of vengeance was completed, advanced to London.

Compared with the innumerable hosts awaiting the commands of modern generals, the forces of the rival roses combined were small indeed, not more numerous, so far as we can gather, than a single army-corps of an European Power of to-day. But what they lacked in numbers they made up for in ferocity, and, moreover, the battles of that time were fought largely hand-to-hand: they were chiefly *mêlées*, always a more sanguinary form of contest than long-range actions, even though fought with weapons of precision.

Four thousand men, led by the Duke of York, in 1451, were sufficiently numerous to overawe the king in the neighbourhood of London, and in the greatest battle fought since Hastings, not more than 120,000 combatants were engaged.

The level meadow-lands that stretch, green and fertile, on either side of Mortimer's Cross form the ideal site for a battle, and the hills of Croft Ambrey, Ivington, Berrington, and the wooded uplands of Aymestry, make a fitting amphitheatre to this tremendous drama, enacted where, many centuries before, the Romans had overcome the Britons and had laid down that road which still exists as a country lane, running in a straight line from Hereford to Brampton Bryan. Near the village of Kingsland stands, beside the road and in front of the Three Horseshoes Inn, a tardy memorial erected in 1799, in memory of that history-making battle.

When we came to it and read the long inscription which recorded that desperate fight; how Owen Tudor, the descendant of Cadwallader, had been taken prisoner afterwards, and how the issue of the day had transferred the crown of England from Henry VI. to the Earl of March, the sun was going down and evening mists wrapped the battlefield in gloom. Its story perhaps, made the field and the evening scene impressive, but as we retired on Leominster for the night through the straggling village of Kingsland, we realized, through being on the actual field of that momentous conflict, much more fully than we had ever done before, the evil passions, the unbounded ambitions, the astonishing personal courage that could bring the men of that age to a hand-to-hand conflict throughout the hours comprised between sunrise and sunset of that bloody February day.

XXXIII.

WE reached Leominster towards eight o'clock, and met, by one of those strange coincidences which make the world seem so small, an acquaintance whom we had last seen in

A COMMERCIAL ROOM.   157

London. He was one who travelled commercially. Not for him were the old-fashioned hostelries of the country, but comfort meant to him the most modern appliances and appointments of the newest commercial hotel in every town he frequented. Yet he was a good fellow in his own way, and so closely does acquaintance draw to friendship in strange places that we yielded to his persuasions and went with him to the chiefest haunt of the "commercial gentlemen" who traded with Leominster town.

We were a very mixed company in this commercial room. One there was who travelled in boots and shoes; another, slender and infinitely long, who sold tea; certain others who dealt in books, ironmongery, groceries, and insignificant miscellanea; and a perplexing foreigner who wanted "wōlls" for dinner. The waitress was at an embarrassing nonplus. "What did you say, sir?" she asked, with just a suspicion of British intolerance of the foreigner and his incomprehensible dietary in her tone. "Wōlls, wōlls," said this outlander, jumping round in his seat, "surely you know what *wōlls* are?"

"The gentleman means rolls, Mary dear," said a gay young traveller, across the table.

There were shouts without during the progress of dinner, and eventually the noise in the streets of Leominster resolved itself into something not unremotely resembling a riot. The occasion was the election of a Town Councillor, and forthwith the conversation at table became concerned with that preposterous form of ambition that prompts a prosperous tradesman, otherwise sane, to incur the peculiar odium that attaches to municipal office. Some there were present who considered the ambition both legitimate and laudable, while others thought that a man who from love of petty eminence would seek a place that held no pecuniary reward was little less than a fool. And so think I.

XXXIV.

LEOMINSTER derives its name from Leofric, Earl of Me[rcia] who founded a priory here in the seventh century. H[e is] better known to Englishmen as the husband of Lady Go[diva] who made Coventry toll-free by her ride round that t[own] "unclothed, save in her chastity." Of Leofric's min[ster] nothing remains at the present day save the record o[f its] foundation and the name of the town which has surv[ived] through twelve centuries, and has certainly for the last [one] hundred years and more been spoken of as "Lemst[er]." It has given a title to a peer—Baron "Lempster,"—[as] the patent of nobility of 12th April, 1692, has it in [its] innocence of proper spelling. And so as Lords Lemps[ter] these barons were known until the title became extinct [in] 1867; for a patent of nobility is a rigid document, and [the] errors made in its execution stand as immutable as the la[ws] of the Medes and Persians.[1]

As for Leominster town of modern times, it cannot, [I] fear, be called very interesting, since its streets are lin[ed] for the most part with long rows of severe red-brick[ed] houses of the brass knocker and classical wooden portic[o] type. One of the quaintest bits in Leominster streets is t[he] little nude statue of a man placed in an alcove in front of t[he] almshouses founded in 1735 by "Hester Clark, widow, an[d] endowed at her death with twenty pounds per annum f[or] four decayed widows." The singular verse placed beneat[h] the statue and seen in the illustration is not sufficient[ly] explanatory, and provoked a curiosity that cannot readil[y] be satisfied. Certainly this is a wretched-looking creature[,] this pious but unfortunate benefactor, who has given awa[y] everything but his hat and his boots : why did he not keep [a] shirt?

But the chief glory of Leominster is its Priory church,

---

[1] Sir William Fermor was created Baron Lempster, 1692, and hi[s] descendants in addition became Earls of Pomfret (or Pontefract) in th[e] eighteenth century.

later foundation than Leofric's minster of Saxon
. It has had so chequered a history and has been so
threatened with destruction at the hands of the Welsh
thers, that it is a wonderful thing to reflect upon its
lan masonry being still in existence. Of course the

> He that gives away all
> before he is Dead,
> Let em' take this Hatchet
> and knock him on y̆ head

"THIS PIOUS BUT UNFORTUNATE BENEFACTOR."

hand of the spoiler has recently been laid upon it, and its mellow tints destroyed to fill some crafty architect's purse with "restoration" funds, but it takes a very great deal of vicarial and churchwardenly mismanagement and ill-taste to wreak much alteration upon such robust and simple early Norman work as we find here.

The Priory of Leominster was a dependency of the great Benedictine Abbey of Reading, and was particularly rich in holy relics, which, if we are to believe in their genuine quality, must have been powerful indeed in the working of miracles. But it is to be feared that the " portion of the linen that was wrapped round the body of Our Lord; the sponge used at His crucifixion; the Rod of Moses; one of the stones with which Stephen was stoned," and " some of the frankincense and myrrh offered by the Magi," were merely old rags, sticks and stones, and drugs that had never seen Palestine, and that the miracles performed at the Priory for the benefit of the credulous were more in the nature of the legerdemain practised nowadays at the Egyptian Hall than supernatural manifestations.

The Bishops of Hereford were as ready to lend themselves to these mean frauds as were the monks of the Priory, for we find them exhorting the faithful to entertain friendly feelings towards the Brethren, and to support them with aid, alms, and good offices. "We know," says one of them, " and have learnt by undoubted proofs that the said Church is loved of God, and that in it are contained the reliques of Saints in greater and more precious quantity than we can find words to express"—being probably pressed for time!

The Chancellor of the Diocese, however, drew up a list of bones and fragments of skulls, by which it would appear that the Priory of Leominster contained almost sufficient relics of saintly or other persons to stock a vault. Here is his return:—

Imprimis.	Twoo peces off the Holye crosse.
Item.	Saynt James hande.
,,	Saynt Phelype scolle.
,,	A bone off Marye Magdalene, with other more.
,,	Saynt Anastasiais hand, with other more.
,,	A piece off Saynte Pancrat's arme.
,,	A bone off Saynt Quyntyn's arme.
,,	A bone off Saynt Davyde's arme.
,,	A bone off Marye Salome's arme.
,,	A bone off Saynt Edward the Martyr's arme.
,,	A bone off Saynt Hierome, with other more.
,,	A bone off Saynt Stephen, with other more.
,,	A bone of Saynt Blaze, with other more.
,,	A bone of Saynt Osmond, with other more.

Item. A bone off Saynt Ursula scole.
„ A chawbone of Saynt Ethelmond.
„ Bones of Saynt Leodigarde and of Saynt Heremei.
„ Bones of Saynt Margarett.
„ Bones of Saynt Arval.
„ A bone off Saynt Aias.
„ A bone of Saynt Andrewe, and two peces off his crosse.
„ A bone off Saynt Fredyswyde.
„ A bone off Saynt Anne, with many other.
There be a multitude of small bonys, etc., wyche wolde occupie iiii schets of papyr to make particularly an inventorye of eny part thereof.

There was also a "Holy Maid" at Leominster Priory whose title seems to have been singularly incorrect, as she was neither a maid nor holy, if all tales be true that are told of her. It seems that the prior, who was apparently a most ingenious rascal, put it about that this sanctified virgin lived on angels' food. She was kept in a room within the choir of the Priory enclosed within an iron grating, and when the prior said mass a third portion of the Host miraculously detached itself from the rest, and flew from the altar into her mouth. These strange doings brought great fame to the Priory, but, alas! for the miracles, some influential sceptics came suddenly and burst open the *pucelle's* grating, when some dogs, which were with them, "straightways fought for bones that were under the bed." Now, as bones seemed, to these inquiring folk, to be an unlikely residue from meals on angels' food, they naturally pursued their investigations farther, when it appeared, on the maid's confession, that she had, with the connivance of the prior, caused her daily portions of the Host to fly into her mouth by means of a long hair pulled from her own head and attached to the sacred element. Nor was this all. We have the authority of Archbishop Cranmer for these facts, and for the statement that the party, headed by Lord Bergavenny, "found a privy door" in the room "where the prior might resort to her and she to him at their pleasures."

So, considering these things, it is perhaps as well that Leominster Priory was presently abolished. The greater part of the monastic building was destroyed, and the portions that were left, including the Refectory, incorporated in 1837 with the buildings of the Union Workhouse. There seems to be a sly, if unconscious, humour about this change. Where those dissolute monks of Leominster Priory belied their Order, and, instead of bringing the spirit into subjection by continual fasting, feasted right royally every day, the Leominster paupers take their skilly, and in grim earnest enact to the letter the vows of abstinence that the religious brethren of bygone centuries disregarded so utterly.

XXXV.

THE existing building is actually two churches: the church of the Priory and the church of the parish, united nowadays under one roof; the whole a singularly haphazard and patchwork relic, but none the less for that an extremely beautiful and dignified example of Norman and later periods. But the great Decorated windows of the south aisle, inserted in the older walls, may be regretted, and the ball-flower ornament that appears on them considered anything but a welcome device; for the whole nature of the edifice is opposed to such large window openings, and as for the ball-flower ornament, it was never a success when applied to exteriors. When thus placed it always destroyed, as it does here and at Ludlow church, the sense of large scale and dignified repose; proving to us that the architects of the fourteenth century were not altogether faultless in æsthetic matters.

WATERSPOUT, LEOMINSTER.

There is a quantity of seventeenth and eighteenth century

LEAD-WORK. 163

lead-work on the exterior of Leominster church, some of it very good indeed. It is chiefly seen in the piping and the rain-water spouts, and such small details. Indeed, lead is a metal readily worked, but its worked examples are, most of them, *in petto:* they fulfil a circumscribed field within whose little bounds the petty ambitions, the ignoble rage for local fame or notoriety of the churchwarden or the builder's clerk-of-works find their satisfaction. As thus: the lead piping that performs the humble but necessary office of carrying the rain-water from off roof-tops is capable of ornamentation, and often, in ecclesiastical buildings, is made to receive some manner of device. In addition to the somewhat low level of design to which these waterspouts are brought, they are frequently made to bear the initials of the churchwardens who during their terms of office have caused them to be erected, together with the date of their achievement (that *annus mirabilis*).

WATERSPOUT, LEOMINSTER.

And herein you will also observe the pride of place reduced to an absurdity, for, in goodness' name, how far and for what length of time does the fame and rumour of a churchwarden fly, let him be never so contentious and obstinate? Such a man, with so frantic a lust for commemoration, would be, as Voltaire said of Habakkuk, *capable de tout.*

The lowest expression of which lead-work would seem to be capable is that instant and peculiarly rough-and-ready method (also a bid for fame) of the restorers' workmen who advertise their devastating passage by cutting or scratching on the leaden roofs of churches a line following the shape of their boots planted there, and inscribing within it the inevitable name and date, by which ingenious device you have (happy stranger!) at once an anthropometrical document in some sort, and conclusive evidence as to the date of restoration. Of course it is dimly conceivable that in the case of a Pompeii or Herculaneum, such artless records would have an interest, but the imagination refuses to journey such problematical lengths.

Occasionally lead-work takes higher levels than these. There are, for instance, leaden-covered fonts of Norman or Saxon date, rich in curious reliefs of ancient mythology, at Lancaut, in Gloucestershire, and otherwise; and in this connection I am mindful of the statue of the fifth Henry—Harry of Monmouth—that stands within an alcove on the frontage of Monmouth Town Hall, in Agincourt Square, over against the sight of his birthplace, Monmouth Castle. It is leaden, essentially unromantic of aspect, and the legs of him are made to bow inwards. Now I am sure Harry of Monmouth was not knock-kneed, the thing is not conceivable; but see to what a dreadful pass so pliable a metal may bring you!

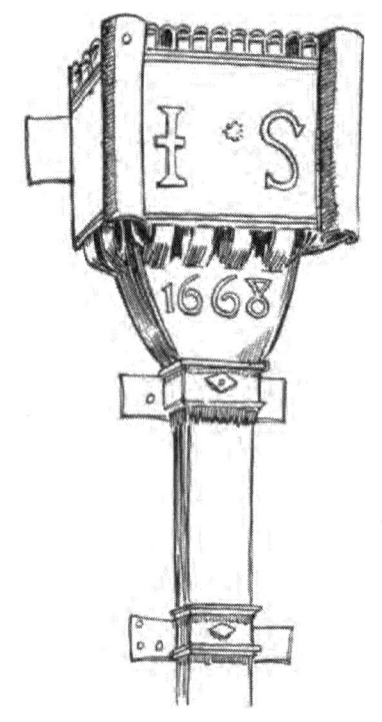

WATERSPOUT, LEOMINSTER.

XXXVI.

But now for a description of another Leominster treasure; one but poorly regarded in that artless town, it is true, but which, had it been in London, we should have kept with loving care. This unconsidered trifle is the building which had from 1634 to 1853 served both as Butter Cross and Town Hall for Leominster town.

It is a most ornate and beautiful structure, composed entirely of carved oak and designed by that famous Herefordshire builder of Town Halls, John Abel, a man whose works were almost exclusively in wood, as indeed a Herefordshire builder's works should be. Abel was a Royalist, who at the siege of Hereford rendered himself particularly useful to the loyal garrison, and his fidelity to the king, together with his professional ability, gained him the title of "King's Carpenter."[1]

He was largely employed, both by the Corporations and the landed gentry of the county, and his work may yet be seen in many mansions and churches; but to the shame of those towns be it said that his Town Halls of Brecon, Hereford, Kington, and Weobley were swept away and utterly demolished to make room for modern "improvements." Leominster was no better than those graceless towns. It was considered by the Corporation that their Market House occupied too much space at the intersection of the streets in the middle of the town, and so they actually put this work of art up to sale by auction, and disposed of it for the ridiculously small sum of £95. Consider the shame of it: the needless vandalism of a Corporation that was not lacking funds wherewith to preserve so precious a relic of olden days.

The purchaser seems to have regretted his bargain, for he sold it to the more appreciative Mr. Arkwright for the

[1] He died in 1674, aged 97, and lies buried between his two wives at Sarnesfield.

price he had given. This gentleman, admirably public-spirited, made the Leominster Town Council a free gift of the building, providing that they would find a site for it—but will it be credited that that soulless body of tradesmen refused to have anything to do with their old-time property!

Mr. Arkwright then rebuilt it just outside the town, where it now stands, scrupulously re-erected in the exact likeness of its old self, and now converted into one of the most entirely charming residences that the mind of man can conceive.

The style of the building exhibits the steady growth of the Renaissance, and throughout all its profuse carvings may be seen the beginnings of that manner of chastened classicism which was afterwards to be known as "Jacobean." The upper storey is supported on a row of sturdy Ionic pillars which enclosed the space on the level of the street, used formerly as the Butter Market, and around the entablature run Latin and English inscriptions, carved in quaint letters in high relief. These are of a piously proverbial nature, and reflect the precepts, if not the practice, of the time. "VIVE . DEO . GRATVS × " they run "CRIMINE . MVNDATVS × TOTI . MVNDO . TVMVLATVS × SEMPER . TRANSIRE . PARATVS × — WHERE . IVSTICE RULE × THERE . VIRTV. FLOW × VIVE . VT . VIVAS × SAT . CITO . SI . SAT . BENE × LIKE . AS . COLLVMNS . DOO . VPPROP . THE . FABRIK . OF . A . BVILDING × SO . NOBLE . GENTRI . DOO . SVPPORT . THE . HONOR . OF . A . KINGDOM × " " IN . MEMORIA . ETERNA . ERIT . IVSTVS . 1633."

A portion of this inscription occurs also on John Abel's handiwork in Abbeydore church; work done for Viscount Scudamore. Possibly Lord Scudamore had also something to do with the building of Leominster Market House; certainly the "noble gentri" contributed largely to the funds for raising it, and their arms were blazoned upon the outward walls. They no longer exist to afford us any clue.

It is quite impossible to understand the action of the Leominster Corporation in this matter. If only they possessed their old Market House now, what a fine public library it would have made, instead of the meagre building that (after all, appropriately) holds their meagre collection of books.

We looked in upon this place for curiosity's sake, but I confess that I enter a free public library with something of a sense of shame, even though the visit be for reference purposes only. Before one, all freely to be read, and some for gratuitous borrowing, are books, the rich products of Brains and Capital, for which you, being a ratepayer, have paid on compulsion some shameful trifle per annum; or, unrated, nothing whatever. Yet here are books, and magazines and newspapers, even to the halfpenny prints, and they, each and all, have their eager readers. I have even seen a shameless creature wait for a quarter of an hour on the chance of a glimpse at the *Echo*, rather than expend a halfpenny; this last a somewhat double-edged appreciation of the best sub-edited paper in London. O healthy shame; O pauperizing Library Acts!

XXXVII.

WE made but a short stay at Leominster, for it is not altogether an attractive town, and its inhabitants are not more prepossessing than their history and their vandalistic record would warrant.

The character of the Leominster people of three centuries ago is shown in their savage massacre of the Protestants upon Cursneh Hill. The adherents of the reformed religion had declared for the Lady Jane Grey, and occupied an old earthwork on the summit of that hill overlooking the town, where their fellow-townsmen fell upon them and slew them mercilessly; earning thereby many grants and favours from the Queen, and the less welcome epithet of "Bloody Lemsters" by which they and their descendants were known for many generations afterwards.

We retraced our steps of the day before, so far, at least,

as Mortimer's Cross, and passed through the wooded hills of Aymestry to Wigmore, whence came that fierce and turbulent brood of the Mortimers whose doings darken the pages of our English history through four centuries.

This indeed is the old-time country of the Mortimers, whose vast possessions extended on every side, including their original holding of Wigmore Castle, the Castle of Ludlow, the town of Cleobury Mortimer and wide spreading tracts of land throughout the Marches. It is a country that to all who care for the history of their native land is especially interesting from its having, through that family, produced the brief line of kings who formed the House of York, whose pretensions to the throne plunged England into that bitter series of quarrels and sanguinary battles, which lasted for a period of thirty years, from 1455 to 1485, known as the Wars of the Roses.

The beginnings of the powerful family of Mortimer are lost in the vague traditions which cling about the immediate ancestors of that Roger de Mortuo Mari who, with his son Ralph, is supposed to have been present at that fatal field of Senlac, usually known as the Battle of Hastings. They came from Normandy, where already they had given their name to a strong castle, near which the valour of their race was proved by a victory gained for their suzerain against desperate odds. It is held that their eke name, de Mortuo Mari, was gained by an ancestor, whose patronymic remains unknown, by some daring feat upon the shores of the Dead Sea, in Palestine, but this must remain uncertain. Certain it is that the Mortimers owned their name many years before the First Crusade.

To Ralph Mortimer was granted the manor of Wigmore with many others. So many indeed were they that when he died no less than one hundred and thirty fell to his son, Hugh, who was possessed also of the castles of Cleobury and Bridgenorth. He built other castles, and quarrelled with Henry II., who lay siege at once to Wigmore, Cleobury and Bridgenorth, which were captured by the Royal troops. Misfortune and an evil conscience broke the spirit

THE MORTIMERS.

of Hugh Mortimer, and he died in 1185, as a canon of that Abbey of Wigmore which he and his father had founded years before.

Roger, his son, third Lord of Wigmore, succeeded him. Thirty years later he died, and Hugh, his eldest son, followed him no longer than twelve years afterwards, dying from wounds received at a tournament. He took part with King John in his struggles with the Barons, held the castles of Holgate and Stratton-dale for him, and intrigued with the Welsh prince Llewellyn.

His [brother, Ralph, succeeded to the family honours. He built the castles of Keventles and Knoclas, married Gladys, the widow of Reginald de Braose, daughter of Llewellyn ap Iorwerth, and was gathered to his fathers in 1246. His son, named Roger, became sixth lord, and had a lengthy and chequered career of thirty-six years, warring now with Llewellyn ap Gruffydd, who took four of his castles, Builth, Melenydd, Keventles, and Radnor; and then fighting for Henry III. He fought for him at Northampton, fled with the remnants of the Royal army from Lewes, aided Prince Edward to escape from custody at Hereford, and brought him to safety at Wigmore. He took part in the sanguinary Battle of Evesham, and thereafter had his reward in receiving the confiscated estates of the Earls of Oxford.

Edmund, his eldest surviving son, had as great a share of glory as his father, although his was but a comparatively short time. He had Welsh blood, and thus became an object of suspicion to the king, but he allayed all doubts on the score of his loyalty by his victory over the Welsh at Builth, and by forwarding the head of Llewellyn ap Gruffydd, the last independent native prince, to London.

He was then received with favour at the court of Edward I., and married a kinswoman of Edward's Spanish queen, Eleanor of Castile. It was at Builth, in 1304, that he received a wound of which he died at his castle of Wigmore.

Roger, Lord Mortimer of Wigmore, the eighth of his line, was but sixteen years of age at the time of his father's death. He was the most notorious and ambitious that had yet held the estates. He succeeded to greatly increased wealth and power, and during twenty-six years continually augmented both. By his marriage with Johanna de Geneville he inherited Ludlow Castle, where his ancestor, Hugh, the second lord, had been kept in captivity. In his thirtieth year he was appointed Lord Lieutenant of Ireland; he captured Cardiff from Hugh le Despencer, and rebelled against Edward II., but was imprisoned. Escaping, he fled across the Channel, where he joined Edward's queen, Isabella, the "she-wolf of France." In the meanwhile, the king's party seized Wigmore, but Mortimer returned, living in shameful intimacy with the queen.

The death of Edward followed, and Mortimer became the most powerful noble, if the most *parvenu*, in the kingdom. He was created Earl of March; the estates of the Despencers became his, together with an astonishing number of other manors, and he, jointly with the queen, became custodian of the young king, Edward III. His progresses through the country were royal in their magnificence, his arrogance excelled the pride of a king, and when he entertained his paramour at his newly-rebuilt castle of Wigmore, the magnificence of the occasion was unprecedented.

For three years after the foul murder of Edward II. at Berkeley, Mortimer's power had been continually flaunted in the face of the nobles. The young king was not yet of age, and the queen-mother and Mortimer practically ruled the land, overawing parliaments and sending even a prince of the blood-royal to the block. The great barons viewed these proceedings with disfavour, and the influence of the new peer with jealousy. They detested not so much the immorality of Isabella as the all-powerful man with whom she openly lived, and they chafed at their own weakness. The king, now eighteen years of age and already married, was eager to assume authority, and designs were laid to seize Mortimer at Nottingham, where the forthcoming session of Parliament was to assemble.

The favourite and Isabella took up their quarters at the

castle, with the king in their charge : the peers, with their followings, lay in the town below. One night when all was quiet, the king, with some trusted companions, entered the stairway leading to the apartments where Mortimer and Isabella, with the Bishop of Lincoln and others, were in council. The door of their council-chamber was burst in, and two knights who guarded it, slain; Edward seized Mortimer with his own hand, and, disregarding the entreaties of his mother, who rushed in from her bedroom, handed him into safe custody.

The prisoner was speedily condemned and taken to London, where he was hanged at Tyburn on the 29th of November, 1330, in the fortieth year of his age.

XXXVIII.

THE character of Roger Mortimer, first Earl of March, exhibited the worst defects of the three races, Norman, Castilian, and Welsh-British, whose blood mingled in his veins. The brutal characteristics of the Norman, the overweening pride and hauteur of the Castilian, and the treacherous nature of the Welsh Celt combined to render him the most insufferable figure of his time. Ambitious in the extreme, and bold to recklessness, his arrogance and display alienated even his friends, while they goaded his enemies to strain every nerve for his destruction. He played for high stakes : to lose meant death, and losing, he paid the inevitable forfeit.

The Earldom of March, forfeited by the treason and attainder of Roger Mortimer, did not long remain out of the family. Edmund, the son of the executed traitor, did not, it is true, recover the forfeited honours, for he died but a few months after his father's shameful death. His son, Roger, was only three years of age at that time, and the remaining estates were the care, during his long minority, of his step-father, the Earl of Northampton. In his twenty-third year, however, he obtained from Edward III.

a reversal of the attainder and the restoration of the title, together with the appointment of Constable of Dover Castle and Warden of the Cinque Ports. He died, youthful, in 1360, a Knight of the Garter and commander of the English forces in Burgundy.

His son, Edmund, was also a minor at the time of his succession to the honours and estates of his forefathers. He was Lieutenant of Ireland, and so highly were his abilities appreciated that to him was intrusted, while he was still under age, the difficult and delicate task of conducting the negotiations that led to peace with France. He died at Cork during his Lieutenancy, in 1381, but he had already married Philippa, daughter of Lionel, Duke of Clarence, a younger brother of Edward III., and thus gave his descendants their claim to the Crown of England.

Roger, fourth Earl of March, his eldest son, was declared heir to the throne during the reign of his childless second cousin, Richard II., but being slain in Ireland he was followed by his unhappy son, Edmund, as fifth Earl of March. In the meanwhile Henry of Bolingbroke, Earl of Hereford, son of John of Gaunt, Shakespeare's "time-honoured Lancaster," had usurped the Crown and reigned as Henry IV. Henry equally hated and feared the family of Mortimer because they could show a better claim to the Crown than himself, and he kept the young Earl of March under close surveillance during the whole of his reign.

His more generous-minded son, Henry V., released him and gave him a command in Normandy, and in the beginning of Henry VI.'s reign he also became Lieutenant of Ireland. He died, however, in 1425, in his twenty-fourth year, and so ended the line of Mortimers of Wigmore.

Shakespeare is singularly incorrect where (*Henry VI.*, First Part, Act II., Scene V.) he makes Edmund Mortimer die, as an old man, in the Tower of London, in the presence of his nephew, Richard Plantagenet, Duke of York, in "loathsome sequestration" of imprisonment.

"Here dies the dusky torch of Mortimer,
Choked with ambition of the meaner sort."

It is not at all probable, however, that Shakespeare was ignorant of Edmund Mortimer's real end. He doubtless contrived the scene in the Tower merely for dramatic effect.

But though names perish, blood remains. His sister Anne was now representative of the family, and by her marriage with Richard Plantagenet, son of Edmund, Duke of York, and grandson of Edward III., she transmitted the Mortimer blood and estates to her son, Richard Plantagenet, Duke of York, the ill-fated protagonist of the Wars of the Roses.

The Mortimers had long been looked upon by the common people as their friends. Richard II. had been unpopular with the people, and their coldness had enabled Henry IV. to secure the Crown, but he had never won their affections. The character of Henry V. had appealed to them, but with his death no worthy object of affection remained to the lieges, and the exhausted condition of the country consequent upon the wars and subsequent defeats in France, together with the rigour of the government directed against the essentially democratic religious reformers called the Lollards, had alienated the masses from the House of Lancaster when its latest representative, Henry VI., began to reign as a child of less than one year's age. The Lancastrian nobles were foremost in the councils of the State during Henry's long minority, and in that time affairs had gone from bad to worse until, of all the English conquests in France, nothing remained but Calais. The blame, if blame there was, could not be laid to their charge, but popular feeling is never rational, and the English people were convinced that the nation's shame could justly be laid to the young king's relatives who ruled the land. To make matters worse, the king's mind not only did not grow with his growth but weakened continually.

These things roused the ambition of the Duke of York, who was cousin to the king and possessed a strong claim to the Crown by both his father's and mother's ancestry. He opposed the king's guardians and fomented the popular discontent and distrust of their authority so successfully that he and his House became now and for long years afterwards, either in fact or in name, the champions of the democracy. The first-fruits of the Duke of York's malignant industry were seen in the popular rising of 1450 in Kent, headed by the Irish adventurer, Jack Cade, who, to gain the sympathy and goodwill of the country-side, had assumed the name of Mortimer. Cade was defeated and beheaded, and his adherents dispersed, but York's plottings went on until by his efforts Henry's ministers had been impeached or merely dismissed and himself appointed Protector during the king's ill-health. But Henry quickly recovered his reason, and the Duke of York's protectorate then ended for a time. The former ministers, or those of them who had escaped the headsman's axe, were restored to their posts and the Protector retired to the Marches to gather strength for further struggles. He soon was in command of an army recruited from his numerous tenantry and augmented by the vassals of the influential Duke of Norfolk, the Earl of Salisbury, the Earl of Warwick and others. They advanced toward London and were met at Saint Albans by Henry and his followers. The Yorkists demanded the surrender of the ministers; Henry refused to yield them up. The first Battle of Saint Albans then ensued, in which the Yorkists were victorious, and thus began the Wars of the Roses.

We are not concerned in this place to follow the fortunes of the White Rose and the Red as they contended all over the kingdom in numerous battles; but have chiefly to note the progress of the Duke of York's ambition from an aspiration to rule the king to an absolute claim to his crown. The battles of Bloreheath and Nottingham were, like the first of the series, Lancastrian defeats, and it was not until five years and six months from the first blow that they scored a victory in the Battle of Wakefield, when the Duke of York was killed in the fight, and his head, crowned in derision with a tinsel crown, set up over the gates of York.

York's eldest son, Edward, Earl of March, a boy of nineteen years, was at Gloucester when news reached him of the Yorkist disaster and the death of his father at Wakefield.

STRUGGLES FOR THE CROWN. 175

Filled with rage and ambition, and perhaps moved to some grief by his father's end—though affection seems to have had little place in those times—he marched on Shrewsbury, where he expected to collect a numerous following. His expectations were fully realized, for the people of the town and country-side were well affected towards his cause and flocked to him in great numbers, so that presently he prepared to advance to meet the king's forces. But a sudden danger appeared in his rear in an army collected by the Earls of Pembroke and Wiltshire and by Owen Tudor, Pembroke's father. He turned desperately at bay and defeated them at Mortimer's Cross, Feb. 2, 1461, capturing Owen Tudor, who was beheaded immediately afterwards with others at Hereford. This victory placed the crown upon the head of the youthful Earl of March. He was proclaimed as king at London on the 4th of March, by the title of Edward IV., and by his victory at Ferrybridge on the 27th of the same month and the terrible slaughter two days later at the Battle of Towton, fought amid falling snow, he settled himself for a time firmly on the throne.

Thirty thousand men fell at Towton, four thousand at Mortimer's Cross, and many more were yet to die in order that the House of York might reign. But though so many crushing blows had been inflicted upon the Lancastrians, and despite the blood of Owen Tudor that had crimsoned the gutters of Hereford, the Yorkists had but a brief spell of power, and the Red Rose was, after all, to survive the struggle for supremacy. Edward IV. reigned with many vicissitudes, for twenty-two years. His two sons were murdered in the Tower of London a few weeks after his death, and the Yorkist line of kings, and with them the House of Mortimer, was finally and utterly extinguished upon Bosworth Field in 1485, in the death of his brother, Richard III. Twenty-five years sufficed to end their dynasty, but the Lancastrians flourished as the House of Tudor for over a century, from the coronation of Henry VII. to the death of Elizabeth.

The personal popularity of Edward IV. was great; manners easy and affable; his face—so they tell us who him—handsome, and he was tall in stature. Licentious self-indulgent, yet with a cool and secret craftiness, he un all the headstrong vices and ambitions of his Morti blood with the diplomatic abilities of the Plantagenets. extraordinary combination of profligacy with the calcu ing nature of the schemer stood Edward IV. in good ste His contemporaries saw him only as a Lothario who sedu the wives of London citizens and the ladies of his court Westminster; who openly lived in adultery with Jane Sho and idled away his time while ambitious rivals plotted oust him from the throne; they knew nothing of the v network of espionage that he devised and kept in su smoothly-working order that he could afford to spend h days in careless riot and luxury, certain that, when t psychological moment had arrived, his agents would la ready hands upon the unsuspecting conspirators of whos plots and hopes he had been cognizant all the while the fancied themselves secure.

Yet it seems strange that his face showed nothing o the sagacity and cunning of his nature to the people whom he daily met. That they should have thought, as they did think, the king but a giddy trifler, without discernment or suspicion, is the more singular in that the portraits we have of him all agree in representing Edward IV. as comely indeed, with the full red lips of the sensualist, but, equally unmistakeably, with a look of craft, and subtle cruelty peering through his eyes and insistent in every line of his face. Moreover, men credited his brother, Richard, Duke of Gloucester, with every wickedness under the sun, combined with a malignant cleverness equal to any emergency; and in so doing they were exercising a sound judgment. How singular then, the fact that they found these qualities (or defects) lacking in one of the same blood!

Of course it would not be wise to deduce the character of a man from the portraiture of that period, supposing only

EDWARD IV.

one portrait to exist; but, whatever discrepancies are to be detected in the several portraits of Edward IV., his able and self-contained character is visible in them all; the greater, then, his assumption of a careless ease that could belie the lineaments of his countenance to those who moved about him during his turbulent reign.

He was a democratic monarch in a peculiar and limited sense. His sympathies did not in reality lie with the people, but he saw, from the history of his House, how powerful for his good the masses might prove. The nobility, to the contrary, were a danger to him, not only from their wealth and numbers, but also from their jealousy of his newly-acquired rank. We can see clearly in the historical perspective that has been obtained in the lapse of years how his mind was working when on the fields of Mortimer's Cross and Towton he bade his soldiers spare the rank and file of the enemy but to single out and strike down the knights and nobles.

The Mortimers were a strenuous race, with qualities and defects that compelled distinction, whether of fame or notoriety. They were able, as their employment as ambassadors and in viceregal positions would assure us; their personal courage had not only never been impugned, but is continually shown in their history, and is argued by the very few of their name who died in their beds: their ambition was unbounded, and their crimes among the blackest of the dark and foul deeds that go to make the history of the middle ages. Richard III., their last representative, was in every respect the culmination of their traits. His ability, his matchless courage, his unequalled crimes, were the outcome of five centuries of evolution, and it is as well that with him the line ended, for though it is unlikely that his excesses could have been exceeded, it was equally undesirable that a chance should exist of their being equalled.

Richard III. was childless, and the only survivor of his race was the Princess Elizabeth, sole remaining daughter of Edward IV. By her marriage with Henry Tudor (Henry

VII.), the rival Roses were united, and those who seek the perpetuation of characteristics may see reproduced in her son, afterwards the magnificently untrustworthy Henry VIII., some of the baleful traits of her ancestors.

It is a most singular fact that of all the many elaborate and beautiful monuments raised to the memory of the lords of Wigmore at Wigmore Abbey and elsewhere, not one remains at this day. The Abbey itself is destroyed more thoroughly than usual, and their chief castle of Wigmore, the scene of the grand displays of Roger Mortimer, Earl of March, paramour of Edward II.'s queen, and "King of Folly," as his son Geoffrey called him, is a complete wreck. Their shield of arms is yet extant, and is described by heralds in the difficult language of "the gentlemanly science" as "Barry of six pieces *or* and *azure*, on a chief of the first, two pallets between as many base esquires of the second. Over all, an inescutcheon *argent*." For those who have no heraldic knowledge, to whom this formula would be unintelligible, the explanation may be seen in the Mortimer shield figured here. The shield within the shield—technically an inescutcheon—is silver, the bars blue, and the field gold.

XXXIX.

WIGMORE village contains little that reminds us of its ancient lords, save the ruins of their great castle, and they, although grim and massive, retain but few architectural features.

The original castle of "Wisingamere" was built by Ethelfleda, a daughter of Alfred the Great, and wife of

Ethelred, governor of Mercia, a tenth-century Amazon, before whose castle-building energies and statesmanship the doings of her husband are pale and ineffectual. She died in the year 912, and the history of the place remains obscure until we hear of Fitz Osbern rebuilding it just before the Conquest. He was one of the Norman mercenaries of Edward the Confessor and was succeeded by a Saxon Earl of Shrewsbury, called Edric Silvaticus, who gave way, in his turn, to the Mortimers. When that family died out and its last representatives perished, Wigmore fell to the Crown in the person of Henry VII., and so remained until granted away by Queen Elizabeth. Thomas Harley purchased it in 1601, and it was demolished by the Roundhead, Sir Robert Harley, in 1642, in order that it should afford no shelter to the Royalist troops who at that time held nearly all Herefordshire. The grandson of this Sir Robert Harley was created a peer of Great Britain in 1711 by the titles of Baron Harley of Wigmore, Earl of Oxford, and Earl Mortimer, the last title being selected in case the distant relatives of Aubrey de Vere, the twentieth and last Earl of Oxford, should claim that ancient earldom.

Wigmore Abbey was founded by a repentant Mortimer—Ralph of that name—in the next years after the Conquest. His son, Hugh, died as a penitent canon of his father's foundation in 1185, and was buried before the high altar; but in later ages this religious retreat seems, like nearly all its fellows, to have become a microcosm of worldly sins, for the charges against the last Abbot of Wigmore include the crimes of simony, peculation, and notorious evil living. Let us hope the charges were false, but I must confess, like the Scot, "I hae ma doots."

We pushed on across country to the village and park of Brampton Bryan, a famous place in the times of the Cavaliers and the Roundheads, when the ferocity of the rival Roses had seemed to come again, and when art and culture of every description gave place to a struggle between those who had and the others who had not a sufficiency of worldly goods. Let us allow that the arbitrary demands of the king precipitated a conflict, but let it none the less be acknowledged that even had Charles the First been of a more yielding and pliable nature, the war would still have broken out. For the lower orders had a bitter hatred of their superiors in those days, even as in our own times the blackguardly paid agitators are stirring up a spirit of strife and discontent which will have to be reckoned with in the near future. The only difference between the two cases lies in the religious cloak which the Puritans threw over their proceedings, while the modern Roundheads are a secular, if not altogether atheistical and freethinking, crew.

The ruins of Brampton Bryan Castle stand in a hollow near the church, and consist of a strong gateway flanked with drum towers of the fourteenth century, with, at the rear, the broken walls and decaying windows of the additions made to this old stronghold of Sir Bryan de Brampton in the Tudor age.

Brampton Bryan owes its fame rather to the last scenes in its history than to any chronicles of its earlier days that have come down to us through the ages; for at a time when the Parliamentary cause seemed lost in the struggle with Charles I. this was the only garrison that held out against the king's forces in the whole of Herefordshire. The owners of Brampton at that time were the Harleys, to whom Wigmore also had come. Sir Robert Harley was the owner at the outbreak of the Civil War and he made himself especially active in the councils of the rebels in London, leaving his wife in residence here with her youngest children. Her eldest son was an officer in the rebel army, and here, far away from aid, she was left to hold this one post against immeasurably superior forces in a country entirely estranged from her party. Many letters from Lady Brilliana Harley to her son, written in the anxious times before and during the first siege, are available, and are well worthy perusal. Here is an extract from one, written shortly before the first siege:—" My comfort is," she says, " that you are not with me, lest they should take you; but I doo most dearly mis you. I wisch, if it pleased God, that I weare with your father . . . . My deare Ned,

BRAMPTON BRYAN CASTLE.

I pray you aduis with your father wheather he thinkes it best that I should put away most of the men that are in my power, and wheather it be best for me to goo from Brampton, or, by God's healp, to stand it out. I will be willing to doo what he would have me doo. I never was in such sorrows as I have bine sence you left me, but I hope the Lord will deleaver me; but they are most cruelly bent against me."

From February 1643, to July, the danger of investment was gradually drawing nearer, until at last the Castle was summoned to surrender on the 25th of July. The siege began the next day, under the command of Sir William Vavasour, and continued for seven weeks. Meanwhile, all the timber in the parks had been destroyed by the besiegers, and the flocks and herds belonging to the Harleys consumed. The whole village was plundered and burnt, and even the church utterly wrecked; and the fury of the Royalists was so senseless and brutal that their very advent was marked by the wanton murder of a blind man who met them upon the road to the Castle.

But so active had been this little garrison of a hundred men, commanded by a woman, that all efforts to take the place failed and the besiegers retired for a while, leaving Lady Harley victorious indeed, but dying from the anxieties of the defence. She died in the October following, when only forty-three years of age; one of that little band of distinguished ladies of either party, who throughout those stirring times won renown by their defence of hearth and home. Lady Bankes, the defender of Corfe Castle; Blanche, Lady Arundel, who held the Castle of Wardour; Lady Wintour of Lydney, and the Countess of Derby's heroic defence of Latham House, are memorable on the Royalist side.

The portrait of Lady Brilliana Harley does not present to us the features of a resolute and steadfast commander, but rather the conventional female face of her time, seen so often repeated in the paintings of that courtly artist, the Hollander, Sir Peter Lely, who surely was the most consummate flatterer and unblushing beautifier of distinguished womenkind who ever lived, and altogether the most un-Dutchman-like Hollander of his or any other age.

Brampton Bryan was, however, not yet done with sieges, for shortly after Lady Harley's death, the Royalists returned and lay closely round the castle for three weeks. At the end of that time the garrison, commanded by Dr. Wright, a physician in the employ of the Harley family, capitulated and were taken as prisoners to Shrewsbury. Sixty-seven prisoners were thus disposed of, and two barrels of gunpowder, together with one hundred stand of arms were captured at the same time. The Royalists, determined that Brampton should never again be a trouble to them, set fire to the castle and destroyed utterly all the books and rare manuscripts which the taste and learning of the Harleys had collected in the course of many years.

This is the extreme north-western corner of Herefordshire. Just to the other side of Brampton comes Shropshire and the rugged country of the Forest of Clun; a district, despite its name, comparatively treeless. Here are small castles, dotted up and down the criss-cross valleys and bleak hilltops; chief among them the ruins of Clun Castle.

Clun Castle is supposed to have been built by Picot de Say, Doomsday Lord of the Manor. In the reign of Henry II., Isabel, the last of the Says, married three husbands in succession, William Fitz Alan of Oswestry, Geoffrey de Vere, and William Botterall. In 1195, while Botterall was holding the barony of Clun, the castle was stormed and burnt by Rhys, a petty Welsh prince, and in 1216, in consequence of the rebellion of John Fitz Alan, King John led an army to besiege it. Again, in 1234, the Welsh, under Llewellyn, appeared before the place and burnt the town. So it will be seen that the history of Clun is not without its dramatic episodes. An Inquest of the date of 1272 says:—" At Clun is a certain small castle, competently built," but its state, so the document goes on to say, was decayed. Leland says that in his time it was "somewhat in ruines. It hath been both stronge and well builded. By Clun is a great forest full of redde dere and rooes."

The Inquisition just quoted contains a passage by which it seems that one William Kempe held a messuage and croft

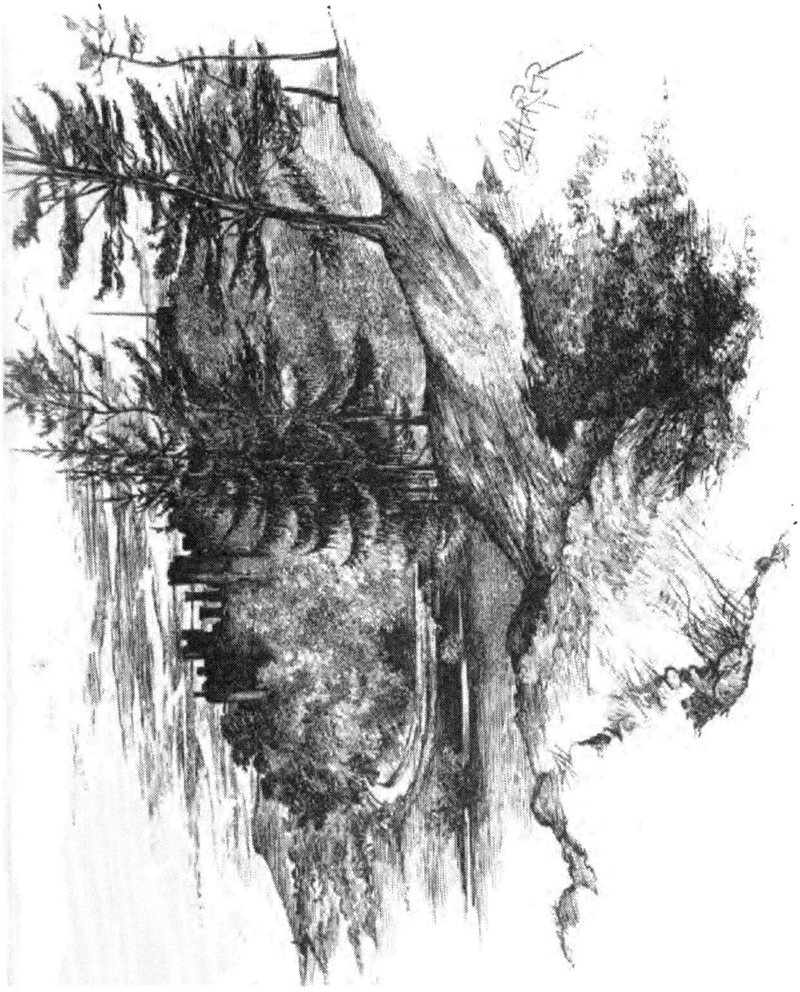

by the tenure of carrying the heads of felons to Shrewsbury. The explanation of this singular tenure lies in one of the peculiar privileges and immunities of the Lord of Clun as a Lord Marcher. A criminal captured in his lordship, and tried and condemned at Shrewsbury, could not by the laws under which the Marches existed, be executed outside that territory in which he was arrested. The Lord Marcher sent his own officer to fetch the culprit for execution, but he was obliged subsequently to send back the head in order to prove that justice had been done. William Kempe and his heirs, therefore, held their croft from the Lord of Clun as carriers of a particularly unpleasant kind of voucher for the good faith of their over-lord toward the law-officers of the Crown, resident at Salop.

Hopton Castle, a small, but at one time strong tower, stands in a singularly weak position in a deep and narrow valley between Clun and Brampton Bryan. Its history was insignificant enough until 1644, when it endured a fortnight's siege by the Royalists, who proceeded from Ludlow Castle under Sir Michael Woodhouse. The defence was desperate and stubborn, but the tower was so small, the garrison so few, and the position so worthless, that no excuse could be offered for the obstinate and misguided refusal of Samuel More, the Governor, to surrender to an overwhelmingly superior force when originally summoned. The garrison was at length compelled to surrender through the approach of starvation to the mercy of the Royalists, but it had been better for them to have died fighting, sword in hand to the last, rather than to have yielded to the merciless and inhuman Irish allies of the Royalists, who seized the unfortunate wretches, tied them back to back, and cruelly murdered every one but the Governor, whom they took prisoner to Ludlow Castle.

We had the good fortune to be offered a lift in a trap all the way to Ludlow, as we tramped wearily back through this rough country to Wigmore. No more tempting offer than this could have been made at the time; we closed with it, and came, as the sun was sinking, in view of the castle, surrounded with lofty trees, its turrets standing black against the sky, and the twinkling lights of the town appearing one by one as daylight died away. And so we came into Shropshire.

XL.

SHROPSHIRE is one of the wealthiest counties in England, and its county society remains amongst the most aristocratic and exclusive of provincial circles. The "proud Salopian" is proverbial here no less than the "Essex Calf" and the "Wiltshire Moonrakers" in their territories, or the Cockney in London.

In Shropshire the Squire died perhaps a harder death than in any other part of the kingdom, and here old usages, old traditions and old dialects have survived even to this day, when London has become the bounds of the Salopian horizon, whether for county magnate or farm-hand, instead of Shrewsbury, which used to be the Metropolis, not only of the shire, but of their lives and thoughts. London, except to a very few, was beyond their ken. For business they went to Shrewsbury, and for pleasure and "a change" to Ludlow. Those were the relative positions of the two towns from three hundred to one hundred years ago. County business was transacted at Shrewsbury, and it was the place whence came most of the out-of-the-way requirements of the moneyed class. The Court of the Marches held its greatest state at Ludlow, and thither flocked the fashionables who knew naught of Bath or any other resort outside their all-sufficient county.

The land of Shropshire is rich and fertile; the scenery varied from plains to mountains; and rivers are in plenty from the Severn, to the Teme, the Onny, the Corve, and the numerous brooks that make Corvedale and Coalbrookdale so green and pleasant. They flow through meadow-lands and through gorges of limestone and sandstone crags, on which, as in some Rhine-land, are perched baronial castles, now for the most part far gone in decay—a rich and pleasant land, indeed, where farmers grew fat, and landlords flourished, and tradesfolk and others thrived in times

DERELICT FARMS.

before agricultural depression fell upon the land and easy and rapid transit took away local trade, and sent every Tom, Dick and Harry up to London.

Times are very changed. Land is going rapidly out of cultivation, both because of foreign competition in wheat growing, and of the growing luxury and laziness of the farming class. Every tenant-farmer aspires to the expenditure, if not the manners, of a gentleman, and delegates to bailiffs and understrappers the work which his father and grandfather would have done with their own hands, or under their direct supervision. When the tenant-farmer of to-day who farms from five hundred to a thousand acres condescends to go to market at all, he drives into the town in a smart dog-cart, attired in the most expensive clothes of sporting cut, and puts up at the first hotel in the town. He attends the sheep and cattle market, where he meets others of his kidney, and after an hour's desultory business the whole crew adjourn to a costly lunch, order champagne in plenty, and damn the expense, like lords. So, with the farm-bailiff growing fat on perquisites and sharp practices; with expensive living, and the dairy-work handed over to hired servants instead of being performed by his wife and daughters, farming does not pay. The farmer clamours then for reduction of rent. He gets a ten per cent. relief and presently calls for more and more, until his landlord, who also has grown more luxurious, finds himself bound to refuse. Then the farm goes out of cultivation, and burdocks, thistles and choking weeds eat up all the goodness of the fallow land. The farm-hands lose their employment and are, some of them, driven to the shelter of the workhouse, while the younger and more vigorous come up to London to swell the ranks of the unemployed and the heavy poor's rates of the long-suffering London ratepayer.

The Census returns are eloquent of these processes of evolution from a cultivated county to a wilderness of weeds and brambles; from prosperous villages to decaying hamlets in whose streets the grass grows and round whose borders the stoat and weasel and vermin of every kind increase and multiply. The hedgerows are creeping inwards upon the deserted fields; the watercourses, drains and runnels are choked up for want of attention, and the meadows of these derelict estates are thus being surely converted into morasses where instead of sweet pastures grow the rank and poisonous grasses that flourish in swampy and undrained levels. Is England to become once more a forest, and is the wolf to come again?

The neighbouring counties of Shropshire and Herefordshire afford an insight to this state of things. The census of 1881 showed a population for Shropshire of nearly twelve thousand more than were returned ten years later, and Herefordshire, which has rather less than half the population of the sister county, revealed a decrease of over five thousand in the same period. The rural districts show a heavy decrease, while the small towns remain either stationary or have slightly decayed, and the two large centres—the town of Shrewsbury and the city of Hereford—have increased very slightly (and, singularly enough, in the same ratio):—

Shropshire	1881	248,022	
,,	1891	236,324	
		11,698	Decrease.
Shrewsbury	1881	26,481	
,,	1891	26,967	Increase 486.
Ludlow	1881	5,035	
,,	1891	4,460	
		575	Decrease.
Herefordshire	1881	121,249	
,,	1891	115,986	
		5,263	Decrease.
Hereford City	1881	19,821	
,,	1891	20,267	Increase 446
Leominster	1881	6,044	
,,	1891	5,675	
		369	Decrease.

XLI.

FOLLOWING our plan throughout this tour of taking up our quarters for a time at an attractive centre and making daily excursions from it to outlying places of interest, we stayed awhile at Ludlow, going forth in early morning and returning when day was done to sit in sweet gossip with friends of old standing. Sitting over the fire (for nights were chill) we were told strange tales of errant townsfolk: how the town toper, Jacky Crucis, possessed of devils and strong drink, had lain down to sleep one night upon the highway at Bromfield and only escaped certain death by the fact of a cyclist upsetting over him in the darkness, who, Samaritan-like, conveyed him home. Also of the great burial controversy that had divided the town into opposing factions; and again, how Benson the curate had eloped with an actress; and how—but these be scandals!

Ludlow occupied a fortified and central position in the Marches, and here and in the immediate neighbourhood were situated the strongest castles of the Borders: the fortresses of Wigmore, Richard's Castle, Brampton Bryan, Bishop's Castle; the strongly defended town and castle of Shrewsbury, and many embattled residences of the type of Stokesay. On every hand were means of defence, and these advanced posts of the Norman were fully needed; for, ever and again, the wild Welshmen, headed by some Llewellyn or Tudor, or Ap Howell, came streaming over the ragged and uncertain frontiers with fire and sword, into that fair land of England from which the Teutonic hordes of the Heptarchy had driven their fathers. This, which had been an outlying portion of the Saxon kingdom of Mercia, was in the forefront of the attack, and suffered periodically from these irruptions.

There does not seem to have been any fortified post established here, either before or at the time immediately following upon the Norman conquest, for there is no mention of Ludlow in Doomsday Book, beyond particulars that are given of three places named Lude in this neighbourhood, one of which is supposed to refer to the future Ludlow. The word Lude is considered to have denoted a ford: thus at this day we have in the village of Ludford a name whose two syllables bear an identical and repetitive meaning. Osberne Fitz Richard held one Lude at the time of the Doomsday Survey, and it was probably in his day that the termination "low" was adopted to distinguish his property from the other two Ludes. This termination came readily enough from a remarkable mound or "low," probably a sepulchral tumulus, that stood in those days and until 1190 on the site of St. Lawrence's Church in the centre of the town.

Fitz Richard had a tenant of his holding at Lude—one Roger de Lacy, who eventually purchased the lordship and erected a castle here in the decade between 1086-1096. He had not long commenced his building when he is found in rebellion against Rufus on behalf of Rufus' brother, Robert Courthose, Duke of Normandy. He seems by some means to have made his peace with the King, only to break out again in 1195, when he was exiled and died in a foreign land. Rufus did not, as usually done, seize upon the estates, but allowed Lacy's brother, Hugh, to succeed to them. He, however, died childless, and the property fell to the Crown, to be granted shortly afterwards by Henry I. to a knight named Pagan Fitz John who already held a portion of the Lacy estates at Ewias Lacy. Some years later he was slain in an encounter with the Welsh.

Stephen who at that time occupied the throne then seized upon the castle and placed a creature of his own, one Joyce de Dinan, in it; and he, having greatly enlarged and strengthened the already formidable fortress, promply lost it to Gervase Paganel, a powerful rebel, who, acting in concert with the border Barons, surprised the King's castellan and held the place successfully against all the forces that Stephen in person could bring to a siege. A tale is told of this obstinate leaguer, by which it seems that Prince Henry of Scotland, who was a hostage in Stephen's camp, was within an ace of being captured by the garrison of Ludlow Castle. He was incautiously walking too near the walls when a grapnel was

Sieges of Ludlow Castle.

suddenly lowered, seizing him by the shoulder. The King by the exercise of his great strength managed to unhook the Prince while the enemy was in the act of hauling him up.

This unsuccessful siege took place in 1139. In 1150 we find that Stephen was in possession of the castle, and shortly afterwards Joyce de Dinan was again installed there. The unsettled conditions of life upon the borders are shown very clearly by the petty warfare that now ensued between Joyce and Hugh Mortimer of Wigmore. The Lord of Wigmore so beset the neighbourhood of Ludlow with his men that Joyce de Dinan could not leave the castle without fear of being made prisoner, so, to end this uncomfortable state of things and to be revenged for certain injuries, he laid an ambush for his persecutor, took *him* prisoner and confined him within a tower of the inner ward that is known to this day as Mortimer's Tower. It was only by the payment of a heavy ransom that Hugh de Mortimer regained his liberty, but, considering the temper of the times, it seems a strange thing that he escaped death within that prison-tower.

But troublous times were in store for Joyce de Dinan. A certain Hugh de Lacy laid claim to lands in Herefordshire held by him, and also considered the castle of Ludlow to be his by collateral descent from that other Hugh de Lacy who had died some fifty years before. These claims led to a succession of sanguinary contests between the principals and friends on either side, and when Hugh was obliged to cross the St. George's Channel to look after his lordships in Ireland, he left his son, Walter de Lacy, to carry on the quarrel.

One morning Joyce de Dinan arose with the lark, as was his wont—if we may believe the lying minstrels who earned a precarious living by grossly flattering the knights at whose board they sat,—and pacing the battlements of his castle of Ludlow suddenly beheld a great concourse of knights and men-at-arms gathered on Whitcliff and threatening his fortress. Among the banners fluttering in the breeze he observed that of Walter de Lacy, and beheld with dismay his advance guard already crossing Dinham Bridge, that then, as now, leads directly up to the castle. Immediately he roused his people and sent a number of horsemen, together with archers and others, to defend the road, while he prepared to attack the enemy in force. These skirmishers held de Lacy's men in check until Joyce at the head of five hundred mounted knights and men-at-arms, reinforced by the valiant townsmen of Ludlow, swept down upon the scene and utterly routed the invaders. Joyce himself pursued Walter de Lacy along the banks of the Teme in the direction of Bromfield and engaged him in single combat in which his opponent was like to have been killed, until three knights suddenly came to de Lacy's assistance and held him at bay.

Meanwhile, the ladies of the castle had been anxiously watching the progress of events from the battlements and made the place resound with their lamentations when they beheld this untoward rencontre. The only man left in the Castle was Joyce's ward, Fulke Fitz Warine, and he was but eighteen years of age. Hearing their cries, he came along the tower where they stood and asked the reason of them. "Hold thy tongue," replied Joyce's daughter, Hawyse; "thou resemblest little thy father of Whittington who is so bold and strong: thou art but a coward and ever will be. Seest thou not where my father, who has cherished thee and bred thee with such care, is in danger of his life for want of help? while thou art not ashamed to go up and down, safe, without paying any attention." This vehement reproof so spurred on young Fitz Warine to action that, rushing into the armoury, he seized a rusty old helmet and a great Danish axe, and, mounting a cart-horse, dashed across the river to where Joyce de Dinan, already dismounted by his assailants, was about to receive his *coup de grace*. Arrived here, he performed prodigies of valour, cleaving in two with his axe the backbone of one knight, and splitting in half the skull of another. The knight of Ludlow was now enabled to regain his feet, and between them they secured Walter de Lacy and the remaining horseman, Arnold de Lisle, who, both severely wounded, were brought to the castle and imprisoned in one of its towers.

THE KEEP, LUDLOW CASTLE.

THE NEW YORK
PUBLIC LIBRARY

ASTOR, LENOX
TILDEN FOUNDATION

These two prisoners were treated with a kindness which, all things considered, seems to have been altogether out of place. They were visited in their captivity by the ladies of the castle, and a certain Marion de la Bruere was so enthralled by the grace and romantic misfortunes of de Lisle that she allowed herself to be seduced by him, and gave aid to both the prisoners in their plans for escape. They swung themselves down from their tower one dark night by the aid of a rope fashioned with towels and napkins tied together, and de Lacy, communicating with his father in Ireland, recommenced the struggle between the two Houses. Peace was, however, restored for a time by the good offices of the neighbouring lords, and the occasion was celebrated by the marriage of Fulke Fitz Warine to the scornful Hawyse. The wedding party departed for Hertland (wherever that may have been) and Ludlow Castle was left in charge of some thirty knights and seventy soldiers, "for fear of the Lacy and other people."

This fear was only too well founded, for Marion de la Bruere, who had been left behind in pretended ill-health, sent a message to her knight, inviting him to visit her in the absence of Joyce de Dinan and his friends. He was to be admitted secretly at night by the window in the tower from which he and his friend had already escaped. She had no thought of treachery to her friends, but the opportunity for revenge was communicated by de Lisle to his friend Walter de Lacy, and a plot was formed between them for capturing the castle. De Lisle charged himself with carrying out the plot. He procured a leathern ladder, and, coming quietly by night into the neighbourhood of Ludlow with a large party of horsemen, he posted the greater number of them in the woods of Whitcliff and concealed a number of foot-soldiers in the gardens beneath the castle walls. When all was in readiness he approached the trysting-place with an attendant carrying his ladder. His lady-love was ready and helped to draw it up to the window; he entered and the ladder was left dangling to the ground. In the small hours of the morning, while Arnold de Lisle and his mistress slept in an adjoining apartment, a hundred men, as previously arranged, ascended the ladder and made themselves masters of the place. The sentinel, asleep at his post, was very properly cast into the fosse, where his back was broken and he perished miserably; the little garrison was slain, even to the last man, as they lay asleep in their beds; and then the castle gates were opened to admit the larger party of conspirators. That was an ill night for Ludlow, town and castle alike, for the townsfolk were massacred without mercy and the town was burnt. Not until daybreak did Marion de la Bruere awake to this foul treachery, but when she realized the horrors that had been wrought, she seized the sword of her faithless lover and slew him as he lay asleep, casting herself in an agony of despair from the window of her room on to the rocks below, where her neck was broken.

When Walter de Lacy heard of this success, he came and took possession of the castle in force, intending to hold it against all attacks. He had not long to wait before Joyce de Dinan came, with a great army of seven thousand men, and opened a determined siege. They established their base of operations at Caynham, two miles from Ludlow, and for a time contrived to draw numbers of the garrison from Ludlow Castle into open ground, where they were continually defeated and numbers slain. These losses compelled de Lacy to shut himself up entirely within the castle walls, but even here he was followed to such good purpose that the great doorway of the gatehouse was attacked and burnt with the aid of a bonfire made of bacon and grease. The besiegers then carried the outer ward, but were compelled to retire before a host of no less than twenty thousand Welshmen, led by one of the Welsh chieftans whom de Lacy, finding himself on the point of surrender, had invited to his aid. They fought at Caynham against these desperate odds, but were defeated. Joyce was taken prisoner and lodged in durance in his own castle of Ludlow; his son-in-law was severely wounded and barely escaped with life from the field. Hurrying to Gloucester, where the king was staying,

Fulke enlisted the royal sympathy, and de Lacy was commanded to set his prisoners free.

With the death of Joyce, which happened shortly afterwards at Lambourne, the castle seems to have been granted to his son-in-law, but in the reign of King John we find Walter de Lacy paying four hundred marks into the Exchequer to be reinstated at Ludlow. This was in 1206. In the next year John seized the castle, and placed successive castellans in charge until, in 1214, he directed Ingelram de Cygoigne to hand it over to de Lacy. Finally Walter de Lacy died (and he must have been a very old man indeed) in 1241, leaving his estates to his grandson, Walter, who died a minor, leaving two sisters to share the property. Matilda, the elder, married firstly Peter de Geneva, and secondly, Geoffrey de Geneville. Geoffrey held the castle and half the manor in right of his wife, and had a son, Peter de Geneville, to whom the estate would appear to have been transferred by deed of gift in his parents' lifetime. His daughter, Johanna, married Roger Mortimer, afterwards first Earl of March, who thus brought the Ludlow property into this already richly-dowered House.

Ludlow Castle remained the property of the Mortimers and their successors for one hundred and eighty years. In the last twenty-four years of this period it became Crown property upon the accession of Edward IV., and when the last representative of the Mortimer blood fell in the person of Richard III. it continued in the keeping of the Crown, and so remained until quite recent times. During the last century the building was leased to the Powis family, and the freehold was finally purchased by the Earl of Powis in 1811, to whose successors it still belongs.

XLII.

THE *political* history of Ludlow Castle, as apart from the merely domestic blood-feuds of these jealous barons, commences with the reign of Edward IV. in 1461. To thoroughly understand the immense importance of Ludlow, we must do no less than trace the origin and progress of the Marches from the Saxon invasion until the Revolution of 1688; which at once saved this country from Popery and wooden shoes, and gave the final blow in a series of attacks upon the semi-regal government of the Marches.

About the year 585 A.D., the Anglian chief, Crida, crossed the Severn, and, subduing the tribes who occupied the lands between that river and the Wye, founded the kingdom of Mercia, the frontier province between the Angles and the British. The village of Credenhill still by its name bears witness to his prowess and to one of many great battles fought in the conquest of this neighbourhood. But here the tide of conquest stayed awhile, for during six generations of constant warfare the British had regained the self-reliance and skill in arms which they had lost during the Roman occupation of the country, and, moreover, they had been at last driven against the wall of these Welsh hills and mountains which enabled them to offer a stubborn and tolerably successful resistance to further aggression.

Thus first arose the name from which, in later years, the "Marches" of Wales derived, whence the English earldom of March sprang and the title of marquis originated. The Kingdom of Mercia was, in the language of the Teutons, the "meorc", or mark between two alien nations; its name was, more than that of any other of the seven kingdoms of the Heptarchy, an expression of political rather than of physical geography.

Not only in this island was the term of "Mercia" known. The political exigencies of Continental tribes and nationalities entailed its use, which occurs in many protean forms in Europe, where the frontiers of hostile races "march" together. The expression meant essentially the mark or margin—the demarcation—between races, and the modern political slang term of "buffer state" very clearly expresses the conditions under which our English Mercia existed when first its name came into use. Applications of the same term occur in other parts of this country; the Staffordshire village of Marchington, for instance, and the Cambridgeshire town of March, which "marked" the boundary-line between the Saxons and the Danes, are but examples taken at random of its widespread use.[1]

In Europe, the provinces of Marche, in France; of Marcia, in Spain; the country of Den*mark*; the districts of Germany, ruled in bygone times by the Markgraves, may be cited. Dukes and Earls of Mercia were known in Saxon times, but it was not until after the Norman Conquest that the Lords Marchers came into existence.

The early Norman sovereigns of England were divided between a care for the Crown of this country and an eager desire to retain the Dukedoms and Lordships that lay over-sea in Normandy. They continually oscillated between England and France, putting down family rebellions and popular uprisings, and the story of their lives is one long tale of harassing endeavours to hold their own. Thus it was that they had no time nor forces available for keeping in check the Welsh, who, pent up beyond Offa's Dyke by the Saxons, used every effort to cross that boundary whose very existence they looked upon as a standing mark of degradation and shame, and lay waste the fertile lands of England that had once been theirs. The Norman kings had not sufficient power to stop these inroads, but they were second to none in cunning, and soon devised a means of protecting the borders without cost to themselves. Their hungry lords and knights had been rewarded for their part at Hastings by grants of manors innumerable throughout England; but the appetite of these earth-hungry soldiers was insatiable, and so, to at once protect the borders against the Welsh and to throw a sop to their turbulent nobles, the kings of England granted to such of them as held lordships on the frontier a license, in general terms, to hold from the Crown "all that they could conquer from the Welsh." The tables were thus turned against the Welsh chieftains with a vengeance. Instead of compelling the

---

[1] Other English examples are Marchwood, near Eling, in Hampshire; Marksbury, and Mark, in Somersetshire; Markington, and Markingfield, in Yorkshire; Markby, Lincolnshire; and East and West Markham, Notts.

frontier barons to take a defensive attitude, they were themselves obliged to be ever on the alert to prevent these rapacio land-grabbers from seizing upon their domains, for th roving commissions thus granted to the barons were nothing less than royal licences for spoliation, robbery and murder, of which they were not slow to avail themselves, nor over particular in the means employed to attain their ends.

The Norman nobles who thus settled on the borders of Wales early acquired the title of Lords Marchers (*Marchiones Marchiae Walliae* in the Red Book of the Exchequer) long before the title of Marquess—introduced in the reign of Richard II.—existed amongst the nobility of England. The ostensible function of a marquess was to guard the limits or frontiers of a kingdom, but the brunt of that not wholly uncongenial duty fell upon the earlier Lords Marchers, who were barons merely. Nominally, they were subject to the jurisdiction of the Warden of the Marches, who held his appointment from the Crown; but his control was necessarily of the feeblest kind. Here, however, the subtlety of the kings stepped in, by the conferment of seats in Parliament upon these powerful lords, who, flattered and blinded by their representative rank, failed to see the hold which their Parliamentary duties gave the Crown over them. Frequently they also held lordships in England in places remote from the Marches, and in those cases the Crown compelled their obedience through pain of forfeiture. But in the Marches they were absolute; whenever one of these adventurers had succeeded in plundering an unfortunate Welshman of his estate, he immediately assumed all, and perhaps greater, power over his tenants or vassals than had been exercised by the native prince. The domestic affairs of the Marches were the particular and exclusive business of these barons; each lordship was autonomous and all internal quarrels were settled before its lord. The Lords Marchers were for many years the most powerful of the English nobles; they married even into the royal family, and, emboldened by their great possessions and their numerous tenantry, who under the feudal system were bound to fight under the banner of their over-lord, aspired even to the Crown of England.

They conferred charters, couched in regal style, upon the towns which grew up around their castles, appointed chancellors and judges within their territories, and in every way conducted themselves as independent sovereigns, not infrequently setting the power of the King at defiance. The King's writ did not run in their dominions, which were not shire-ground: consequently, every rogue and assassin who could escape from English justice, made at once for shelter there and remained safe from arrest, moving from one Lordship to another as occasion required. Extradition was not even thought of, for the Marchers were exceedingly jealous of their privileges, and if by chance one of them had been prepared to hand over a criminal to the King's officers, that felon had only to cross into the estates of another Border ruffian to evade pursuit; for although the Lords Marchers were at one in resistance to kingly authority they were not less ready to resent a neighbour's interference. In this way the Marches became an Alsatia where no man's life or property was safe. These lords paramount were lords of life and death, and entitled to the goods of their tenants who died intestate; what then, more easy, when inclination and interest served, than to provide for sudden and mysterious deaths and for intestacy?

Petty warfare between rival Marchers added to the horrors of the times, for the disputes that were continually occurring, instead of being submitted to the suzerain for settlement were put to the arbitration of the sword whenever the contending parties felt themselves strong enough to treat this authority with contempt.

The Lords Marchers erected a chain of castles along the borders, from the Severn to the Dee, both for defensive and aggressive purposes; to fulfil the different functions of shelters and advance-posts whence they might with impunity blackmail the Welsh. These strongholds of the Norman are exceedingly numerous, and were originally of a strong but extremely simple character, consisting merely of a single square tower of immensely thick walls, the entrance and the windows placed at a considerable height from the ground, and the basement of such cyclopean solidity as to defy all attacks upon it. This keep was the entire castle of the early Norman period. To this early type of fortress many additions were made in the great castle-building era of King Stephen, but it was not until the Edwardian period that the spreading wards, curtain-walls and outward towers, the great fosses and earthworks, were introduced that brought the mediæval castle to its highest development.

The castles of Gloucester, Shrewsbury, and Chester were representatives of the main line of important strongholds erected by William's barons. These formed a rear-guard; in advance of them stood the castles of Striguil (or Chepstow), Monmouth, Hereford, Chirk, Hawarden, Flint, Montgomery and others, all erected within fifty years of the Conquest, and each originally consisting of the typical early Norman keep, built on a mound and surrounded with a fosse.

The limits of the Marches were for ever fluctuating. Even so late as 1263, towards the end of Henry III.'s long reign, the Welsh invaded and laid waste all the lands almost as far as Weobley, Eardisley and Wigmore, capturing the Marchers' castles and bringing fire and sword even to the walls of Hereford.

Our Afghanistan experiences, and our constantly-recurring little wars with the hill-tribes who make the northern frontiers of India a continual scene of strife, furnish us moderns with an exact parallel to the thirteenth-century Border warfare between the English and the Welsh. In both cases the stronger power had to contend with not only a fierce and fearless race, but with the rugged impediments which nature had strewn so thickly in the debateable lands. The Welsh had great advantages in their inhospitable mountains, and, so long as they were cunning enough to keep away from the lowlands, success was not wanting.

Their valour, however, on this occasion led them too far afield, and so their success was only temporary, for Henry III. advanced against them, aided by the Lords Marchers, who were for the time glad to co-operate with the King in order to save themselves. Roger, sixth Lord of Wigmore, was prominent in his loyalty and his son approved himself as loyal by sending the head of Llewellyn to London, where, crowned with a tinsel crown and carried on horseback to the city, a prophecy that he should ride into the capital crowned, was fulfilled in an unexpected way.

But the Marchers had for some time past looked askance upon the vigorous efforts made by the Crown to reduce the Welsh to subjection. Intriguing at one time with the Welsh princes, at another firmly allied to the King, they held— like an Irish party in Parliament to-day—the balance of power, and held it always for their own aggrandisement. They foresaw that the final subjugation of the Principality would mean the extinction of their own peculiar privileges, and therefore, even while outwardly aiding the King they were secretly in traitorous communication with his foes. This appeared upon the death of Llewellyn at Builth, for on the body of the Prince was found a note concealed in his sleeve and couched in obscure terms, with feigned names; from which it might be plainly gathered that certain noblemen on the borders of Wales were not well pleased with the King's proceedings.

With the death of Llewellyn ended the independence of Wales. The unhappy Welshmen, divided one against the other when not engaged with the Normans, had been unable to offer an adequate resistance to these lawless marauders. Had the native princes cordially united, they might have protracted the struggle and preserved their independence awhile,—if the anarchy and confusion in which the country was involved under so many petty tyrants could be called an independence worth possessing. Although we may admire the desperate valour and the heroic qualities of the Welsh chieftains, and regret the fate of Llewellyn, yet every impartial person who has studied the history of Wales cannot but acknowledge that its final subjugation by Edward I. was a blessing in disguise for the people at large, by rendering their despotic and turbulent rulers amenable to the King of England, and finally to the English laws, and thus ending the party feuds and petty mountain warfare which had for long kept the country in a welter of blood and ruins.

Upon Llewellyn's death Edward, by the Statute ot Rhuddlan, divided the country into shires, and into these newly-formed provinces introduced many English laws and customs. The acquisition of new Lordships Marchers was rendered impossible, since the Crown had assumed authority over Wales, and consequently no more land remained for the barons to win by force of arms. One hundred and forty-one of these lordships existed at this date in the strip of country extending from Chepstow to Chester, and even penetrating in some places to the heart of Wales.

From this period (1284) dates the ruin of many of the Border castles, especially of those which had been built purely for strategic purposes. They served no longer as outposts against an independent power, and so had outlived their usefulness. But the case of fortress-residences, such as those of Chepstow, Wigmore, Monmouth and Ludlow, was very different. Within castles of this type was now concentrated the Marchers' strength, unimpaired, and indeed consolidated by the new departure of the Crown in conquests; for the advanced line of defence now beginning to prove unnecessary, the energies and treasure expended in keeping large garrisons in outlying places were husbanded or employed in rendering still more formidable the fortress homes of the several Marcher Lords. This, indeed, was a new period in castle-building, and all the great residential castles show many additions and improvements made at this particular time.

The singularly bold and crafty policy of the English Crown had by the Statute of Rhuddlan finally put a limit to the extension of the Marches, but the power and wealth of the Lords Marchers were to continually increase for many years to come; for the Crown, though willing to strike at the independence of the class whom its necessities had in former reigns created, was not in a position to make away with their local jurisdiction. They continued to enjoy their almost sovereign privileges and immunities unimpaired for a further period of one hundred and eighty-five years, and not only suffered no curtailment of their authority, but waxed fat and powerful enough to dictate terms to their suzerain on occasions neither few nor far between.

Indeed, we see in the history of the Mortimers the gradual growth of the power and pretensions of the Marcher class fully shown. That family, the foremost and most thoroughly representative of their order, had come, first by conquest, then by inheritance, and lastly by marriage into the royal family, the richest and most powerful, the haughtiest and most influential of all the nobles whose ancestors had carved out estates for themselves by the sword drawn and used against the Welsh. They held their possessions, it is true, of the Crown, but the cruel irony of fate at length rendered this tenure not only nominal, but brought the Kings of England to that unlooked-for pass that they wore the Crown in fact, though not in theory, by favour of the House of Mortimer. Their relative positions were exactly reversed, and the successive blows inflicted on the Lancastrians by Edward Plantagenet, the heir of the Mortimers, at Mortimer's Cross and Towton shattered even the theory.

When, in 1461, the victor of Towton ascended the throne as Edward IV., the day of the Marchers had reached its apogee. He represented in his person the interests of those powerful lords, and his success was in great measure owing to them and to his tenantry, collected from the wide-spreading manors in the Marches that owned him as feudal chief.

But there is no such thing as political gratitude. The interests of Edward Plantagenet as king were altogether different from those of the same man as Earl of March. As King of England, he saw how inimical to him would be a continuance of the much-abused privileges of the Lords Marchers, and at the earliest possible moment he determined to undermine the power of the class from which he sprang. Deprived of his support, the Marchers could make little active protest against reform, for with his elevation to kingly rank, the Mortimer estates, at least one-third of the Border lordships, had become Crown property. The psychological moment, however, had not yet arrived, and it was not until eight years after his accession that Edward felt his position strong enough to set about a cherished scheme by which the king should be not only nominally but actually sovereign lord of England. The opportunity came in 1469, and in that year the office of Warden of the Marches was abolished and merged into a newly-constituted body called the Court of the Lord President and Council of the Marches of Wales, a powerful authority whose jurisdiction, extending through the hitherto lawless marchlands, was more firmly exercised than ever the Warden's had been. The good faith and loyalty of the Council was well assured, for its chief Court was held in Ludlow Castle, a princely building that stood in the very heart of the Mortimer country; and this assurance was redoubled when Edward's two sons were sent there under the guardianship of their maternal uncle, Earl Rivers, in 1472.

It was in great measure by the goodwill of the people rather than of the nobility that Edward had been able to obtain and hold his crown. To retain their affections and to flatter his own numerous tenantry into an enthusiastic loyalty, he created Edward, his eldest son, Prince of Wales in his earliest infancy, and to Ludlow he was sent, as an old chronicle says, "for justice to be doen in the Marches of Wales, to the end that by the authoritie of hys presence the wild Welshmenne and evill disposed personnes should refrain from their accustomed murthers and outrages."

For two hundred and nineteen years this Court existed, presided over by great nobles and many militant bishops from 1469 to 1688, in all the splendour and circumstance of royalty, but its real utility disappeared at an early stage of ts existence, in 1535, the twenty-seventh year of Henry 'III.'s reign, when the incorporation of this *Imperium in*

THE COURT OF THE MARCHES.

Imperio, the Marches, with the adjoining English and Welsh counties was effected, thus finally ending the misrule of the absolute and evilly-despotic Lords Marchers.

But though now in great measure merely ornamental, the Council of the Marches made a brave show of authority for many years afterwards, and the Court of Ludlow was kept up in great style far into the times of the Puritans. The

LUDFORD BRIDGE AND THE CLEE HILLS.

superior members of the Court were, the Lord President, the Vice-President, and the Chief Justice, and among the Council were many of the nobility of the counties bordering on the Marches. The subordinate officers were, the Clerk of the Council, Clerk of the Signet, Keeper of the Castle, Gentleman Porter, Sergeants-at-Arms, messengers and others. The Court was held alternately at Shrewsbury and

Ludlow. This was at that time quite a metropolis, to which resorted wealth and fashion when the Court was in residence, and to this day, the reflex of its ancient state may be seen in the fine old mansions with which the town still abounds; plain even to severity in their frontages of Georgian red brick, but beautiful within by reason of their fine old English woodwork, much of it as old as the times of the Tudors. There is one house in especial, a corn-chandler's, in Castle Street; uninteresting outside, but with rooms panelled from floor to ceiling with carved oak, black with age.

Ludlow Castle was held for Charles I. by Sir Michael Woodhouse, but was surrendered, with but little fighting, to the Roundheads, and the Council of the Marches was suspended until the Restoration. From 1661 to 1688 it was revived, but its authority had been greatly weakened by the corrupt practices of its law-officers, and the almost fruitless efforts of suitors in its courts to obtain redress from the injustices of the powerful and wealthy nobles who bribed its officials of every rank with the most shameless and cynical publicity. The pitiful petitions of dwellers in the Marches for better government were at last acceded to, and among the first public acts of William III. was the abolition of this ancient Court.

XLIII.

LUDLOW is a town of memories, of historical wraiths and shadows and moving visions. Also it is a place wherein the tongue of gossip and scandal never ceases out of the land. Therefore, you who delight in social signs and portents should not fail of becoming well acquaint with this typical English county town of an era before railways were dreamed of. It will entertain the cynic hugely, it will afford a calm retirement to the philosopher; to the antiquarian it will—but why recount the varied interests of it? See Naples and die (of its intolerably bad sanitation): visit Ludlow and live

A Town of Character.

a life which has no excitements and few worries. If I were so ill-advised as to set about the writing of a novel in which little social peculiarities were to find a place, I would, for choice, make Ludlow a social observatory from which to note the lives and habits of its inhabitants. Or, to change the figure, I would subject them to the searching investigation of the mental microscope! Then should I be the literary Lubbock of Ludlow! What joy to classify their infinite variety of mental attitude! With what scientific rapture one would embark upon their docketing and the division of them into classes and sub-classes! For Ludlow is a town of character. Not the coarse and vigorous character that impels to the doing of wild and fearsome things, but the character of the finer and—if you will have it so—the pettier shades: the feminine character.

Now, the consideration of these things fills the contemplative man with a mild surprise, for if he has read the history of the town he will know that its story is not only vigorous, but filled with all manner of lawless and fierce and savage doings, and its records are stained with many and most sanguinary spots and splashes. The Castle, whose many towers overlook the river Teme, has been in its time the scene of happenings that are, many of them, recorded in the history of this realm; but of the valour, the savagery of the deeds that have been wrought here, and of their untoward results of battle, murder and sudden death, we can, who live in this nineteenth century, form but the haziest of notions, who compass our enemies' destruction by other means than those which obtained with our delightful ancestors in the days when—as the shallower historians remark—"Might was Right!" as if Might would under any conceivable circumstances ever be anything else! Ludlow was excellently well situated for the purpose of defence before the invention of gunpowder and the introduction of ordnance. Since the conditions of warfare have become changed, its position is altered from strength to weakness; for from the heights of Whitcliff a shower of shot and shell could be poured into the town with such precision and certainty that it could not hope to hold out for an hour. The town and Castle are built upon a rocky eminence rising gradually from Corve Dale, and increasing in height until it reaches the banks of the river Teme, which flows past the town in a deep gorge, worn by the water through uncounted centuries in the limestone rock. The site upon which Ludlow is built is situated in Shropshire; the tall cliffs of Whitcliff that overlook the town are in the county of Hereford. All around are lands of great beauty and wonderful fertility, and numerous lesser streams flow into the greater Teme, which in its turn empties into the Severn, many miles away, below the City of Worcester. The Onny, the Lutwyche Brook and the Corve all fall into the Teme in the neighbourhood of Ludlow, the confluence of the Corve and Teme being situated just below the lofty Castle rock, which rises to a height of over one hundred feet directly from the level water meadows. Two bridges connect the town with the Herefordshire shore—that of Dinham, below the Castle, and Ludford Bridge at the Herefordshire village of Ludford, situated at the other end of the town. The town was walled and entered by strongly defended gateways, of which one only is left—that of Broad Gate—and in a much disfigured condition, being restored and plastered and finished with trumpery battlements in the sham, finicking gothic of the last century. The Teme, although a considerable river, is not navigable here, as it is normally too shallow, for one thing, and, for another, there are no less than four substantial weirs upon it within the space of half a mile. The roaring of these weirs upon still summer nights fills the air with a continual murmur, which in time of flood rises to an insistent angry shouting that fills the streets and alleys of the old town with strange and wonderful reverberations.

The greater part of Ludlow is comprised within five streets, Corve Street, Broad Street, Old Street, Mill Street, and Gaolford, this last now spelled Galdeford, for the proper satisfaction of modern and qualmish susceptibilities. Behind the timbered or Georgian red-bricked frontages of these streets there are, for the most part, quaint and fertile gar-

BROAD GATE, LUDLOW.

THE
PUBLIC

ASTOR

dens where, on sunny afternoons of summer and early autumn (but not in the early months of the year, for spring comes slowly down this way) the semi-rural dainty Phillises of this rustic town disport them with tennis; or, with an ineffable purring content to which neither you nor I, my friends of London, can ever attain, devote the happy hours to the due unravelling of the love-lorn plots of the lady novelist. For this old town and its like are the strongholds of storytellers of the sentimental cast. Ludlow is a Town of Girls, a place where it is always afternoon, a little world that wags not fiercely with bursts of hard work and the strong excitements of the metropolis; rather is it a spot in which to sport with Amaryllis in the shade. Ambition, the race for fame and gain, have no place here. For the ambitious, the suitors on fortune, and those who are in any way impatient of advancement, have hurried off to where these things may be struggled for by the strong with some chance of achievement. Hot blood, quick pulse, are scattered to all points of the compass, and Ludlow holds but little young manhood. Those who remain are of a phlegmatic temperament, and the many spinsters use them chiefly as blocks on which to sharpen their wits. Thus it is that the maidens of this idyllic town are adepts at flirting; indeed, it is to one of them that I owe a perspicuous definition of the term, and an enlightened differentiation between the two arts of flirting and spooning, far beyond the powers of lexicographers even of Doctor Johnson's calibre. Said she, "flirting is looking, spooning is touching." Need I say aught but that I was properly grateful for so luminous an explanation?

The oldest portion of Ludlow Castle is the Norman keep, probably the work of Roger de Lacy, built about 1090. It guards the entrance of the inner ward of the Castle and overlooks an extensive outer ward, now covered with a smooth lawn, but at one time a busy courtyard where knights exercised, and the hazards of the tourney were encountered. It is a grim and grey old building, this storied keep; with dungeons deep down in the basement, where many a wretched prisoner has ended his days in times gone by, and where many others have endured the milder rigours of the Lords Presidents of the Marches in more recent times.

Some of the curious Norman windows of this keep are still to be seen, but the character of this particular building was much altered in the sixteenth century. The chief apartments of the inner ward were built by that most haughty and flamboyant of all the Mortimers—Roger, first Earl of March. All of them are roofless now, and owe their ruin to that day when orders came from the Government of George I. in London, to strip the lead from the roofs. Decay soon set in upon the exposed timber, and the townsfolk, seeing how unregarded was the old place, plundered it of all its wainscoting and valuable fittings; and even did not hesitate to despoil the Norman chapel of its panelling, painted with the arms of the Presidents. That panelling is now to be seen in the peculiarly secular dining room of the Bull Inn.

In these roofless towers, all open to the sky, the haunt of owls and bats, and the chance pastures where ferns and wallflowers grow luxuriantly, the two Princes, Edward, Prince of Wales, and his younger brother, the sons of Edward IV., were residing under the care of their maternal uncle, Earl Rivers, when their father died. Their tragic deaths in the Tower of London, where they were murdered to gratify the ambition of their uncle, who thereby became Richard III., are well known. Here also lived Prince Arthur, eldest son of Henry VII., who held his princely Court here where the Mortimers once ruled. It was the most cherished wish of Henry, that this son should reign after him and revive the legendary glories of the famous British King after whom he had been named.

Henry Tudor, a Celt by his father's side, was, like all his imaginative and impulsive race, a dreamer of dreams, a builder of airy castles, where his Yorkist predecessors on the throne of England had been ruthless men of action, skilled in warfare, but devoid of any powers of idealization. His tastes were literary and artistic; under his care artists and men of learning flourished, and gothic architecture reached the flower and ultimate expression of its long growth. His gorgeous chapel in Westminster Abbey shows at once its culminating point, and the first strong evidences of the coming Renaissance. To him and his sympathies with all that was intellectual, we really owe the mental activity of Elizabeth's time, acknowledged to be the Augustan age of literature in England. Had he not fostered the Renaissance in this land, that brilliant period would have come in a later reign, and the Puritans had then deferred their coming to a time when a Cromwell had been impossible, and regicides guiltless of a monarch's blood. But these are speculations in the shadowy land of "might have been."

Prince Arthur was married at the age of fifteen, his bride being his senior by three years. The wedding ceremony took place in London, and immediately afterwards this youthful pair proceeded to Ludlow, where they held a splendid court, the like of which had never before been seen here. The wedding was described by a contemporary writer named Hall, and although it took place away from the town, a portion of his work may be quoted in this place, both to show how magnificent was the occasion and how ancient that high-flown style of writing of which the *Daily Telegraph* of our day is an exponent. Omitting the archaic spelling and the quaint terms of expression, one might be reading the morning paper's description of a modern Royal wedding. But hear him :—" Because I will not be tedious I passe over the wyse devices, the prudent speeches, the costly workes, the conninge portratures pratised and set forth in VII. goodly beautiful pageaunts erected and set up in diverse places in the citie. I leave also the goodly ballades, the swete armony, the musicall instruments, which sounded with heavenly noyse on every side of the strete. I omit farther, the costly apparel both of gold smythes worke and embroidery, the ryche jewelles, the massy chaynes, the stryvinge horses, the beautiful barbes, and the glitterynge trappes, lode with belles and spangles of golde. I pretermit also the ryche apparelle of the pryncesse, the straunge fashion of the Spanyshe nacion, the beauty of the Englishe ladyes, the goodly demeanoure of the young damosels, the amorous countenance of the lusty bachelers." And so forth. Do you not seem to have read this manner of thing at your breakfast table?

But the King's scheme for a glorious England to be ruled over by another Arthur was doomed to failure, for in his sixteenth year, and within four months from his marriage with Catherine of Aragon, Prince Arthur died in this Castle of Ludlow, and the seventh Henry was succeeded, seven years later, by Henry VIII., whose enthusiasm ran in other channels than those of his father. Prince Arthur lies buried in Worcester Cathedral, but two shrines which bear no inscriptions are shown in the nave of Ludlow Church, said to be in memory of him and of one of his esquires.

XLIV.

SOMETHING of the methods by which the lords of these mediæval castles inflicted punishments or extorted confessions may be guessed by a sight of the instruments of torture that are to be seen in Ludlow Museum. Here, among other devilish contrivances, are spiked iron collars, heavy fetters, and the terrible "branks"—an iron mask or helmet, moulded roughly to the shape of the head, with a screw affixed by which it could be drawn tightly upon the skull and frontal bones of an unhappy prisoner, crushing the head sufficiently to produce horrible agonies, though not forcibly enough to kill outright. Unlike an ordinary mask, the branks had no holes for the eyes, but contained simply concavities into which the wretched victim's eyes started under the violent pressure which a turn of the

WINDOW, LUDLOW CASTLE.

A License to Torture.

screw produced. When we come to consider that the hard-fought battles, the famous victories of the warfare of the middle ages, were followed by wholesale executions and such tortures as these instruments suggest, the chivalry that permitted such practices wears rather a sorry aspect. Even in great Elizabeth's time, that spacious and more enlightened age, tortures were freely applied. There still exists a significant document, the "Instructions to Sir Henry Sydney," which shows abundantly that moral suasion

LUDLOW CASTLE, 1789.
(*From an old print.*)

was not approved of then. It recites that "The said Lord President and Council, or those of them at least whereof the President shall be one, upon sufficient ground, matter, or cause, shall or may put any person accused and known, or suspected, of any treason, murder, or felony, to tortures when they shall think convenient, and that the cause shall apparently require, by their discretions."

The wording of these instructions, though singularly involved, is not sufficiently obscure to hide their full meaning. They prove the existence in the Castle of engines for maiming and torturing, and the discretionary power for their use seems thorough. But it is difficult, from what we know of Sidney, for us to believe that he took advantage of the latitude allowed him. He governed the Marches in the wise and firm spirit of his great predecessor, Roland Lee, Bishop of Coventry and Lichfield; he punished, with due severity, the malefactors and ruffians from whom the borders were never free; but his was no tyrannical rule, and he did not regard his discretionary powers, as others might have done, as commands to kill and maim without mercy.

Indeed, one of the most brilliant periods for Ludlow came in those comparatively recent times, when Sir Henry Sidney held this important and dignified post of Lord President of the Council of the Marches of Wales. Sidney was a wise counsellor, a just and valued officer of State, the holder of many other posts of power and responsibility, yet his seems to have been a no less gentle than lofty spirit. The yet more famous Sir Philip Sidney was his son, and a letter written to him by his father while he was at school at Shrewsbury remains to us:—

"I have received two letters from you," says he, "one written in Latine, the other in French, which I take in good part, and will you to exercise that practise of learning often; for that will stand you in most stead in that profession of life that you are born to live in. And since this is my first letter that ever I did write to you, I will not that it be all empty of some advices, which my natural care of you provoketh me to wish you to follow, as documents to you in this your tender age.

"Let your first action be the lifting up your mind to Almighty God by hearty prayer, and feelingly digest the words you speak in prayer, with continual meditation and thinking of Him to whom you pray, and of the matter for which you pray. . . . Be humble and obedient to your master, for unless you frame yourself to obey others, yea, and feel in yourself what obedience is, you will never be able to teach others how to obey you. . . . Well (my

SIR HENRY SIDNEY,
*Lord President of
the Council of
the Marches.*

little Philippe), this is enough for me, and too much, I fear, for you.

"Your loving father, so long as you live in the fear of God,
"H. SYDNEY."

It is a charming letter, better by far than any of those famous epistles—the Earl of Chesterfield's letters to his son, cynical, worldly, and hollow. But Sidney's mind was not of the cold and calculating nature that peeps from between the lines written by that mincing man of fashion, Philip Dormer.

This pious and courtly gentleman was trusted and employed alike by Edward VI., Mary, and Elizabeth—no mean tribute to his worth when we bear in mind the terrible vicissitudes of politics and religion in those three reigns. He held this appointment for twenty-seven years, and died at Worcester in the fifty-seventh year of his age. During his occupation he rebuilt and altered the structure of Ludlow Castle very largely, and an allusion to "the ingratitude of man," which he caused to be inserted in the inscription that appears over the great doorway, is supposed to have some reference to the bad faith of the Government which allowed him to undertake this work but refused to pay for it. The inscription is surmounted by the arms of Queen Elizabeth and of Sidney, and runs thus :—

"HOMINIBUS INGRATIS LOQUIMINI LAPIDES.
ANNO REGNI REGINAE ELIZABETHAE 23.
THE 22 YEAR COPLET OF THE PRESIDENCY OF
SIR HENRI SYDNEY
KNIGHT OF THE MOST NOBLE ORDER OF THE
GARTER ETC. 1581"

He was buried with his people at Penshurst, in Kent, the Queen whom he had served so well granting him a State funeral. His body was taken with much pomp and a numerous gathering of heralds and dignitaries to Worcester Cathedral, where it lay in state. Thence to Penshurst, accompanied by the officers of the Court of Ludlow and the principal domestics. It speaks something for the difficulties of travelling in those times when we learn that he died on the 5th of May and his funeral *cortège* only arrived at Penshurst on the 21st of June.

His heart was buried in the same tomb with his infant daughter, Ambrosia, in Ludlow Church. The leaden urn which contained it was shamefully stolen at some unknown

CASKET CONTAINING THE HEART OF SIR HENRY SIDNEY.

period, and was in the possession of some Leominster people many years ago. It was figured in the *Gentleman's Magazine* so far back as 1794.

A portrait of Sir Henry Sidney, robed and wearing a chain of office, hands down to our day the likeness of as loyal and high-spirited a gentleman as his age could show.

THE LORDS PRESIDENTS.

One can see in this portly and dignified presence the honest, straightforward character of the man, whose bluff and cheery features proclaim the typical Englishman; courteous without affectation, loyal without protestations of loyalty, and God-fearing in all his doings, caring not so much for creeds as for the dictates of his individual conscience.

Sir Henry Sidney was followed in the office of Lord President by his son-in-law, Sir Henry Herbert, Earl of Pembroke, who was succeeded by Lord Zouch, in 1601. Ralph, Lord Eure, held the post from 1607 to 1616; Lord Gerald, of Gerald's Bromley, to 1618; the Earl of Northampton, to 1630; and the Earl of Bridgwater from 1633 to his death in 1649. The last years of this nobleman's term of office were, however, passed in the time of the Commonwealth, and his was but an empty post during that period. The first years of his Presidency had been marked by great magnificence, and to them belongs the celebrated production of *Comus*, written by Milton for the Earl. The masque was founded upon the adventures of the Earl and his party, who, coming to Ludlow for the first time, were benighted and lost in Hay Woods. It was set to music and acted in the Great Hall of the Castle on Michaelmas Eve, 1634, by the Lord President's children and guests.

Ludlow seems to have been at this time, and after the return of Charles II., quite a notable literary centre, for when the Earl of Carbery was appointed Lord President in 1661, he brought with him as secretary and steward, Samuel Butler, who wrote a great portion of *Hudibras* in his rooms over the gateway beside the keep. Richard Baxter, the divine, lived for awhile at Ludlow when under the altogether worldly and inadequate tuition of the chaplain to the Council. Jeremy Taylor wrote his *Holy Dying* for the Earl of Carbery, plunged in grief for the death of his wife, who, years before, had been Lady Alice Egerton, daughter of the Earl of Bridgwater, and had acted in the gay scenes of *Comus* within these walls.

The Earl of Carbery died in 1672, and was succeeded by

the Duke of Beaufort, whose magnificent progresses through the Borders are recounted exhaustively by Master Thomas Dingley, one of his train on those sumptuous occasions. The Duke died in 1687, and the Earl of Macclesfield took his place.

In the person of Charles Gerard, first Earl of Macclesfield, this long line of governing peers and bishops came to no

MORTIMER'S TOWER.

unworthy end, for Gerard was a man of great parts and unshaken loyalty, and had been throughout his long life a commander of distinction. It was he who was for a time the scourge of the Parliamentarians in Wales and the Borders; before whom the garrisons of Cardigan, Cardiff, Kidwelly, Laugharne and Newcastle Emlyn had melted away, and who would surely have changed the issue of Naseby had his

CHARLES GERARD,
EARL OF MACCLES-
FIELD.

NEW YORK

forces reached that disastrous field in time. He had been twice severely wounded during the Civil War, but carried his restless energy and enthusiasm through the failure of the King's cause, and, flying to the Netherlands with others of the Cavaliers, plotted there continually for the Restoration. He was the author of a scheme by which his cousin, John Gerard, was to assassinate Cromwell; a plot that failed and ended in the beheading of John Gerard in the Tower.

When Charles II. returned to claim his own, Gerard took a prominent place in the King's progress to London, and his estates, which had been forfeited under the Commonwealth, were restored to him, together with the grant of a pension and many lucrative posts. He had been created Baron Gerard of Brandon, in Suffolk, in 1645, and chose that title, says Clarendon, somewhat curiously, for the reason "that there was once an eminent person called Charles Brandon, who was afterwards made a duke." This may afford a key to Gerard's character, which seems to have been both aspiring and tenacious. His portrait, if we may judge by the portraits of the seventeenth-century painters, shows him to have been thoroughly British and dogged in appearance, and one who, once embarked in a project would not readily withdraw. If he ever thought that the title of Brandon would eventually bring him a Dukedom, he was doomed to disappointment, for his creation as Earl of Macclesfield in 1679 marked his highest step in the Peerage.

But no sooner was he settled in his estates after the Restoration than he changed the scene of his combative qualities from the field to the courts of law and the House of Lords; and the legal battles that he fought were not less numerous than his military exploits. He was a friend of the Duke of Monmouth, and James II. issued a warrant for his apprehension, but he escaped in good time and passed three years of outlawry on the Continent only to return again with the winning side at the Revolution of 1688. In that year his sentence of outlawry was reversed and he was made a Privy Councillor, with the Lord Lieutenancies of Hereford, Monmouth, Gloucester, and North and South Wales, and was appointed

Lord President of the Marches. This last, however, he held but for a few months, for the office of Lord President and the Court of the Marches were abolished during the same year upon the petition of over twenty-eight thousand inhabitants of the Principality. Five years later, Jan. 7, 1694, he died, at a very great age. We do not know the year of his birth, but the date at which he was entered at Leyden University has come down to us, by which it seems that he was admitted as a student in 1633.

XLV.

For the rest, Ludlow town is interesting enough, apart from the Castle, and its great church of Saint Lawrence is one of the largest parish churches in England. There have been many buildings on its site, some destroyed to make way for larger edifices, others burnt and pillaged by opposing factions. This last fate befel the building of which the present church is the immediate successor, for it was in great part destroyed by fire when the Lancastrians entered the town in 1459. The church was formerly collegiate and was an appanage of the Palmer's Guild, a religious body which flourished in Ludlow for centuries, until its dissolution in the reign of Edward VI. To that wealthy and earnest corporation, and to the gifts and favours of Edward IV., who rewarded the attachment of his Ludlow people in many ways, we owe this magnificent cruciform building, with stately nave and transepts and rich choir, its windows filled with ancient stained glass and its stalls carved with many curious devices. There are thirty miserere seats in these stalls, fifteen on each side, nearly all elaborately carved with the humorous and satirical groups usually found in such situations: cooks joking in kitchens; Reynard the Fox, cowled as a monk, preaching to a congregation of geese; grotesque representations of the fashions, and so forth. Here are sketches of two, representative of their kind. In the first is the humorous figure of a man in the act of drawing liquor from a tiny barrel into a flagon of the most gigantic proportions; the second shows a hideous mermaid with her traditional comb and

MISERERE, SAINT LAWRENCE'S.

mirror, and the most dreadful leer, probably meant by the old religious brother who carved it for a seductive smile.

MISERERE, SAINT LAWRENCE'S.

Many monuments of Chief Justices and other dignitaries in the government of the Marches are to be seen in Saint

Lawrence's. On the apex of the gable of the north transept stands an iron arrow, the mark of the Fletchers' (or arrow-makers) Company, who built this part of the church ; but traditionally held by the country people to be the last arrow shot by Robin Hood from a spot near where Bromfield race-course now stands.

The Reader's House

Old houses abound in the town. Among them, the Reader's House, a seventeenth-century building of timber and plaster, standing in the churchyard, is the quaintest, and the picturesque Feathers' Inn is perhaps as fine an example of a black and white timbered building as may be found anywhere. Queer old shops, cavernous and gloomy, are to

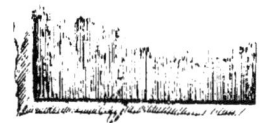

THE COUNTRY SHOP.

be seen everywhere; many of them with richly decorated ceilings, and others contrived in the most unlikely places. One, comparatively modern, in Corve Street, occupies the front of an ancient timbered house whose massive beams are quite needlessly covered over with recent plaster, leaving only two grotesque corbels grinning out from a frontage covered with the gaudy trade marks and insistent advertisements of modern commerce.

Plate glass and elaborate frontages have not yet made any great mark upon the town, for the agricultural interests upon which it chiefly depends in these days are not so flourishing as they might be, and local trade languishes in these days of easy communications and competition with London. All the old tradesmen's guilds have died out and their books and money-chests have found at last a resting place in the local museum. The two great trade-guilds of Ludlow were the Hammermen and Stitchmen. The first comprised all those industries in which the hammer was used—the trades of the carpenters and joiners, the smiths, the masons and others; the second included the glovers, the tailors, and the shoemakers. These societies were duly incorporated so far back as the sixteenth century and had powers by which they could forbid those whom they termed "foreigners,"—that is to say strangers, or tradesmen not natives of the town—from carrying on their occupations within the borough. And these powers were freely exercised for the protection of their interests, as may be seen from their old books which record how "foreigners" were fined and expelled the town, or admitted only upon a heavy payment. All the interests of the allied trades were carefully looked after, and every Sunday the members went to the parish church with their families, and occupied a certain part of the building especially reserved for them. They were no less charitable than rigorous in the due ordering of their affairs, and the wardens lent money and gave in alms to deserving craftsmen as occasion arose. Every year the members of either guild met to audit the funds of their respective corporations, and afterwards feasted at some favourite inn.

But as time went on, the officers of these guilds found their governing powers frequently assailed and the laws of their forbears continually disregarded. " Foreigners," with all the impudence imaginable, came and settled in the town and refused to recognize their authority; members even refused to be brought to order or to pay subscriptions, and actually unauthorized persons appropriated their seats in the church. The history of the decline and fall of the guilds is plaintively evident in the papers relating to the last years of their existence. Relying upon their charters, they brought actions at law against recalcitrants, only to be worsted after repeated struggles, and their privileges declared obsolete and useless in the eyes of the law-officers of the Crown. Yet for a few years longer they held together, more in the nature of clubs or voluntary associations of good-fellowship; until, one by one, the old members died and the younger generation, which cared nothing for old associations unless they offered substantial advantages, held aloof. The usefulness of the guilds had died out and they had to pass into the limbo of all worn-out institutions. The Stitchmen's Guild was the first to dissolve, and was followed within a year or two by the Hammermen's Guild, some thirty years ago.

XLVI.

Broad Street, Ludlow.
Oct. 7.

DEAR JACK,—So you're returned from the gaieties of your Belgian *plage;* from the toilettes, and from the eternal cigars whose scent neutralizes the healthy ozone that comes from off the North Sea. Ah, those fashionable seaside resorts, how I loathe them and their dressy crowds! Yet you seem content with your experiences. Well, well, it takes all sorts to make a world. I wonder how you would enjoy such a holiday as mine, here amid the wilds of the Welsh borders, where a stray newspaper is rare and folks know nothing of the questions that agitate your world. (I would have said *our*, were it not that this tramping tour of these last few weeks appears to have placed an immeasurable gulf between us, sufficient almost to make you seem to me the inhabitant of another planet.)

I and the Other Man are staying for a few days in this old town which, since the days of the Georges, has neither grown nor decayed. The red-brick architecture of that period is the very latest novelty the streets of Ludlow are acquainted with, and although the railway reaches us, and we have a station hidden away in a remote part of the town, one would never guess from appearances that the Coaching Era had given way to steam. What have we and the five thousand inhabitants (more or less) of Ludlow to do with steam and railways?

The knoll upon whose sides the town is built commands Corve Dale and the Clee Hills. Those two hills—Titterstone and Brown Clee—are distant from us some nine miles, and our horizon, geographical and mental, is bounded by them. They say that coal is mined there, and that Dhustone comes thence; but these be rumours, for although I have inquired of a goodly proportion of the aforesaid five thousand, yet have I not encountered one who has penetrated to those far regions. MEM.—You may not know it, but Dhu-stone is familiar to you by sight, if not by name. The macadamized streets of London are made with it. . . .

Strolling up Broad Street this morning, early, I noticed an old man weeding the pavement and roadway, with a semi-circle of five entirely-absorbed spectators, and no one else visible in all the street. Broad Street, I may tell you, is one of the chiefest streets of Ludlow. There's life and movement! But there was some stir in the town a few days ago. The Shropshire County Council and the University Extensionists have contrived, between them, to institute a series of lectures on subjects that no one here cares the least little bit about. "Basket-making" was the subject of one, "Botany" and "Geology" those of others. All the girls in the place—that is to say, all the unmarried women between the ages of sixteen and thirty—rushed to attend the first two *séances*, for the one lecturer was a likely-looking young fellow, and the other was an Oxford prig of the first dimensions—you understand his kind. Why is it—psychological query—that women are so fond of prigs?

As for the geological lecturer—old, and wizened as a dried zoophyte—he held forth on Murchison and the Ludlow series of rocks to a row of empty benches. I give you my word that the next day all the girls were basket-making or botanizing—it was the case of the crew of the *Hot Cross Bun* and Lieutenant Belay over again. The basket-maker and the botanist went off in a blaze of glory, accompanied to the station by a bevy—good word, bevy—of rapturous pupils, and the geologist, having partaken of a recent *stratum* of Ludlow rocks, miscalled cake, prepared by his landlady's daughter, departed with a bad attack of indigestion. Meanwhile, the botanizing and basket-making *furore* has subsided. It is understood that the geologist has recommended the Corporation to obtain a good plain cook for a course of practical lectures on housewifery.

Yesterday was market-day. Such an assemblage ot curious country people I have never seen before, nor, I think, shall ever again. Their style of dress that of two generations ago, their speech like no other dialect. Two old dames, each with a huge bonnet, large plaid shawl, print dress, and a great market-basket, I heard disputing, one with another, by the Buttercross: "Ye wunna?" said one, "No, I shanna," replied the other.

I think I hear you ask, "What is the Buttercross?" It is a fair-sized stone building in the classic taste of the last century, with an open piazza on the ground floor for the butter-market, the Corporation muniment-rooms above, and over them a clock. At night-time the clock dials are illuminated. Now that the Ludlow Corporation have a Jubilee market hall in the place of the old barn that formerly did duty for a market, they don't quite know how they shall contrive to spoil the Buttercross. They offered it to the postal authorities for a post office, but Saint Martin's-le-Grand did not approve, fortunately. It is from here that the Corporation walk in their robes to church on Sunday mornings, headed by the mayor and two mace-bearers: this church of Saint Lawrence, by the way, as handsome a building as one could wish to see, with a tall pinnacled tower that is a landmark for miles around, and, in the belfry, a set of chimes that play a different tune for each day of the week. To-day they played "Home, Sweet Home." Their programme for the remainder of the week is "Hanover," "See! the Conquering Hero Comes," "The Blue Bells of Scotland," "The Old 113th Psalm," "My Lodging is on the Cold Ground," and "Life let us Cherish."

There is no lack of clergy here, from the rector, "a particularly haughty and exclusive person," with a double-barrelled name which commences with two small f's in place of the more usual (and plebeian) capital letter, down to a posse of curates and "readers." They say—*whisper*—that the rector married a Clive and has walked the clouds ever since; but country folk *will* gossip. What's that I hear? "So do you." Nay, but I have done. To all friends, greetings. To yourself, good-night.

XLVII.

AT length we left the capital of the Marches for Shrewsbury, walking out of the town down Corve Street, and so into the country road, over Corve Bridge, where the last ravellings of Ludlow finally cease in squalor and potsherds.

Two miles walking brought us to the picturesque village of Bromfield, where the river Onny crosses the road under a substantial stone bridge, and clatters over its shingly bed to join the Teme lower down in Oakley Park. A row of twelve tall poplars, called the Twelve Apostles, stood here until a few years ago when all but three or four were blown down or felled in anticipation of decay. The survivors are still the " Twelve," no less than Wordsworth's "little maid" who, with her six brothers and sisters deceased, was "seven." One of the prettiest views conceivable is formed by the parish church of Bromfield, once a Priory, that closes the perspective, looking down the stream.

Three miles further is the village of Onibury, and, in another two miles, the road brings the pedestrian to Craven Arms.

BROMFIELD.

Half a mile on this side of Craven Arms Junction stands the fortified thirteenth-century manor-house of Stokesay, an almost unique example of a domestic building of that period. Stoke Castle, as it was once called, has had a long and varied line of owners, from the Lacys to the Allcrofts, its present proprietors. The Says, who were tenants of the Lacys through many generations, took their name from Sez in Normandy, and conferred it in turn upon this manor

STOKESAY CASTLE.

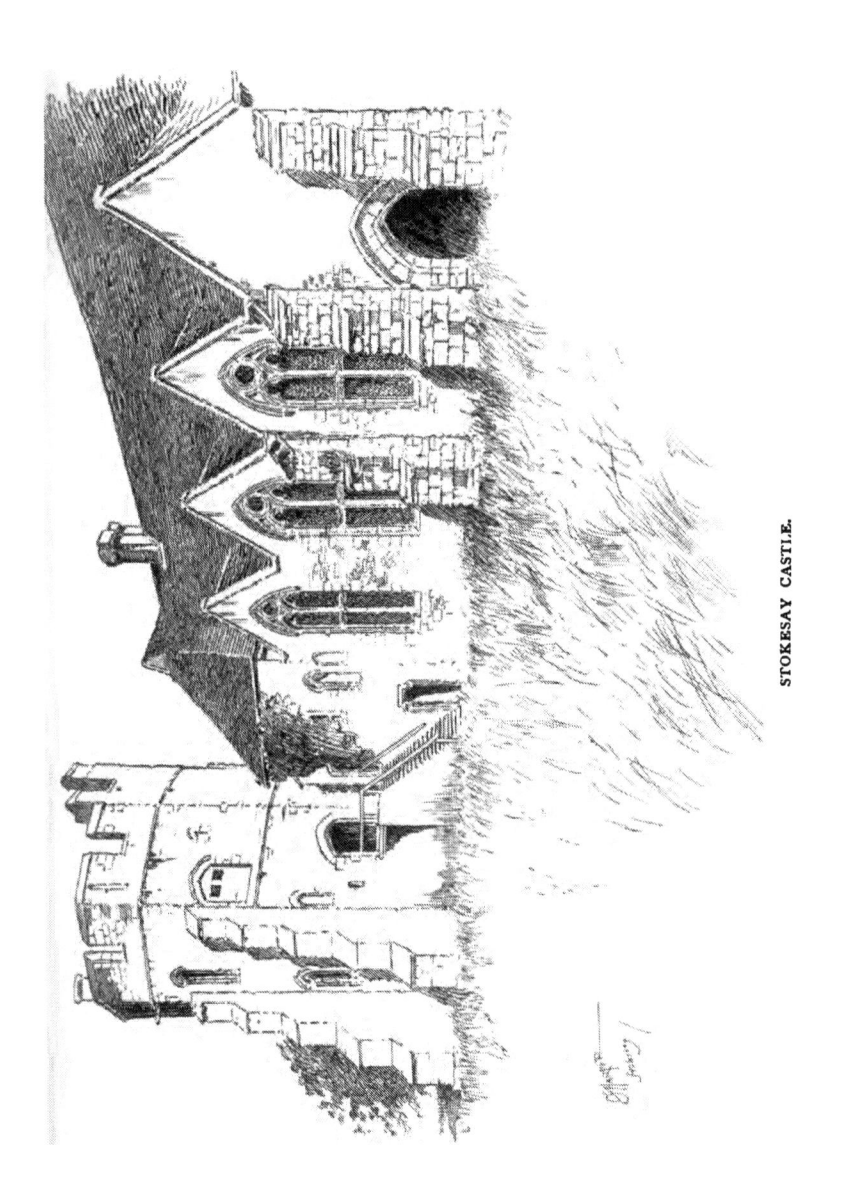

STOKESAY.

——hence this second name, which, through a succession of lords, has continued to the present time. They held Stoke Say for two hundred years, and were at the same time lords of other manors, among them that of Hope Say, which also retains their name. We see another instance of a manor taking the name of its lords in the neighbouring village of Stanton Lacy, and can at the same time trace many other similar instances throughout Shropshire, in Moreton Corbet, Acton Burnell, Acton Scott, and other villages.

John de Verdun held Stokesay for a time, in right of his wife, daughter and heiress of the last of the Lacys. In 1281 we find the manor in the possession of a certain Laurence de Ludlow, who is supposed to have been one of a family of wealthy merchants, eager to give his newly-acquired wealth the dignity of a landed interest—what our fathers called a "stake in the country"—in precisely the same manner as Mr. J. D. Allcroft, the wealthy tradesman of the gloving firm of Dent and Allcroft, invested his money in this very estate some few years ago. Thus do we find the history of manors repeat itself throughout the centuries; and, to go backwards to the ancestors of the late Earl of Craven, from whom Mr. Allcroft bought Stokesay, we shall find that the Sir William Craven, who purchased Stokesay from the Mainwarings in 1616, was himself a rich trader, being indeed a Merchant Taylor and sometime Lord Mayor of London. He died in 1618 and was succeeded by his eldest son, William, who became afterwards the first Earl of Craven, a title created in 1664. The neighbouring station of Craven Arms takes its name from an old coaching inn that stood close by, on the high road to Shrewsbury, before ever railways were thought of, whose sign bore, swinging in the wind, the arms of the Cravens: *or*, five *fleurs-de-lis* in cross sable; a chief wavée *azure*; crest, a crane or heron rising, *proper*.

Laurence de Ludlow obtained in 1284 a royal licence to crenellate his residence, and to him we owe the present hall and great tower. For ten generations the descendants of this Ludlow merchant held the manor, and then, when at last the male line of their family failed, it came by marriage to the Vernons. Their successors were the Mainwarings, who, as we have seen, parted with the estates to William Craven. He leased Stokesay to the Baldwyns, during whose tenancy the manor-house was held for King Charles against the Parliament; for both landlord and tenants were staunch Royalists.

But the Governor of Stokesay—a certain Captain Dawsett—was a prudent man. When the enemy came marching down the Dale from Shrewsbury in force, he, for honour's sake, refused to surrender at the first summons, but, observing the preparations that were going forward for taking the place by storm, he promptly complied with the second, and admitted them. If we cannot admire his easy compliance, we must at least thank him for that course of action which doubtless saved this most interesting old building from destruction; for had he resisted, the place would certainly have been taken and ruined afterwards by the malevolence of the Roundhead soldiery. The Royalist governor of Ludlow, hearing of this capitulation, gathered a force of two hundred mounted men with a large number of infantry, and advanced to within a mile of Stokesay, where he was defeated with great loss, Sir William Croft, of Croft Castle, being killed with one hundred soldiers. Four hundred prisoners were taken, including sixty officers and gentlemen, with all their baggage and ordnance.

Stokesay Castle was inhabited by the Baldwyns until 1727, since when it has been deserted.

The plan of Stokesay Castle is an irregular square, surrounded by a moat and defended by a wall of stone on three sides. The fourth side, across the courtyard from the gatehouse, is occupied by the hall and domestic buildings, with a massive tower at each of the two angles. This hall, a beautiful Early English building, is fifty-three feet long, thirty-one feet wide, and thirty-four feet high. It is lighted with a range of Early Pointed windows, with mullions and transoms and simple tracery, which rise above the springing of the roof in delicate stone gables. The roof is

A Shropshire Legend. 247

supported by stone corbels placed low down in the walls, and rises from them in bold and massive curves of open timber-work, blackened with the smoke from log fires that burned in the centre of the hall, before fireplaces and chimneys came into use. The smoke found an outlet through the "lantern," an ornamental ventilator in the roof, which has long since disappeared. The towers are pierced with loopholes, and in the smaller one, a well, fifteen feet deep, assured the household of an abundant supply of water should disturbances or dangers of any sort forbid their resorting to the larger well that stood outside in the courtyard. Several rooms in these buildings are fitted with panelling and carved fireplaces, dating from Tudor to Jacobean times, and a small tower has a singular wooden upper storey projecting from the stonework.

But the beautiful timbered gatehouse of Elizabethan age is the gem of the place. It forms the only entrance to the courtyard, and is a strongly defended building of two floors, the lower storey built firmly on a foundation of massive stone, the upper a singularly rich and interesting example of sixteenth-century wood-carving, provided with a lattice-window and a gabled roof of ideal picturesqueness: the archway provided with strong doors and freely loopholed for musketry. Indeed, Stokesay Castle has not its fellow anywhere. More strictly military-buildings are thickly scattered about England, but a fortified *dwelling* of such age and excellent preservation is rare indeed.

Shropshire folk-lore has (or had; for all folk-lore is dead now and the Folk-lore Society sits on its corpse and dissects it) a legend about two giants who lived on a hill upon either side of this valley—Norton Camp and Yeo Edge to wit—and kept a great chest of treasures buried beneath the moat of Stokesay Castle. Why they should have been so foolish as to hoard their wealth in so damp a place is neither here nor there; but it seems that when one of these giants wished to draw upon the treasure-chest he would shout to his fellow-capitalist across the valley of the Onny for the key, which was thereupon thrown over to him. But one day, when this call was made, the giant who held possession of it happened to have rheumatism in the arm so badly that he only succeeded in pitching the key half way across. It fell into the moat where the chest itself was hidden, and with all their searching, the giants never found it again. The chest also disappeared. Alas! poor giants; like a lofty house, ill-furnished at the top, how did you fare when all your treasure was thus lost?

When the key is found, then will the treasure-chest appear also; but, although in bygone times the country-folk were credulous enough to believe this tale and to search eagerly for the missing key, it has not yet been brought to light. The age has grown wiser and correspondingly unromantic since then: like a child who grows up from the glorious dreams of childhood to the hard facts of this workaday world, where fairy legends and foolish giants have no place.

Romance fades with time, and its tattered fragments look tawdry in the light of heaped-up years, even as pantomime spangles stand revealed in the searching daylight for the poor things they are, belongings of a realm of sawdust, and of painted canvas that apes the aspect of solid stone. Our fancies do not busy themselves with buried gold or hidden treasure after tender years are past and gone—years tender, physically speaking, for, mentally, none others are so robust as our earliest, when the imagination can assimilate anything in the way of flamboyant invention, however improbable.

There is a common-place plastered wall in a very ordinary London house behind whose plebeian stucco my childish fancies buried untold treasures. Had I been allowed my own way, I would have demolished that wall and revelled in boundless wealth, but (fortunately, it would appear) one is not in those early days permitted to put these vain imaginings to such tests as this. The sight of that wall only the other day recalled that early romance to my mind, but in the colder and less generous light of these later days I realized, together with a shock at the loss of romance, that the only results of having been accorded that ardent desire of my heart would have been a disillusionment all too early, and, subsequently, something substantial in the shape of a bill for builders' reparations. Only that, and nothing more. Recently I revisited, under happy circumstances, the site of that apocryphal hoard, as I knew it must be; yet I turned away with a sigh for the loss of an exuberant imagination that, had it not vanished with added years, might have proved the making of a successful novelist. Indeed, the exquisite edge of all one's senses becomes dulled too soon, and the imaginings and the affections of aforetime had a keener zest than they can have now.

There is, behind that same house of unsubstantial treasures, a garden, where, beneath the boughs of a spreading tree, lies buried a goodly array of domestic pets, cats and dogs, and birds of varied feather, companions of a *vie intime* long by-past, all laid in the dank mould of that sunless corner, with many childish tears for the untimely fate that befel them. Not again, I think and hope, shall I sound the depths of such grief as was my lot when the best-beloved of these my friends passed away in my arms, dumbly, but with a moist, glistening eye that, I thought, was eloquent with an understanding of my sorrow at our parting. Dear dead friend, the memory of you comes back to me as I write, with a poignancy of regret astonishing after all the years that have ensued and all the things that have befallen since you passed away into that eclipse which (we are told) is the pre-eminently distinguishing feature between your intelligent but soulless race and we inheritors of immortality. The remembrance of your hot and jealous affection comes back to me across the wrack of time as bitter-sweet, since you are gone, and the undesired memory of my ill-humours towards you cuts me, even now, with the sting and smart of whips.

But here I find myself on the brink of moralizing: that besetting sin which accompanies most reminiscences, good or ill, joyous or sorrowful. Back, Muse, from the flowery way of irresponsible speculation, and let us tread the hard macadam of an itinerary!

XLVIII.

CRAVEN ARMS JUNCTION is a great centre of railway traffic, and the growth of travel has created quite a large village in the neighbourhood of the station. Branch lines radiate from it to North and South Wales, to Wellington, Hereford, and to Bishop's Castle: this last an unfortunate independent company, with a total mileage of ten miles and a traffic insufficient to pay its working expenses. It is only three years ago that the rolling-stock of the Bishop's Castle Railway was seized for debt.

We pushed on, through modern Craven Arms, to the pretty village of Wistanstow and so towards Marshbrook, where the mountainous scenery of the Longmynd comes in view. We had already walked about twelve miles from Ludlow, and were thinking of a wayside halt, when "a strange thing happened," to quote the formula of Mr. William Black. Loathsome odours, borne for some time fitfully upon the breeze, at last poisoned the air on every side. Blue-bottle flies of a prodigious bigness, and in great numbers, became annoyingly evident, and presently they grew, together with the smell, quite unbearable. A little way ahead of us slouched a meagre tramp, sniffing the air like a pointer, and when we were come close behind him, we observed a something in the ditch beside the road that caused this all-pervading scent. It was the very much decayed carcase of a cow. The tramp glanced over his shoulder in our direction upon catching sight of the noisome object, and, whipping out a knife from his pocket, ran, and kneeling down beside the thing, hacked away an immense kibob of flesh, purple with decay. The myriad flies buzzed off with loud protests, but the tramp smacked his lips, exclaiming as we hurried past, "Fresh as a daisy!"

We would have laughed had we not felt so ill, because his theatrical instinct for exciting compassion for the

Death on the Hills.

"starving poor" was altogether too obvious to be a genuine expression of hunger. Mem: *Summum ars est celare artem.*

We hurried off, and came at tea-time to the little town of Church Stretton, set down amid the great rolling hills of the Longmynd, and close to that old Roman road, Watling Street, whence comes its original name of Street-town, together with the hamlets of Little Stretton, All Stretton, and Stretford Bridge. Church Stretton is a beautiful little place; a modern township, with tiny gasworks; a mineral-water manufactory, fed with the locally celebrated water of the Cound Spring; and a pretentious hotel. The Longmynd affords some of the wildest and most secluded scenery in Shropshire, and the bracing mountain air has made Church Stretton quite noted as a resort for invalids and the overworked.

But those healthful hills have their tragic as well as their recuperative side, for when the summer has gone and the visitors all departed, that bracing air which puts new life into the limbs of townsfolk becomes cruelly rigorous, and snow falls earlier here than anywhere else within the county. Church Stretton fair, held on Saint Andrew's Day, has acquired the title of Dead Man's Fair, from the many unfortunate people who have perished of cold, lost in the snows and fogs of these hills, on their way home. Indeed, there is a place, called the Mill Glen, beside the winding road that leads up to a deserted carding-mill, which is a veritable Golgotha, so many have been the fatal accidents at that spot. Narrow gorges between the hills, known in Shropshire as "gutters," have in the wild weather of mid-winter entrapped many people into the snowdrifts collected there, and these ominous places still bear the significant names of "Dead Man's Hollow," "Dead Man's Beach," and "Deadly Gutter." But in summer-time the carding-mill is the scene of many picnics, and gay parties go strolling up to the summit of the Longmynd range, 1700 feet above the sea, and across to the pretty waterfall called the Light Spout, reckless of these dreadful records, or else with a greater appreciation of the scenery because of them.

In January, 1865, the Reverend Donald Carr, vicar of the neighbouring villages of Woolstaston and Ratlinghope (Woolson and Ratchope in Salopian mouths), set out one Sunday afternoon for Woolstaston, with the intention of conducting evening service at that place. He had crossed the summit of the Longmynd in the morning, but returning the same way in the afternoon, he was met by a violent wind and snowstorm, so furious that he was frequently thrown down in his efforts to climb the hillside. At length he was successful in reaching the crest of the hill where he had in his morning journey remarked the dead body of a pony. This served as a landmark, and assured him that, so far, he had not missed his way. Renewed efforts brought the clergyman across the level summit of the hill to a well-known feature of this region, a dark pool in a little hollow frequented by curlews and other wild-fowl. After a short rest here to regain breath, Mr. Carr started again. The way now lay up a steep ascent for rather less than half a mile, and afterwards across a level flat for another two or three hundred yards, which would have brought him at another time, to a fir plantation situated upon the confines of civilization, and within easy reach of the village. But the storm had now increased to such a degree, that it was become quite impossible to look up in the face of it, or to see a yard distant. In this manner he lost his way and turned off at a right angle from the proper course. After proceeding for some distance onwards he became aware that the ground was unfamiliar, but thinking that he had only slightly missed the path, he continued walking as fast as he could amid the gloom and the pelting snow, when suddenly his feet flew from under him, and he found himself shooting at a fearful pace down the side of one of the steep ravines which he had supposed were far away to the right hand. In an attempt to stop himself he was turned over, and continued the descent head downwards; until, at last, by using one leg as a hook, he succeeded in reversing this unnatural toboggan. He now descended with great care to the bottom of the ravine, intending to walk along the course of the stream, but found this impossible, owing to the deep snowdrifts which choked it up!

It was now quite dark, and the clergyman was uncertain which of the numerous ravines intersecting this part of the mountain it was into which he had fallen. Having extricated himself from the drifts at the bottom, he mounted the opposite bank, struggling with the snow, which was at times as deep as his waist, and, having reached the top and traversed some distance along the ridge, he suddenly lost his footing again. "This," he says, in his little book, "A Night in the Snow; or a Struggle for Life," "was, if possible, a more fearful glissade than my previous one; it was a very precipitous place and I was whirled round and round in my descent, sometimes head first, sometimes feet first, and again sideways; rolling over and over, till at last, by clutching at the gorse bushes, and by digging my feet into the snow as before, I once more managed to check my wild career, and bring myself to a stand; but I had lost my hat and a pair of warm fur gloves, which I had on over a pair of old dog-skins. The loss of these fur gloves proved very serious to me, as my hands soon began to get so numbed with the cold that they were comparatively useless. At the bottom of the ravine into which I had now fallen, I found myself again involved in snowdrifts, and had still more difficulty than before in getting out of them. I had tumbled into a very soft one, far over my head, and had to fight, and scratch, and burrow for a long time before I could extricate myself, and became more exhausted than at any other time during the night."

In this manner, wandering amid the snowdrifts, Mr. Carr passed the whole night on the Longmynd. Fortunately, as it happened, he had taken a small flask of brandy with him, and this helped to warm and sustain him through the weary hours. When at last morning broke over the whitened hills, it brought with it a thick mist, and the clergyman at the same time began to feel the effects of snow blindness. He fell frequently, and often from great heights. At length, finding himself upon the brink of a ravine of great depth, he descended it painfully, and heard the sound of running water below. This proved to be the valley just above the Light Spout waterfall. Unaware of this at the time, Mr. Carr fell over the upper fall, and narrowly escaped breaking his neck over the other. He walked for a long while in a circle round this place, and soon afterwards lost his boots, which had become sodden and fell to pieces. He was now so helpless and fatigued, that he was unable to button his coat which had become torn open, and was sinking into utter exhaustion, when he heard the sound of children's voices in the valley. They were children of the cottagers who lived beside the carding-mill, and thither he was carried and revived, after having been for twenty-four hours wandering on the hill-sides.

XLIX.

We stayed at Church Stretton for two days, and departed on a Sunday morning, shouldering our knapsacks and marching off from the hotel much to the disgust of the curates and pious young ladies who frequent that place and while away the intervals between church services and the dinner-gong, by flirting over hymn-books and the discussion of church discipline.

All the milestones hereabouts are inscribed with so many miles to "Salop," that is, Shrewsbury, even as those round about Winchester show "Winton" to the astonished gaze of the stranger. At the seventh milestone we came to Dorrington. Dorrington is a place of little or no interest, and had nothing to show except a quaint seventeenth-century cottage-tablet, done in plaster upon an old and bowed tenement beside the road. We had made a collection of drawings of these singularly varied devices, met from time to time on this tour, and added this to the number.

The art of the cottage-tablet is a casual, promiscuous and home-grown art; having no principles and no canons whatever. That is why it is so naïve, so interesting and so rich in the unexpected. But what, you ask, is the cottage-tablet? Let me explain to you.

When the bucolic cottager had built him a cottage (generally, in other times, with his own hands), he very naturally and with a pride which, though amusing, is surely pardonable, desired to commemorate that very important event, the completion of his new dwelling. Generally, he adopted the fleeting but convivial practice of celebrating the great occasion by holding a house-warming whereat the metheglin flowed copiously, and the guests, blessed with immense and unsophisticated appetites, did wonderful execution upon the plain and solid English fare of roast beef and Yorkshire pudding.

But sometimes he felt that this was not a sufficiently enduring method of commemoration: also, perhaps, he was not always convivially natured, but cursed with the melancholy and contemplative nature of the artist! In that case, it would occur to him that a tablet inserted in the wall of his house would be a better and a more sure way of handing down his achievement to posterity, than by giving a feast to ungrateful fellows.

TABLET : DORRINGTON.

The simplest form of cottage-tablet is just a slab of stone with the cottager's initials and those of his wife inscribed upon it, together with the date of that *annus mirabilis* which saw the building of their home. The disposition of these initials, usually follows one fashion. Supposing John and Ann Jones had builded for themselves a little house, in which, of course, they had a proper pride; then would in all probability be seen a tablet with inscription something in this wise:—

```
┌─────────┐
│    J    │
│  A. J.  │
│  1790   │
└─────────┘
```

The surname always occupies the apex of this pyramidal arrangement, the place of honour; and the stone bearing the inscription is generally to be found over the doorway.

Of course, the workmanship of these home-made tablets was often singularly rude, and their spelling (when they run to more elaborate examples) is ofttimes peculiarly archaic; but those qualities or defects give them an interest which the primly correct name-tablets of the speculative builder and his like always lack. A terrace of workmen's cottages, for instance, whose centre house bears the inscription "Alma Terrace, 1854," is not even mildly interesting, and "Providence Place" more often attracts attention from the obvious improvidence of the British Striker than by reason of any other attribute.

But indeed it is not in the outskirts of towns, or in the mean modern ravellings of great cities that one looks for these things, but rather in the villages and hamlets where agricultural Phillises and Corydons most do dwell, in more or less poetic content. Thus it is that in the remote, romantic places of the Severn Valley and the valley of the Wye, one comes upon many instances of this pretty fashion. It is seen in the deserted settlement of Old Furnace, near Tintern, where three simple tablets done in cast-iron, with date and initials, remain upon as many ruinated cottages; and in the neighbouring hamlet of Trelleck Grange an admirable example is let into the wall of a tiny cottage whose sole ornament it is. Who he was, or who they were who bore these initials (for I suppose the three letters, together with the heart, are somehow symbolical of love in a cottage), I cannot say, for it is a far cry to that century-old *fin de siècle*, 1799. But, certainly, Corydon, when he inscribed this record of his achievement here and painted his design in black paint, fashioned something individual and notable, despite that little error of the reversed 9's.

This shield-shaped device, from high up in the plastered

gable-end of the "Sloop Inn" at Llandogo, is a matter of some ninety-two years older than that loving emblem at Trelleck Grange. Here again, I, the moral Autolycus of these generally unconsidered trifles, cannot pierce the veil which hides the identity of those whose initials appear on this design, and can form no sort of idea what the star-fish symbolizes, or whether it be only a meaningless whimsy.

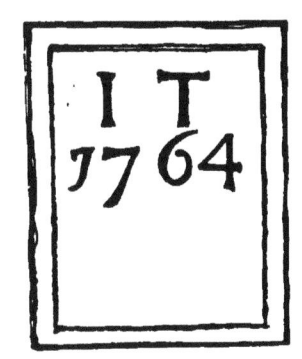

COTTAGE TABLETS, OLD FURNACE.

Nor can it be said what that shapeless lump in base had been when the eighteenth century was young: let us be thankful for what the gods have given and what the weather has left us.

Now observe the old tablet from Tintern that caps so unconventionally this fine old stone doorway of the "Royal George Inn" at that place. How singularly one-sided and unconventional, and how irritating to the orderly mind of the modern Briton! That British love of mathematical

COTTAGE TABLET, TRELLECK GRANGE.

TABLET, "SLOOP INN," LLANDOGO.

balance is, indeed, essentially modern, and is typified in a very remarkable and unpleasing way by (for instance) those prides of the middle-class householder's eye, the cut-glass

Cottage Tablets Again. 259

lustres that flank with such deathly precision the mantelpieces of Philistine and unregenerate suburbs. Everywhere we see this bugbear of the T-square and the *pendant*, do we not? Here, then, is rue for your matter-of-fact and mathematically-precise wayfarer!

A DOORWAY OF THE "GEORGE," TINTERN.

The immediate neighbourhood of Tintern is rich in these cottage-tablets. At Coedithel Farm, beside the Wye, this singular device is sculptured upon a stone-built outhouse, and directly across the river, at the little decayed village of Brockweir, occurs perhaps the most charming of any I have seen. It is inserted in the gable of the "New Inn," and gives that old building a quite distinguished air. It has somewhat the appearance of a playing-card, with its two inverted hearts; but what sentimentalist *posuit* this emblem of love in a beer-house?

COEDITHEL FARM.

"NEW INN," BROCKWEIR.

Monnow Street, Monmouth, is enriched with one of these tablets upon an otherwise uninteresting house, and a very neat early example is carved deeply in stone upon the front of Welsh Newton Farm.

The cottager whose tableted dwelling had attracted our attention at Dorrington came out and looked on while I made the drawing.

"No," said he, "I canna tell ye nothen about it. 'Tis

MONNOW STREET, MONMOUTH.

WELSH NEWTON FARM.

main old, sure. Yes, 'tis wonderful old, an' strange it han't been pulled down before this. But in these here quiet places things 'll last for sentries."

We could scarcely fail to hear the shouts and howls of the cottager's numerous family which made the house and the greater part of the village street answer to the Shakespearean stage directions of "alarums and excursions," but we agreed with him, to save argument, that "the place was that quiet you might be dead, as you may say." Meanwhile, the cottager's wife had appeared with the youngest of her tribe in her arms, gurgling and pawing the air.

"Ah!" said she, dropping H's freely in a manner most strange and unusual in these parts, "ain't 'e a little progeny? Look at 'im a-setting straight up in my arms an' smilin' at me like a little gamboo cane."

"How do you manage to pass your time on Sundays in this *quiet* place?" we asked, with involuntary sarcasm. "You can't go to church more than twice in the course of the day, and—"

"No, master," said the woman, "church don't trouble *he* much: he goes to church where prayer-books have handles."

L.

SOON after Dorrington was left behind the spires of Shrewsbury came in sight, and when we came within three miles of the town, groups and single parties of the lieges were to be seen walking along the road in the due performance of their Sunday after-dinner walk. It is really surprising, however, to notice how few are they who, in a large town like this, numbering some thirty thousand inhabitants, find sufficient energy to carry them two or three miles beyond their thresholds. Do you not know the Sunday of the British lower middle-class? The late rising; the graceless Sunday paper at the eleven o'clock breakfast; the solid one o'clock dinner; the plethoric after-dinner nap, announced to the startled ear by stertorous snores in awful diapason; the choked awakening, with the early tea, and the deadly dull "constitutional." Evening service, perhaps, if your Briton be not altogether Godless; supper; yawns all round; bed at an early hour, with the consciousness of having spent a dull day, and a very great satisfaction that it is at last done with. The Sunday clothes are put away for another six days' rest, the Sunday religion, too, for a like period: while the thoughtful sigh and the cynics chuckle at the idea of these Sabbath suits for body and soul.

At length Shrewsbury's suburbs encroached on either side upon the fields, and we passed from Abbey Foregate into the town, over the English Bridge. The first street within the town walls is Wyle Cop, hilly, ancient, and crowded with old inns. We regarded all these inns doubtfully from the middle arch of the English Bridge, and observing an old man, dressed in the blackest and glossiest of Sunday best, lounging along and gazing pensively at the yellow waters of the Severn, sought of him what we considered would be the specialized opinion of an old inhabitant of the town as to the individual merits of these numerous hostelries. But he turned a sour Puritanical face toward us and said,—

"I canna tell ye nohow, I dinna frequent no sich places myself."

We wished him a convivial day, and turned upon our heels, rebuked, but not contrite, for our preferences for licensed houses over temperance hotels or private dwellings.

We were, without a doubt or question, travellers, and readily found suitable quarters at an old-fashioned inn, bearing the most incongruous sign of the "Lion and Pheasant," in Wyle Cop. Here we stayed for a few days while we made ourselves acquainted with Shrewsbury, and came in and went out, day by day, rubbing shoulders with market people and strange characters from the outlying villages. We took our meals in a little slip of a room, looking out upon the courtyard of the inn, where carriers' carts and farmers' traps rattled in over the cobble-stones under the archway that led from the street. The most striking feature of this room was a china mantel-ornament that purported to be a likeness of Louis Napoleon, seated apparently on a humorous carthorse. You can see at once from the accompanying illustration how near a likeness this is to Napoleon III., but perhaps it is as well that his name has been placed on the pedestal, so that there can be no doubt about the identity of this warrior bold, who looks like some gay Lothario of mediæval times, or an Alonzo from the romantic and Italian pages of Mrs. Radcliffe.

But if our inn was quaint, how shall I describe the quaintness of the old timbered shops of Shrewsbury? the mediæval Butcher's Row, the tottering tenements of the old suburb of Frankwell, or the crazy stalls of Mardol? These things are to be seen, and not to be adequately pictured in prose. But, tell me, are you becoming *blasé* with the restricted circle of the picturesque, in the common acceptation of that misused word? Have you had your fill of glens and gorges, cathedrals, waterfalls and all the other well-worn subjects of the guide-book? Yes, surely. Descend, then, from the contemplation of your castles, from the craggy pinnacles of rugged cliffs, and seek the picturesqueness of the domestic side of life.

It is not, indeed, far to seek, but is on every side, ready to your view. Take, for instance, the old-fashioned country shop, with its surprisingly incongruous stock and its haphazard methods of construction. It is well to note the type now, for its day is done, and the more curious examples are growing fewer, day by day, as business centres more and more in large cities, and, together with the Parcel Post, destroys the custom and connection of the country shop.

I like the old-fashioned shop of the little country town

THE
BAR BER'S
SHOP.

the wayside village, or the rural hamlet, although it must be owned that the cosmopolitan blast of its very comprehensive stock is, on first acquaintance, somewhat trying. But one soon becomes used to the warring scents of tea and coffee, of strong, home-cured hams and yet stronger cheeses, and then this rural mart is not without its own peculiar interest. The space within is, as a rule, restricted indeed, what with biscuit-boxes, piles of pails, barricades of brooms, and shining arrays of bright tin goods; but the cavernous little place makes a picture—unconventional, of course—but filled with spots of colour and great rich shadows which send you at once harking back to Rembrandt to point the force of your impression.

Within all is peaceful, for customers do not crowd the country shop, save of Saturday nights. The white cat on the well-scrubbed counter of plain deal seems all innocent of canaries or mice, and has never a thievish thought of the herrings exposed in the window; while as for the tempting butter—it is only the reprehensible town cat that does these things. This cat, on the other hand, sleeps on the counter all day, except when one of the village urchins comes in to buy, with much hesitation and dubious choosing, a pennyworth of sweets of the sort that yields the heaviest weight for two half-pence. Then the cat gets his tail pulled, not weakly but too well, and retires hastily, while the boy, whom retribution has overtaken, sucks his clawed hand, and the shopkeeper, roused by the tinkling of the shop-door bell, emerges from his little parlour. If you look into the little window, crowded with all manner of goods, you will see some half-dozen faces, more or less, pressed against the panes, and distorted horribly by the faulty glass. They are all goggling anxiously at the purchase being concluded within: for this is a joint-stock transaction, and the buyer, entrusted with the capital of the syndicate, has only been chosen after much earnest council. The merits and respective cost of various luxuries have been duly canvassed, you may be sure.

The shop-bell rings furiously when, the purchase duly

completed, the buyer bangs the door after him. I think it is only in the country that shop-doors have bells on them that ring when one enters or leaves. This opens a field of inquiry whose glories I leave to any enterprising philosopher

who may have time hanging heavily on his hands: *e.g.* are shopkeepers more cautious and less trustful in the country than in town; or does the countryman respect the Eighth Commandment less than townsfolk?

CHANGES IN THE COUNTRY SHOP. 269

You may purchase many and diverse things at the typical village shop: things so antipathetic as notepaper and envelopes; bacon, herrings, or oranges; patent medicines and penny novelettes. Blushing Dutch cheeses, red and fiery, like so many suns on foggy mornings, jostle pallid skins of lard, horrid to the touch, and these are next-door neighbours to vast lumps of glittering white loaf-sugar, for the most part wrapped round with wrappages of blue paper.

Alas! it is only in the country shop, and in few of these, that one still sees the sugar-loaf: the cube and centrifugal sugars have deposed the loaf, and is not the name of Tate a power in the land?

The "march of progress" has brought other changes than those in the shape of sugar to the country shop. They are changes that remind one of Carlyle and his denunciation of the Seven Foot Hat; for they all belong to the order of that monstrous growth:—that is to say, they are in the shape of elaborate advertisements, upon which money has been expended that might more reasonably have gone toward an improvement of the goods advertised. Consider what enormous sums have gone toward the making of those enamelled plates that nowadays one finds fixed upon the frontages of shops—town or country!

This is not to say anything against the pictorial value these things lend to a sketch in oils or water: indeed, if one but suppresses the advertisement, the result is an added piquancy in a colour scheme. In the original, of course, there is always a barbaric orgie of colour, for blue, red and yellow are not harmonious neighbours; but in your sketch it is always possible to sort them out, unless you are possessed of the devil of uncompromising truth—a sorry possession for an artist.

Here you shall see an earnest of these things, in sketches of country shops, the fruits of walking tours taken in the remotenesses of England, where commerce comes but fitfully, filtered through many miles intervening between the capital and their situations: the barber's shop, where the stubbly chins of country joskins are reaped at painful weekly intervals; the shop under the piazza, and the gabled house where the general shop has a carven seventeenth-century facia which arouses the passion for possession in the breast of the Londoner, wearied of the endlessly-repeated mouldings and decorations of modern times.

LI.

SHREWSBURY is the capital of Shropshire and a mediæval town of many and most intricate annals. Its site was, like so many of our towns and cities, originally selected from its strategic value and capacities for defence. It stands, therefore, upon a strong position formed by a bold bluff round whose sides the Severn bends in such a manner as to all but convert the town into an island. Only a very narrow neck of land remained in times before the Severn was bridged, by which Shrewsbury might be entered, and this point was defended by the castle, originally but an earthwork, protected by palisades, at the time when Offa drove out the Britons and founded Scrobbesbyrig on the ashes of the British Pengwern.

This British settlement was formed at the destruction of Uriconium, when the Picts and Scots descended upon the Romano-British city and massacred all whom they could find there. The long train of fugitives streamed across the country until they came to this defensible spot, on which they sought refuge from the barbarian hordes. They and their descendants remained here, continually retrograding from the state of civilization in which the Romans had left them, until the conquering spirit of the Saxons brought Offa to the Severn and drove them backwards upon the rugged and inhospitable hills of Wales. "Pengwern" was the British descriptive phrase for the situation of their settlement, and signified "Head of the Alderwood"; and if we select the most likely of the derivations offered by antiquaries and philologists for the Saxon "Scrobbesbyrig," we shall find it exactly fit the nomenclature of the people they drove away. For "Scrobbesbyrig," translated into modern English, means Scrub-bury, the Town in the Bush, and it is singular to remark even at the present time, the alders and other shrubs that grow so profusely on the little islands in mid-stream of the Severn, opposite the town.

Other theories take the derivation of "Scrobbesbyrig" from the name of a Norman knight who held lands in Shropshire and Herefordshire in the time of Edward the Confessor; one Richard Fitz Scrob, the terrible builder of "Richard's Castle," whose malignant individuality was sufficiently marked to confer his Christian name upon his stronghold for all time. But in the multitudes of plausible origins for the names of Shrewsbury, Shropshire, and Salop, it is impossible to arrive at any positive statement of fact. The ingenuity of philologists bent upon discovering the origin of a place-name is inexhaustible, and is well shown in the theory by which the alternative name of Salop for town and county is derived from the ancient Erse words, *sa*, a stream, and *lub*, a loop—a physical description of the site of Shrewsbury, almost wholly encircled by the loop of the Severn. However correct or scientific they may be, these warring theories cannot fail of amusement, so varied are they, and so irreconcilable one with another.

To the Saxons succeeded in due time the Norman adventurers in " Civitas Scrobbensis," as the old Latin charters term Shrewsbury. Then was built the frowning castle that even now looks down from its rock in its majesty of eight hundred years upon the station-yard and the railway, the cabs and carriages, the portmanteaux and Gladstone bags of modern life. Roger de Montgomery, Earl of Shrewsbury, built it, and his son, Roger de Belesme, commenced the Town Walls, finished sometime afterwards by Henry III. The keep of the Castle is all that is left of Roger de Montgomery's building. The outworks have long since disappeared, and the walls of the keep itself have been repeatedly re-faced. The interior is now a modern residence, but the height on which the towers stand, and their deep-red walls of sandstone, give a fine effect as one comes from the suburbs of Shrewsbury, low-lying amid the meadows beside the Severn. More impressive still is the Castle when the sun is setting and the lights of the Railway Station begin to twinkle down below its ponderous turrets. Its deep-red walls then take on a silhouetted blackness that effectually hides all these innovations and modern touches only too visible in the broad eye of day.

Few towns have so many relics of their mediæval existence to show as Shrewsbury, both in actual stone and timber and in the curious old-world names of its streets. These are still numerous, in spite of modern changes, and the use of the word " street " is even now of rare occurrence in the old town. Wyle Cop is the singular name of a steep thoroughfare that leads down to the Welsh Bridge; its meaning is simple enough, being just " Hill Top "; but the un-English words have a strange sound and a fascination

T

Shrewsbury Street Names.

that seems to have not been lost upon Tom Ingoldsby in his legend of " Bloudie Jack of Shrewsberie":—

> "Your trunk thus dismantled and torn,
>   Bloudie Jack,
> They hew and they hack and they chop;
>   And to finish the whole
>   They stuck up a pole
> In the place that's still called the Wylde Coppe."

Mardol Dairy Fold, is the name of another thoroughfare;

WYLE COP.

Dog-pole, or Duck Pool, the title of a street near Saint Mary's Church; Murivance, the survival of a mediæval term applied to the neighbourhood of the Town Walls; and Shop Latch is an extraordinary corruption of Shutte Place, once the residence of an old Shropshire family. Bellstone, Belmont, Mardol Head, The Dana, and Pride Hill are other unusual names.

The dedications of Shrewsbury churches are not less remarkable than the names of its streets: Saint Alkmund, Saint Julian, and Saint Chad are saints rarely honoured in this country. The church of Saint Alkmund was founded so far back as the year 912, but all except its tower and spire was destroyed in 1794, to make way for a "carpenter's gothic" building that is almost as dreadful an example of architectural incompetence as the church of New St. Chad's, built just two years before. This is a Doric building, circular in plan, with the gaudy and meretricious internal ornament of a music hall and an exterior resembling a corn exchange or a town hall. Yet this pagan-like exhibition of bad taste accommodates the most fashionable audience in all Shrewsbury. Old Saint Chad's fell in 1788; indeed the latter half of the eighteenth century was a period when Gothic architecture in Shrewsbury seems to have been peculiarly unfortunate; for in 1750 the Norman church of Saint Julian was entirely swept away to make room for the unsightly building that now offends the eye, and the fine old embattled gateway that guarded the Welsh Bridge was pulled down. But, despite ecclesiastical vandalism, there are still some exquisite Gothic churches left to Shrewsbury; foremost among them being the church of Saint Mary's, and the Abbey church of Saint Peter and Saint Paul, across the river, in the suburb of Abbey Foregate. The first is a large and extremely handsome building of all Gothic phases, ranging from Norman to Perpendicular, and has a lofty and most beautiful spire of 220

THE REFECTORY PULPIT.

SHREWSBURY ABBEY.   277

feet in height. It was this notable eminence that tempted a steeplejack named Cadman to his doom in 1739. He had been employed to repair the weather-cock, and having successfully performed this sufficiently hazardous feat, was led to essay the foolhardy experiment of sliding down a rope fastened at the top of the spire and descending to the other side of the Severn, where it was secured to an oak-tree, still pointed out in a riverside meadow. The rope broke and the stupid fellow was thrown into a street called Saint Mary's Fryars, where he was, of course, instantly killed. Saint Mary's is a cruciform church, filled with elaborately carved oaken roofs and stained-glass windows of thirteenth, fourteenth, and fifteenth-century workmanship. It also contains several monuments, including one to that sturdy native of Shrewsbury, Admiral Benbow, who, however, is not buried here, but at Kingston, Jamaica, where he died of his wounds received in action with the French at Cartagena, in 1702.

The Abbey church, built of ruddy sandstone, is a conspicuous object to the traveller who enters Shrewsbury by rail. Although so large and stately a building, it is not, as now seen, more than half its original size; for at that time of spoliation and ruin, the period of the dissolution of the monasteries, the choir and all the eastern portion up to and including the great central tower was demolished; while the clerestory of the nave fell at a later period. All the extensive monastic buildings were at the same time utterly destroyed, with the single exception of the graceful stone pulpit, once occupying a position in the refectory, but now standing amid the coal-trucks and goods-sheds of the Abbey Foregate railway-station.

Much judicious restoration has been going forward here of late years, not in any effort to rebuild the choir, but simply in an attempt to round off the present eastern end in a creditable manner. Shrewsbury Abbey is memorable as having been the scene of the first English Parliament, held in the Chapter-house here in 1283. Here also died the great Roger de Montgomery, Earl of Shrewsbury, in 1094;

like so many other warriors, a monk of the very Abbey himself had founded. His mutilated effigy lies here in a gloomy recess, among other monuments; some brought from the rebuilt churches of Saint Chad, Saint Julian, and Saint Alkmund, with one removed from Wellington, and others originally erected here.

Shrewsbury School is one of the most striking features of this old town. It rises, tall and grey, within sight of the railway-station, and with its handsome approach, is one of the chief ornaments of the borough. It was founded in 1551 by Edward VI. and has been the *alma mater* of many distinguished Salopians and others, from Sir Philip Sidney to the notorious Judge Jeffreys. Of late years, the old school-building has been superseded by a much larger modern range of schools built at the suburb of Kingsland, on the other side of the Severn, and this old Tudor pile has found a new usefulness in its present state of museum and public library.

An old manuscript book still preserved in Shrewsbury Museum, contains many notes of local happenings, recorded year by year from the time of Henry VIII. to the death of Queen Elizabeth. A perusal of it shows how God-fearing were the citizens of the town and how credulous of supernatural agencies in the storms and evil happenings that from time to time visited them. The most trivial things were not too minute for this sixteenth-century journalist to note. He chronicles with equal gusto the coming of the Court of the Marches to Shrewsbury, the accidents of every-day life, and the two-headed sheep and the six-legged calves that were occasionally brought as curiosities from the farms and villages round about. Here are a few extracts to show his quality :—

"This yeare 1533 uppon twelfft daye in Shrewsbury the dyvyll apearyd in Sainct Alkmonds churche there when the preest was at highe masse wth greate tempest and darknes so that as he passyd through the churche he mounted up the steeple in the sayde churche teringe the wyer of the sayde clocke and put the prynt of hys clawes uppon the iijth bell and toocke one of the pynnacles awaye with hym and for the tyme stayed all the bells in the churches wth in the sayd towne that they could neyther toll nor rynge.

"1537. This yeare also in the moonthe of January a servingeman of Master Styrries of Rossall by Shrewsberie repayringe to a howse at St. John's hyll in Shrosberie desperately thrust hys owne dager throughe hys throte and by chance myssyd hys wesand pype by helpe wherof it is curable and good hope to lyve thys mans name ys Yevan.

"This year one Yevan ap Davyd alias Yevan Wever of Franchvill in Shrewsberie beinge a man above 7x yeares in the X'ras hollydayes goinge up a tree uppon his backesyde wth a ladder to plucke downe a pyeametts neast fell downe and broosyd hys braynes that he nev' spacke but dyed wth in an howre after the fall.

"1550. This yeare and about thys tyme were seene dyv' strange and monsterews things as iij soonns iij moones somtymes pale somtymes bloodye in marvellows fryghtfull order.

"1583. This yeare and the 17 of Marche one John Rawlyns of Ratly choppe in the countie of Salop beinge a beggar hangid hym sellfe in an old coate or cowe house wth a lease cast ov' a beame in the same cote and there was founde in hys house bills of debt owynge him for the soom of 50^li or ther abouts a just reward by the dyvill uppon sutche dyssymbli^ng beggers."

It goes against one's inclination to call so apparently ingenuous a recorder by harsh names, but his imagination seems to have been of a high order when he could in all seriousness write of the Devil printing an impression of his claws upon a church bell. Yet a liar of malice prepense would not have rested content with saying that the Enemy "toocke one of the pynnacles awaye." He would not have been satisfied with so inconclusive and tentative a statement, but would have told us that the Devil made away with bells and steeple also. Therefore, though we reject his "facts" as being fancies merely, let us believe in his good faith.

LII.

THREE miles to the north-west of the town is Battlefield. Here the great Battle of Shrewsbury was fought on the twenty-first of July, 1403. In the beginning of that year, according to that worthy chronicler of history and the marvellous, Richard Grafton, there appeared in the heavens a "comete or blazing starre of a great and huge quantitie, which some expounded to signify great effusion of man's blood." And so it happened, for the Battle of Shrewsbury was the most sanguinary of any since Hastings. The influence of the House of Mortimer can be traced here, in the causes which led to this contest. Henry IV. had but recently usurped the throne of Richard II. and imprisoned the Earl of March, the rightful heir, in the Tower, for fear of his strong claims upon the succession. Owen Glendower, who had been a warm friend of the late King, had risen in revolt in Wales, goaded to armed resistance by the injuries he had received at the hands of Lord Grey of Ruthin, and the refusal with contumely of the English Parliament to redress the wrongs of one whom they contemptuously styled a "barefoot knave."

Rarely was contempt less justified, for Glendower raised a large force, assumed the title of Prince of Wales, and, burning the town of Ruthin, advanced upon the English troops of Sir Edmund Mortimer, uncle of the imprisoned Earl of March, and defeated him with the loss of one thousand men, slain at the Battle of Brynglas. Sir Edmund Mortimer was taken prisoner and held to ransom, but Henry regarded the defeat of Brynglas but lightly, as it had resulted in this notable capture of a man, loyal, so far, to himself, it is true, but next heir after his nephew Edmund to the crown. He refused to ransom Glendower's prisoner and thereby gave a pretext to Henry Percy (the famous Hotspur, son of the Duke of Northumberland) for revolting from his service against the Welsh in these Borders. For Hotspur had married the sister of Sir Edmund Mortimer and regarded it as an affront that his kinsman should be thus neglected. But more potent causes joined this sentimental reason for throwing off allegiance to the *parvenu* king. Henry had afforded Hotspur little support in his services against the Welsh, and had also unwarrantably delayed payment for those services, and of the great amount expended by the House of Percy in his aid, nothing had been refunded. Hotspur had taken the Earl of Douglas prisoner at the battle of Homildon Hill in a purely domestic quarrel between himself and the Scots, and the King aroused his anger still further by a demand that the earl should be given up to him.

A great conspiracy was now formed out of these causes for discontent, and the Percies—Hotspur; his father (the Duke of Northumberland); and his uncle, Thomas Percy, Earl of Worcester—joined hands with Glendower in an attempt to place the Earl of March upon the throne. Sir Edmund Mortimer recovered his liberty by espousing a daughter of the Welsh chieftain, and the allies, further reinforced by the following of the Earl of Douglas, negotiated for aid from France to hurl Henry IV. from his place. A French fleet hovered in the Channel; Hotspur; the Earl of Worcester, and Douglas led their forces from the north to effect a junction with Glendower, while the Earl of Northumberland gathered a supporting army in their rear. The King had learned very little of these great preparations for his destruction, but knew of the discontent of the Percies, and invited them, with the promise of protection, to a conference at Windsor, for a redress of their grievances. But the malcontents insolently declared that they could not trust his word for safe-conduct and the negotiations were broken off. Worcester was in London, acting as spy for his fellow-conspirators, and when the King set out on a progress through the west country, he hurried off to join his friends in the north. The King, however, had altered his course, and marched rapidly toward Scotland on learning that a Scots rising was contemplated. By the 16th of July in this year of 1403, he had reached Burton, when news came that the Percies and the whole of the North of England was in arms, and that an army was marching to join the Welsh under Glendower. He turned and reached the walled town of Shrewsbury on the 19th, just in time to occupy the place, when Hotspur's banners came in sight from the battlements as the sun was setting. The royal standard waving from the walls warned the insurgents that they were too late in their design to seize the town, and they retired to a strong position by the Shelton Ford, to await daybreak and the arrival of Glendower. The next day witnessed well-meant attempts by the King to secure peace. He had no reason to anticipate defeat, for he held the strongly defensible town of Shrewsbury, and his forces largely outnumbered those of the enemy: 20,000 against 14,000. But although promises of pardon with a general amnesty, and an offer to comply with any reasonable demands on the part of the rebels were made, they were rejected, chiefly at the instigation of Worcester.

On the morrow of that day the armies faced one another, the King marching out to give battle; and as they lay confronting in the field of ripe peas which then occupied the site of this church of Battlefield, a last appeal was made by Henry to the Earl of Worcester, who seems throughout to have been the prime mover of these conspiracies.

"Put thyself in my grace," entreated the King, earnestly.

"I trust not in your grace," replied Worcester.

Then said the King, "I pray God that thou mayest have to answer for the blood here to be shed this day, and not I."

The armies then engaged, the battle being begun by a detachment under the command of Henry, Prince of Wales (afterwards Henry V.), who had attained his fifteenth year that day. Hotspur roused hurriedly from his headquarters at the village of Berwick, and so hastily did he come that he left his favourite sword behind him in his tent, not missing it until he was close upon the field. When he called for it he was told where it had been left.

The Battle of Shrewsbury. 283

"'I perceive then," he replied, "that my plough is drawing to its last furrow, for a wizard told me in Northumberland that I should perish at Berwick, which I vainly interpreted of that town in the north."

Here, under the beautiful Haughmond Hill, the armies closed. Hotspur made an address to his men, and then according to Holinshed, "he suddenly blew the trumpets, the King's part crying *Saint George* upon them, their adversaries raising their battle-shout of *Esperance Percy*." Glendower had not come on to the field with his promised reinforcements. He had reached the ford of the Severn at the opening of the battle, but hung inactive there, awaiting Fortune's decisive turn before joining in the *mêlée*. "Glendower's Oak," a tree into whose branches this unusually cautious chieftain is said to have climbed to watch the issue of the fight, stood until recently on the Oswestry road, and was a venerable stump forty-two feet in girth and perfectly hollow.

Glendower held aloof during the whole of the battle, and withdrew without striking a blow. Northumberland, too, was far off, beyond call. The battle raged furiously for three hours, and the King's forces were suffering severely. The Cheshire bowmen plied their yews, "laying on such load of arrows that many died and were driven down that never rose again." Douglas and Hotspur, charging at the head of their knights, made a great alley in the armed men around the King, and the Prince of Wales was wounded in the face by an arrow. The royal standard-bearer, Sir Walter Blunt, was struck down, and the onrush pressed hard upon the King. Douglas sought all over the field for him, and thrice slew figures bearing the royal armour, but no sooner had he despatched one than another met his astonished gaze.

"I marvel," said he, "to see so many kings thus arise so suddenly, one on the neck of another;" or, as Shakespeare makes him say, "Another king! they grow like hydras' heads."

The King had clad several knights in this distinctive

dress, for he well knew that his life was specially sought; and this was seen in the fact of all those devoted men being slain.

But at the moment when, to the King's friends, all seemed lost, the tide of battle turned. Hotspur was struck by a random arrow which pierced his brain, and he fell dead in sight of the King. "Percy is dead," shouted the King, in a voice heard above the din, and the allies broke and fled, discomfited. Their loss was five thousand men, together with two hundred knights and esquires, thirty-six of whom, it is said, were slain by Henry with his own hand. Of the Royalists, one thousand five hundred were slain, and four thousand "grievously wounded."

The English rebellion was at an end, and Glendower, watching from his oak, half-hearted and treacherous—a true Welshman—turned back to his Welsh mountains, where Nature did most of the fighting for him.

Douglas was taken prisoner, but unconditionally released, and the body of Hotspur was given to a kinsman for decent sepulture; but the Earl of Worcester, with two other prisoners of rank, was executed at Shrewsbury by Henry's orders. Says Grafton: "He first rendered his humble and hearty thanks to God Almighty and caused the Earl of Worcester the next morrow after to be drawn, hanged, and quartered in the town of Shrewsbury, and his head to be sent to London and there set upon a pole upon London Bridge."

The King afterwards caused a votive chapel to be erected over the place where the slain were buried in one great pit, and on the site of that Golgotha, its successor, the present church of Battlefield, now stands.

When Wellington revisited Waterloo his first exclamation was "They have spoiled my battlefield"; and so they have. It were, then, too much to hope that Shrewsbury battlefield, incomparably older than that of Waterloo, should have escaped disfigurement. The scene of this great fight is cut in halves by the lofty railway embankment of the branch line from Shrewsbury to Whitchurch, and it thus becomes im-

THE BATTLEFIELD. 285

possible to take in at one view the scene where Hotspur fell and Henry IV. became still more a king.

The place is a flat and fertile tableland, just three miles from Shrewsbury town, which lies almost within sight, in the hollow by the winding Severn. All round are distant hills, the Wrekin, the Longmynd, Caer Caradoc, and the striking Breiddin Hills. The pleasant eminences of Haughmond=*Haut Mont*—high mount—rise nearer, and are interesting to the historian from the fact that it was here that Douglas, wounded and weary, flying from the fight, was captured while urging his horse up these wooded slopes.

It was a singular coincidence that when we visited the battlefield we noticed that peas are still grown on the site of the field of peas in which the armies faced one another four hundred and ninety years ago.

Battlefield Church, the memorial of this great event, stands quite apart from any village. It is a beautiful Perpendicular building, erected about 1460, as a successor to the votive chapel which arose here immediately after the battle was fought. The building consists of a square embattled and pinnacled tower, and a nave without either aisles, chapels, or chancel arch, but with a handsome openwork roof. The whole was well restored in 1862, and the remarkably fine gargoyles renewed. These represent armoured knights and men-at-arms, and are exceptionally good in design and execution.

LIII.

ONE of the most varied and interesting excursions from Shrewsbury is the walk of five miles to Wroxeter, a village built beside a long-forgotten Roman city that sleeps beneath fields now covered with waving corn and green pastures. Antiquaries have dug trenches and probed the earth here and there on its site, and have been rewarded with finds dear to the antiquarian heart, but with little of any intrinsic value; and the smallness of the funds at the disposal of archæological societies, together with the very natural desire of the farmers to use the land which they have rented for agricultural purposes, have hindered operations on a large scale, which alone could yield a satisfactory exploration of so large a site as this old city occupied.

The Roman city of Uriconium—the City of the Wrekin—took its name from that great isolated hill of North Shropshire which is the pride of the proud Salopian and the origin of the patriotic county toast: " To the health of friends all round the Wrekin," that attained its greatest favour in the days of the port-drinking squires and no heel-taps.

It was about the year 48 A.D. when the Roman General, Ostorius Scapula, drove out the British tribes and founded here the largest and most important station on the Severn, standing where the Watling Street and the Ikenild Street met. He selected a strategic point in the angle of land formed by the confluence of the Severn and the Tern, and surrounded at that time by meres and extensive marshes; and he Latinized the British name—Wre-kin, meaning chief hill—of the most distinctive feature of the scenery for the title of his new city. The Wrekin has ever been the dominant feature, both to eye and mind, of this neighbourhood. When Ostorius Scapula advanced into the district, that swelling height of 1370 feet was the first thing to attract his attention, both from its bulk and singular isolation, and from the embarrassing fact that in an entrenched camp on its summit lay a native force which it became necessary to dislodge before he could call himself master of the lands beneath. We have no account of how he set about this task, nor how long it took him to reduce that force, but that he eventually overcame is made manifest by the existence of the splendid city of Uriconium for a period of four hundred years.

The period of the Roman occupation of this island is so remote that we are accustomed to think of it merely as a passing political phase, but when one considers that—taking thirty years as a generation—thirteen generations of Romans lived their lives here and died and were forgotten before Uriconium came to an end, it will be seen that the Roman rule was not like the swiftly-fading glory of a summer's day. Put in another way, this period represents as lengthy a range as from Henry VII.'s reign to our own time.

Uriconium was indeed no mean place. Its prosperity arose from the position which it occupied, a vantage-point in course of time for trading with the Welsh tribes who brought from their mountains native gold, and skins, and other raw products, and thus rendered it a mart probably second to no Roman settlement in Britain. Its walls enclosed a space of three miles in circumference—an area more than one-third larger than the famous town of Pompeii; and it was greater beyond comparison with *Deva*—Chester, to the north; or *Magna Castra*—Kenchester, near Hereford, to the south.

Thus this Roman city stood until their great Empire, weakened by the inroads of barbarians who threatened the Eternal City itself, could no longer spare the army of occupation that kept Britain in subjection. The legions were recalled from outlying colonies to defend the heart of the Empire, and by the end of A.D. 410, no Roman soldier remained in Britain.

When the country was left to itself after four hundred and fifty-three years of firm rule, the civilization that had been established fell rapidly into decay. Grown effeminate themselves and weakened by many generations of wealth and luxury, the Romans had by their example degraded the once valorous and heroic Britons to so low a level that they became absolutely helpless against the savage northern tribes that, when the legionaries had departed, descended in numberless hordes from the wild country beyond the Tweed. These Picts and Scots, crossing Hadrian's Wall, overran the northern provinces, and to the southward appeared swarms of Teutonic pirates who rapidly lay waste the coasts of what were afterwards to be known as Essex, Kent, and Sussex.

The Romanized Britons were thus assailed on either hand. They had grown unaccustomed to the use of arms; their appeals to Rome for aid could not be answered, and thus they were abandoned to their fate, which was speedy and cruel. The country offered a tempting prey to savage invaders. The long years of Roman rule and prosperity had left the whole face of the island dotted over with great cities and luxurious villas, where lay great treasures of gold and silver, after which the poor and savage, but fierce and fearless, Teutonic marauders lusted; also many triumphs of art and decoration remained : but for these things they cared nothing. At this time a large portion of the land was under cultivation; smiling fields yielded rich harvests, and splendid roads traversed the country in every direction. Of these the principal were Watling Street, which crossed the country diagonally from *Rutupiæ*—Richborough, near Ramsgate—to London, and thence to *Segontium*, near Carnarvon, passing through these very ruins of Uriconium; the Foss Way, from Cornwall to Lincoln; the Ikenild Street, from Tynemouth to Saint David's; and the Ermine Street, from Saint David's to Southampton.

The helpless Britons did the very worst thing possible to be done : they employed their Teutonic foes as mercenaries against the northern invaders. The Saxons, Jutes, and Angles certainly drove back the tribes from Caledonia, but, eventually, they also ousted their employers. In the space of forty-seven years from their first landing, the kingdom of Kent was founded by Hengist, and in a hundred and seventy-six years from the departure of the Roman legions, nothing remained to the nerveless Britons but the tract of land—now Wales—westward of the Severn, and, in the south of the island, the district of "West Wales," that is to say, the counties of Devon and Cornwall.

Uriconium was destroyed by the Picts and Scots, or by the North Welsh tribes, about the year 450, and its inhabitants massacred; and since that time no attempt has ever been made to inhabit its burnt and shattered ruins. When the Saxons came, they found a deserted site, with grass and shrubs already growing in the streets and upon the walls; with pestiferous swamps and pools dealing death and agues and fevers, exhaling the most loathsome effluvia, and all aglow at nights with the phosphorescence arising from a soil poisoned and saturated with the wreck and refuse of an ancient and populous place. Wild beasts and obscene birds alone inhabited here, and it is small wonder that the Saxons shunned its site with superstitious dread, believing it to be the home of evil spirits. They founded the present village of Wroxeter, on new ground, outside the walls of this haunted spot, whose name is simply *Wreakenceaster*, the Sassenach for Uriconium. Their settlement of Wrockwardine—*Wreaken-worthen* = Wrekin village—is another instance of how largely the looming Wrekin bulked in the minds of the English, Romans, and Britons.

The ruins stood for six hundred years, sinking deeper and more deeply into the earth created by the growth and decay of the vegetation which grew rankly in the marshes, until the Normans, who were not over-timid when anything was to be gained by boldness, dug up and carried away the wrought stones of the Roman buildings as materials for their churches and castles. The Norman church of Wroxeter was built of the spoils of Uriconium.

During the Middle Ages, legends were continually current as to hidden treasure to be found here, but it was not until 1702 that we begin to hear of any antiquarian discoveries on the site of this dead-and-gone civilization. In that year a mosaic pavement was found, and curiosity began to be aroused as to the origin of the only other visible relic of a forgotten city—that stretch of massive wall, three feet in thickness, seventy-two feet long, and twenty-one feet high, called by the country people the Old Wall. This was the very centre of the city: the grassy mound, which forms in places quite a striking object as it runs in a wide circle through the surrounding fields, covers the remains of the city wall. Within its compass lies whatever still is left of the streets, the temples, the shops and residences of the Roman City of the Wrekin.

Traces of a Roman cemetery have been discovered without the walls, at a spot skirting the narrow country lane that bears the name of Watling Street Road. The plough has turned up tombstones that prove the present cornfields to have been, once upon a time, a great burial-ground, and their carvings and inscriptions bring the days of the Cæsars nearer to us than the stones of secular buildings can do. Epitaphs lie, doubtless, but what pious frauds they are: love and grief are the pleasure and pain of every race, and the sorrow of the mother for the child, of the husband for the wife, of the children for the parents, as seen recorded on these gravestones of eighteen hundred years sithence, is full of tears even now.

Here is a simple example. It commences, like all these pagan memorials, with the initials D.M., an invocation to the Gods of the Manes:—

D.M.	Diadumenus erected this to Antonia Gemella, a most affectionate wife. She lived thirty-three years.
ANTONIAE	
GEMELLAE	
DIADVMENVS	
PIENTISSIMAE	
FECIT.	
VIXIT . ANNIS . XXXIII	

Another, with many abbreviations, reads, translated:—

"Marcus Petronius, son of Lucius, of the Menenian tribe, lived thirty-eight years, a soldier of the fourteenth legion called Gemina; he served as a soldier eighteen years, and was a standard-bearer: he lies here."

One other may be quoted. It runs, in its mutilated form:—

D.M.
DEVCCV
S. AN. XV
CVR. AG
RATRE

Diis Manibus	To the Gods of the Manes,
Deucco	Deuccus, aged fifteen years;
S, annorum xv,	raised by the care of his brother.
curam agente	
fratre	

In 1858 a sum was subscribed towards the excavation of Uriconium, and operations were begun in the following year by the North Shropshire Archæological Society. But they were interrupted by a surly and aggrieved farmer, who pre-

EXPLORATION OF URICONIUM.

ferred the welfare of his turnips to hypocausts and tesseræ. This unscientific agriculturist was disgusted at the number of people who came tramping over his fields and treading down his young wheat, and thought that folks who came so far out of their way, just to see a few old walls, were little better than lunatics. A committee of archæologists then rented two acres of land, which they had permission from the owner, the Duke of Cleveland, to dig as they pleased. The immediate results were the discovery of the basements of buildings, which were laid open for inspection, showing the method employed by the Romans for warming their houses.

Fireplaces were unknown to them: they constructed instead a basement chamber, floored with cement and usually three feet in height, with numerous little pillars of bricks and tiles to support the floor above. Flues led up inside the walls and distributed heat from the burning wood or charcoal, with which this underground "hypocaust," as it was called, was filled. It was in one of these hypocausts that the explorers discovered three skeletons, crouched up against the wall. Two were those of women, the other was the skeleton of an old man. Within his grasp was a pile of Roman coins, 142 in all, and beside them lay some fragments of wood and the rusty remains of nails, all that was left of the cash-box which their owner, his ruling passion strong in the last hour of his life, had carried away with him when the city was pillaged and its inhabitants exterminated by the tribes. None were spared when Uriconium was taken, and the citizens, realizing that this would be the case, made in great numbers for the underground hypocausts of whose existence, they thought, it was unlikely that the savages would be aware.

Probably they were correct, but it is evident that these poor wretches, at least, were suffocated by the fumes of the burning charcoal which filled their hiding-place. Other evidences of the fury of the attack are visible, among them the skeleton of a child, murdered and thrown over the wall of a courtyard.

Relics of domestic life are constantly found in the dust-bins of the ruined houses; bone and ivory hairpins, still greasy with the pomade used by the Roman ladies; brooches, nails, glass, oyster-shells, and fragments of pottery, all signs that the world wagged then in much the same manner as it does now. Even patent medicines were known and medical quacks plied a no less lucrative trade than our own pill and syrup empirics, as may be judged from the engraved stone label of an eye-wash found in these ruins, similar to many others discovered in Roman settlements elsewhere.

LIV.

By the Welsh Bridge, "the reddie waye to Wales," we left Shrewsbury for Oswestry. Nearly eighteen miles lie between the two places, and all the way there is not one considerable village, but only a few roadside hamlets of little or no importance. This is the Holyhead road, Telford's great achievement of over seventy years ago, when the high-roads were the only routes between one town and another; but nowadays its great width, like that of most of the great highways, is far too roomy for the diminished traffic that in these railway times finds its way upon the roads, and only the crown of the highway is kept in repair by the various county councils through whose territory it runs.

Directly across the Welsh Bridge from Shrewsbury is the ancient suburb of Frankwell, a long street lining the highroad. This was formerly outside the jurisdiction of the Mayor and Corporation of Shrewsbury, and here, when strangers and "foreigners" were not allowed to pursue their callings within the town, they were suffered to settle in this liberty, and earn what livelihood they might contrive without the walls. Here, too, the proscribed Welshmen of bypast centuries, who were not allowed to live within the town, passed a precarious existence. Thus arose the suburb of Frankwell, the first syllable of which name derives from the franchise or freedom accorded to these outlanders. There is a hamlet of Welsh Frankton, near Oswestry, whose name derives from similar circumstances.

But Frankwell has a more recent fame as having been the birthplace of Darwin, who was born at The Mount, on February 12, 1809. He was entered at Shrewsbury School in 1818, in the time when Doctor Butler was Head Master. Shrewsbury people are somewhat tardily proud of him, and the local papers have not yet done with discussing the unprofitable question of whether or not the author of the " Origin of Species " was a Christian. He was certainly a sad stumbling-block to the orthodox, and like other innovators and leaders of thought, had his period of probation, when his views were not accepted so readily as now, when everyone talks glibly of evolution and heredity, and the survival of the fittest in the struggle for life. It is from Darwin's works that the French have taken their ideas of what an eminent French author has curiously termed the "strugforlife"; and "strugforlifeurs," has become quite a well-known Gallic term for those who live from hand to mouth in the battle for existence.

Darwin was himself a striking instance of heredity, for his grandfather, Erasmus Darwin, had been a man of great distinction in medicine and biology, and was in the front rank of the men of science of his day. He was, like his more celebrated grandson, an agnostic, and of great independence of thought and habit. It is related of him that George III. offered him the post of King's Physician, if he would give up his country residence and live in London, but he refused the honour.

It is astonishing what storms of clerical vituperation were aroused by Charles Darwin's works on Evolution and the Descent of Man. His views were diametrically opposed to the literal interpretation of the Bible, and though he expressly disclaimed any intention of invading the realms of theology and preferred the passive attitude of " know nothing " to the aggressiveness of the atheists, his labours as a naturalist and the new ideas at which he arrived were the occasions of much abuse from the religious people of that day, who regarded Holy Writ as not only inspired, but its periods of time as to be taken with the fullest belief. They held that the Creation was accomplished in six periods of twenty-four hours each, and that those six days mentioned in the Book of Genesis were actually six days of our reckoning, rather than arbitrary terms given to cycles of uncounted thousands of years.

The new and startling theories of Darwin exasperated some of these believers in the literal accuracy of the Bible and pained others who desired to retain their whole-souled faith in its account of the beginnings of the world, while they could not help admitting the logical views of this heterodox naturalist. The two views would not square with one another, and the anguish of mind was great which Darwin unwittingly caused these good people whose unquestioning faith was rudely shaken by the force of his hard facts. But his blameless life and his purely scientific ends, entirely removed from any question of religious polemics, gained him at last the respect even of those who would not be converted to his views. He sleeps in Westminster Abbey, now that his work is done.

Just beyond Frankwell comes Shelton, where Glendower is supposed to have watched the issue of the Battle of Shrewsbury from the branches of an oak-tree. He may certainly have beheld Shrewsbury Castle from here, but the field of battle is far beyond the view from this point. However that may be, Glendower's oak has been pointed out for many years, and may conceivably be as old, and older, than four hundred and ninety years. It is hollow now, and decrepit, and the interior space is paved with cobble-stones. The giant trunk measures in circumference forty-two feet, and the measurement from the ground to the top of the main trunk is forty-one feet six inches.

Shortly after we passed the "Four Crosses Inn," the Breiddin Hills came in full view to our left, blue in the distance and impressive from their isolation. The Hills of the Robbers, as their Welsh name implies, are a landmark for many miles. Presently the Severn crossed the highway at the pretty hamlet of Montford Bridge, and on the bridge we rested.

It was hot, intolerably hot. Great fissures appeared in the parched earth, as thirsty as ourselves, and the grass, even by the streams, was gone brown and dry, and the streams themselves trickled insignificantly within their beds, like the rivulet of type that flows through the ample margins of an *édition de luxe*. It was, of all the heated days of this fervent year, the hottest. Although we are by no manner of means frequenters of taverns nor amongst those to whom an ale-house sign is the cheeriest sight in all the landscape, yet it must be confessed that the appearance of successive "Red Lions" and "Ships and Anchors," was grateful indeed, and that their cool, stone-floored parlours were not to be exchanged just at present for the most luxuriously carpeted of drawing-rooms.

It was a day when the heathen, vine-crowned Bacchus, astride upon his barrel, seemed a less preposterous god, when Silenus was excusable, and their vinous attendant cupids less to be reprobated as youthful candidates for some Inebriate Asylum; a day on which an aspiration for two gullets would have become even a Blue Ribbonite; when the parched versifier might have been excused the perpetration of such doggerel as this :—

> ' O! give me foremost, first
>   A swallow like a six-inch main
> And then a god-like thirst ;
>   Then rivulets of dry champagne,
> And let me drink till I am dry again.
> " Then give to me capacity
>   Of hogsheads ten or twenty,
> And floods of liquor let there be :
>   Yea, seas and lakes in plenty.
> Yes . . . . . ."

Alas! here the bacchanalian bard, overcome by emotion and potations, becomes unintelligible, smiles upon his fingers, and babbles of green fields, like a celebrated prototype. But the realization of such aspirations leads infallibly to the haunts of the Stipendiaries and, even in jest, is anathema to the devotees of the pump.

While we rested here, there came along the road a working-man, bronzed and bearded, a Salopian evidently, by his face. He, too, leaned over the parapet of the bridge, and gazed into the water as a relief from the white and dusty road.

"'Tis hard work, walking," said he, and we agreed with him.

He had walked from "Salop," as he called Shrewsbury, to "Odgerstree" the day before, on the chance of finding work which was scarce at the former place, but had not succeeded in his object, as too many men at Oswestry were in the same plight as himself. A job was promised him in five days' time, and he would walk back in time to secure it.

"But why," we asked him, "don't you stay in Oswestry till then, on the chance of finding work?"

"Ah," said he, "but how am I to keep myself in the meantime? I asked everywhere in the town for work, and got a job of unloading coals, sufficient to pay for my breakfast this morning, but that leaves me without a penny. Anyhow, my home is in Shrosbury, and I may pick up a shilling or two there before the job commences at Odgerstree."

"But," we said, "do you mean to say that you tramp to and fro such long distances on these slight chances?"

"Yes, sir," replied this stalwart, "I do. I'd get a lasting job if I could, but they're not easily got, and there's many like me as tramps about the country on these off-chances. I've walked to Bromwicham [1] and into Wales, and to Hereford, but times is terrible bad and little work is going."

I never earned a blessing so cheaply as that bestowed upon me by this poor fellow, who did me the honour to accept a small present which I made him out of what God in His goodness has vouchsafed me as a recompense for less labour than his. Consider, you who go about from day to day with a sufficiency of food and raiment, with never a troubled thought as to whence will come your next meal, how many are they who honestly wish for work and rarely find it, and then only at the cost of infinite exertion and many disappointments. Think of this unfortunate man's

[1] Birmingham.

tramp of thirty-seven miles, from Shrewsbury to Oswestry and back, and of its result in earning but the price of a breakfast! Give then of your plenty to them that deserve an alms, nor count it as a drought for drying up the springs of your benevolence that your largesse be occasionally bestowed upon the undeserving and the professional tramp. But, indeed, you need rarely be under a misapprehension as to the character of the wayfarers you meet, for the loafer and ne'er-do-well bear the stamp of their order most unmistakably, and solicit alms with a brazen effrontery which clearly comes of long practice. The honest man is not so ready to beg. He makes no shame of recounting his misfortunes, for their narration lightens his load, whether your sympathy be sentimental or practical. But relieve his needs with delicacy and with his permission first asked and obtained; for, however poor and necessitous a man may be, charity should not be thrust upon him as if he were bound to accept of you and so render himself under an obligation.

Nesscliff was the next place marked on our map, and its name prepared us, long before we came in sight of it, for the kind of situation it occupied. The two syllables of the name are repetitive, for "ness" and "cliff" have both the same meaning, and, true enough, a great precipitous rock arose from beside the road where the hamlet of Nesscliff stood. Further on, a sign-post directed to Llan-y-Mynach, literally Monk's Church; but we kept along the highway to Oswestry, resisting all allurements of these finger-posts, which directed to places of singular names, like " Ruyton-of-the-Eleven Towns," whose very strangeness invited exploration.

The only other place before Oswestry was reached, was the uninteresting but apparently well-to-do village of West Felton; like all the places on this road, of comparatively modern growth. But if the settlements upon this road of recent make were insignificant, the country was lovely. The distant Welsh hills bounded the view, and the lands between were obviously rich, even to the unpractised eyes of us Londoners. Great parks, beautifully wooded, and coated with the most luxuriant turf, every now and again bordered the highway, and noble mansions peeped grandly from woodland drives.

It may well be imagined how wrathful were the Welsh, who, cooped up amid the hills and less fertile lands of Cambria, overlooked the smiling meadows which had once been theirs, but were in turn occupied by "the coiling serpent" as they termed the advancing Saxons, and afterwards by the Normans, who advanced with the quick spring of the panther rather than with the serpent's more gradual movement, and built great castles in the Marches at every step. Yet the hatred of the Norman seems never to have found such constant expression among the Cymry as their intense loathing of the Saxon. If you speak in English to an unlettered Welshman at this day, he will probably reply "dim Saesoneg," with a surprising energy of vindictive intonation that would seem to be entirely uncalled for at the present time, when the Marches are free to Saxon and Briton alike, and when the races are become so largely intermingled.

LV.

THE Marches afford endless delight to the holiday-maker who has a vocation for tramping. Castle succeeds unfailingly to castle along these debateable lands, and Sunday comes not more surely once a week than this picturesque iteration of old-time fortresses. No overgrown towns and miscalled pleasure-resorts mar the wild beauty of the Borders; and, unlike the tourist-haunted coasts, the drone of the wild bees has not yet given way to the bray of the German band.

Homely inns, with honest country fare, are the rule when once the tramper leaves the sophisticated districts that fringe the Wye below Monmouth, and anglers are the usual company one meets at these places. If it were left to the angler to speak of them, we should go in ignorance of these old-world places for ever, for your true fisherman is the most shy and secretive of men, and prefers to keep his streams and pleasaunces to himself.

Touring: In Several Sorts. 299

But there is no sort of community between the angler and the pedestrian. The one fleets a contemplative day with cunning but leisured devices for the due ensnaring of the silver trout or grayling, and so home, when evening falls, to the "Angler's Rest" or "Fisherman's Home" that stands upon the banks of his fishful stream: the other is consumed with a noble rage for many milestones,

A RIVER IN THE MARCHES.

and none so pleased as he when, after an exhausting itinerary of some thirty miles, he drops, all dusty, grimed, and sharp-set, into the most comfortable chair of some village inn, where the tripper is unknown.

No banquet so rich and rare as the pedestrian's evening meal in such a place. A sweet exhaustion creeps upon his every sense; a gentle glow pervades him; this is become the best of all possible worlds, into which blisters enter only as piquant reminders that he has walked an unconscionable distance this day. And of their piquancy on the morrow there may be no doubt. But to-night the world is rosy; and after all, the meal's the thing!

And what manner of meal should this be but high tea? Heaven send you to an inn where the hostess has a pretty taste in teas, for a horrid brew of that best of herbs is the very devil—no less!

And so, Providence having led you to where a right cup of Congo or Bohea may appear upon the evening board, and giving you, moreover, a companion in travel of a like mind with yourself, you shall be more happy than—being but mortal and full of all manner of conflicting prejudices—you have any right to be. For the rest, it matters nothing that you have no refinements and delicacies of the town to grace the board withal. You fare sumptuously, and recognize no lack, upon simple country produce; and you who have been dyspeptic in London can now digest with the best ostrich that ever thrived on scrap-iron and tenpenny nails.

No optimists so cheery as the roseate philosophers you find yourselves on these occasions, and you strike sparks of keenest wit from one another in a fashion entirely unpremeditated and foreign to your usual habit, which, it may be, is stolid enough. It has chanced, perhaps, that the day has not passed without its memorable incidents, whether pleasant or untoward, but they are all one to you who feast so royally on simple fare, and thereafter bid the world good-night, to sleep between lavender-scented sheets in bedrooms contrived in strangest wise with sloping ceilings, queer recesses, and floors that incline sharply and unexpectedly.

When morning comes, with sunbursts and scent of flowers through the open casements, you are famished for an early breakfast. You arise gingerly and with deliberation, for though the spirits may be light, your blistered feet forbid an unconsidered bound on to the hard boards. You descend toward the dressing-table beneath the window with a sudden and entirely unpremeditated rush along the Alpine slopes of the flooring, and behold your sunburned face with a supreme satisfaction in the glass, distorted and absurdly out of drawing though it be in that cracked and wavy mirror. To shave from your wry-mouthed reflection is an operation that calls for all your skill, patience and courage, but, achieved at length, you feel that at least your breakfast has been honestly earned, and not even the mowers in the hillside meadows opposite your eyrie, whose scythes swish so pleasantly through the morning air, have laboured so resolutely for a subsistence.

Your inn, if it be that ideal hostelry to which I have often attained, has a garden wherein grow all manner of simple fruits and vegetables, and rich-scented, old-fashioned flowers, one with another, in most informal concourse; where raspberry canes, gooseberry and currant bushes, red, white, and black, nestle under old apple and pear trees, and again, beneath these, marygolds, agrimony, the pungent "old man," and a hundred other favourites of the cottage garden; and no more pleasant ten minutes while breakfast is a-brewing than those you while away in their fragrant company. And presently, breakfast being despatched and your knapsacks strapped, away you go to repeat your programme of the previous day.

But the pedestrian is of rarer occurrence than he was used to be. Never a popular method of holiday-making, tramping has lost many of its enthusiasts to cycling. You may deplore their taste who pedal to and fro upon the highways, and still more may you contemn those who lounge their holidays away upon esplanade or sea-front of a populous watering-place, but in practice you approve their choice, for it leaves the countryside free and unfrequented for the true padder of the hoof.

"In the Spring a young man's fancy," as the poet might have observed, "lightly turns to thoughts of tours." *Then* does the pedestrian look to his boots, and the cyclist to his wheel, and they, both of them, have out their Reduced Ordnance maps, and fall to scanning routes and distances, to consulting road-books and weather forecasts, and, if they be socially inclined, to securing congenial companions for holiday travel. And to this last consideration, too much attention cannot be paid, for, O, my brothers! an uncongenial spirit with you, a-touring, is the very Evil Spirit himself; nothing ever tries friendship nearly so much as the chances and mischances of touring together, in whatever sort; not even the maleficent power of borrowed money shall so effectually sever you from your life-long friend as a difference on the road. And few are they who are so admirably fitted for touring companionship that they have

SOMEWHAT HARD OF HEARING.

never any quarrels. Why, with one who is not absolutely your other self, they begin even with the day. You are given, let us say, to early rising and breakfasting while yet the dew is fresh, and so off upon the road. The other man is almost sure to be one who likes his bed, and *will* take his money's worth (and more) out of the hotel sheets, though breakfast becomes cold downstairs, and the day already well-aired; and although you implore and entreat him to be up and dressing, he would almost rather you went on your way alone, so only he be left in peace and slumber; and, indeed, he says as much and in so many words.

You, my friend, being, even as myself, long-suffering

and slow to wrath, bear with the lazy wre—, I mean your companion, and at length you are (say) at eleven a.m., or thereby, upon the highway. You manage tolerably well all day, I will assume, with, of course, the exception that when one of you wishes to halt the other wants to go on! but it is when the showers of an uncertain day come on that you begin to realize the hideous selfishness of your mate. *He* has brought with him a waterproof; *you* have left your own at home. It is then, I suspect, that you really begin to dislike the man.

And after such a dull and tiring day, when clouds lower and you wish to rest, should you mistake the road and land the two of you in some trackless waste, then does the other man's wrath descend upon your devoted head in winged words of scornful import. "Here's a mess," says he, "all through *you*. If we'd taken the road *I* said, we should be all right by this time: now we've lost our way altogether. Next time I go away with you, may I be hanged. I've a good mind to go on by myself."

"LOOKS OF FIRE AND HATE."

"GO ON THEN BY YOURSELF," you shout, in, so to speak, capital letters, "and *be* hanged to you!" Then you exchange looks of fire and hate, and *exeunt* severally into the darkness of a wet evening. It befalls, however, that, after a certain time of independent wanderings, you meet accidentally at the same inn. There you have your tea, or supper, or dinner—what you will—each man to himself, strangers yet; each with a newspaper propped up before him at table for a proper and dignified seclusion. But, during the evening, when there is nothing else to do but stare at your maps, you foregather again, and pass both that night and the remainder of the holiday amicably. But you never go touring again with *that* man.

So powerful for evil or for good is companionship on a walking tour. Professor Wilson—the dread Christopher North of the *Edinburgh Review*—was a prodigious walker and courageous enough to take his wife and sister with him on his tramps; but that born tramp, George Borrow, was a solitary: and there are worse ways of touring than that. But for a powerful irritant commend me to the countryman, who, replying to the exhausted tourist's inquiry tells him that "it is rather better nor three mile" to the next village—for, to the weary wayfarer, the surplusage is rather worse than better.

LVI.

AND on the day that we walked from Shrewsbury to Oswestry, we felt the truth of this last remark. At "a little better than" two miles from Oswestry we grew footsore and came with halting step into the town, expectant of interest and beauty from a perusal of Churchyard's eulogistic verse :—

> "This towne doth front on Wales as right as lyne,
> So sondrie townes in Shropshire doe for troth,
> As Ozestrie, a priettie town full fine,
> Which may be lov'd, be likte, and praysed both.
> It stands soe trim, and is mayntayned soe cleane,
> And peopled is with folke that well doe meane,
> That it deserves to be enrouled and shryned
> In each good heart and every manly mind."

But however truthful these lines may have been at the time they were penned, they scarcely hold good now; for, however praiseworthy the Oswestry folk may remain, the town has been well-nigh denuded of old buildings and is to-day a crowded place of some nine thousand inhabitants, penned up in the space usually occupied by towns of half its population; and the result is not pretty.

But Oswestry is wonderfully prosperous and a place of very great antiquity. It derives its name from Oswald, King of Northumbria, who was slain here in battle with

Penda, King of Mercia, in the year 642. Penda caused the dead body of Oswald to be cut in pieces and stuck on poles, as trophies of victory.

> "Whose head, all black with gore, and mangled hands,
> Were fix'd on stakes, at Penda's curs'd commands."

But we need waste no sympathy upon Oswald, although at the time he was accounted a Christian martyr. By all accounts, he was the aggressor in the war between himself and the King of Mercia, and had he been fortunate enough to secure a victory, it seems very likely that portions of Penda would in that case have decorated the neighbourhood. But Oswald had been a great benefactor to religious houses, so he was canonized very shortly after his death, and the field in which he was slain became celebrated for miracles, and subsequently the site of a monastery, of which not a single fragment remains. Oswestry was formerly a walled town, with a castle and four defensible gates: the Beatrice Gate, Black Gate, Willow Gate, and New Gate. Castle, walls, and gates are now all gone, having been demolished in the last century, and their materials applied to the building of a gaol. The town was formerly the great market for Welsh flannels, but that distinction has for very many years passed away. It subsists, nowadays, upon a variety of trades, and being upon the borders of the Denbighshire coal-field, derives much trade from the wants of colliers and collieries. Machine works, and iron and brass foundries are numerous, and the Cambrian Railway has its engine and carriage works here. Some of the more recent buildings are large and handsome, especially the hotels and banks, of which latter there are a great many.

The parish church, dedicated to Saint Oswald, has been restored, and is rather uninteresting, except the venerable-looking tower, which has been left untouched since its reparation after the close of the Civil War. In the contest with the Parliament, Oswestry was held for the King, and the church standing outside the walls, the Royalists pulled down the upper stages of the tower, lest the Puritans on their appearance should use it as a point of vantage whence to fire upon the town. The town was besieged on the 22nd of June, 1644, by the Earl of Denbigh and General Mytton, with a detachment of the Parliamentary army from Market Drayton. A breach was made in the walls and the enemy entered, the defenders and the townsfolk fleeing to the castle. A youth named Cranage had rendered himself very conspicuous in the attack, and the Parliamentary officers " enlivened him with wine " and then induced him to go up to the castle gate, under fire, and fix a petard to it. He succeeded and returned unhurt; the bomb exploded, the castle gate was blown open, and the garrison surrendered.

The Welsh have always been numerous here, from the position of the town just within the English shires, and Jones and Owen are the most frequent patronymics that one sees gracing the facias of its shops. Owen is, after Jones, the commonest name in Wales. Both mean John, and it is supposed that the Christian name of John became so popular because of its having been borne by the favourite disciple of Jesus Christ.

About the distance of a mile north from Oswestry is a hill crowned by an ancient earthwork, called Old Oswestry, whence the country people believe the town to have migrated. The Welsh call it Hen Dinas (old place) or Caer Ogyrfan, from a legendary chief named Ogyrfan, contemporaneous with Arthur. Watt's Dyke, which runs through it, is a parallel earthwork with Offa's Dyke. It commences near Basingwerk Abbey, on the coast of Flintshire and runs by Pen-y-Ffordd, Hope, Wrexham, and through the grounds of Wynnstay at Rhuabon, to Llan-y-Mynach, and the Severn, where it becomes lost. Indeed, it is, throughout, most difficult to follow, because the plough has levelled it in many places, and villages have sprung up on it, tending to obliterate all traces of its course. Watt's Dyke is a mysterious vestige of Saxon times and much less understood than the longer, larger and more famous Dyke of Offa. It has been held that Watt's Dyke was also the work of the Mercian King, and that it was constructed at a later period than its fellow. The supposition is that the ground enclosed between the two dykes was neutral land, but no records exist as to its making or the reasons that led to it, and so everything about the history of Watt's Dyke must remain conjectural.

Churchyard, the Elizabethan poet, speaks with an unwarrantable certainty, born perhaps of poetic necessity:—

> "There is a famous thing
> Called Offa's Dyke, that reacheth farre in length,
> All kind of ware the Danes might thither bring,
> It was free ground, and called the Britons' strength.
> Watt's Dyke, likewise, about the same was set,
> Between which two, the Danes and Britons met,
> And traffic still, but passing bounds by sleight,
> The one did take the other pris'ner streight."

LVII.

OFFA'S DYKE commences near Prestatyn, on the north coast of Flintshire, at a place called in the Welsh tongue " Uffern " (which, being Englished, means Hell), overlooking a dangerous sand-bank where wreckers in other days plied their dreadful trade. It runs, roughly, in a southerly direction, by Caerwys, Mold, Minera, and Ruabon, to Chirk, Selattyn and Llanymynech, where it crosses the Severn to traverse the rough country of the Long Mountain, and then past the town of Montgomery and the hilly Forest of Clun. It leaves Shropshire to enter the county of Radnor at Knighton, anciently called by the Welsh Tref-y-Clawdd—the Town on the Dyke; and thence, passing through the village of Discoyd, comes into Herefordshire at Knill. Through Herefordshire its course lies by Lyonshall, Upperton (or Offa's Town), and Mansell Gamage, to Bridge Sollars, where it meets the Wye, which, for the most part, formed the boundary between Welsh and English for the remaining distance to the Severn estuary at Tidenham in Gloucestershire. The Dyke was made about the year 784 by Offa the Terrible, King of Mercia, from 759 to 794. The earliest mention of it is made by Asser, who says:

"Offa made a rampart between Mercia and Britannia, which stretched *de mari usque ad mare*," and so, from the Bristol Channel to the Frith of Dee it remains to this day; not now, indeed, a political boundary, but a testimony to the energy of the Angles. That it certainly was no handiwork of the Romans can be seen by the fact of their having penetrated far beyond its bounds and thoroughly subduing Wales, centuries before, and from its having been constructed, in one place at least, above late Roman remains. Moreover, even after the lapse of eleven centuries, the English and Welsh names of towns and villages ranged on either side of its course are still very reliable evidence of the particular era when this great rampart first was made.

Thus, to this day, the place-names on the Welsh side are almost exclusively Welsh, and those on the English side unmistakably of English, that is to say, of Teutonic, origin. Those Welsh names that still remain on the eastward, or English, side of the Dyke, bear testimony to the later policy of the Angles, who rose from the ferocity and thirst for blood that first characterized them, to a degree of civilization in which earth-hunger, the greed for land, certainly still provoked aggressive wars—as it must ever do—but whose rise from savagery rendered their conquests not so much a signal for the extermination of the conquered as an opportunity of retaining them as slaves or tillers of the soil who should work for the victors and minister to the luxuries their success demanded. The Welshmen who chose to remain as peaceable subjects of the Mercian kings were allowed to do so, and to those who took advantage of this option the Welsh place-names within the pale owe their survival.

Of these Welsh names, given by Welsh-speaking people to places within Mercian territory, examples are neither many nor important; for although it was good policy to allow individuals to remain, it would have been imprudent to suffer settlements and communities to form, sufficiently large to maintain national traditions and to confer Welsh appellations upon their residences. Moreover, the antipathy between the races forbade a general acceptance of the liberty given the conquered to settle on the Mark.

So they are only hamlets and farms which bear Welsh names within the Dyke. Some names of mountains and rivers still retain Celtic features, and a few towns and villages possess singularly composite names formed by an amalgam of the two languages; but a singularly sharp division of tongues still marches with the Dyke, and without its interposition would be sufficiently obvious to draw attention to the fact that here, from the Severn to the Dee, two hostile races met.

Besides these linguistic differences, there are some few places whose names show their position in ancient political geography in the most obvious way. English and Welsh Bicknor, two villages a few miles above Monmouth, are situated on either side of the Wye, that "scientific frontier" of eleven centuries ago; and just in their rear stands Welsh Newton: Welshpool and Welshampton again are notable examples.

But another class of place-names occurring on the Welsh side is neither Welsh nor English. These are of a much later date than the Dyke and are, in fact, Norman-French of the eleventh century. The great kingdom of England, united for the first time under Egbert in 827, was conquered by the Normans in 1066, and then the Dyke as a military boundary became obsolescent; for the conquerors, pressing westward, soon overpassed the old barrier and founded Norman lordships where the Mercians had failed to penetrate. Of this class are the names of Grosmont and Mold, places sixty miles apart, but whose appellations have almost exactly the same meaning, Grosmont being, simply enough, Great Mountain, and Mold deriving, in more esoteric manner, from the Norman Lords of Mont Alt=High Mountain. The name of the Haughmond Hills, by Shrewsbury, has the same origin.

Antiquaries have continually disputed as to the precise use and purpose of Offa's great earthwork. That an earthen wall of this character would suffice to keep an enemy from invading the lengthy frontiers of these sparsely-settled districts of the Mark is improbable; that it was a mere political boundary is equally unlikely. To come to a more correct view of its function, the Dyke must be carefully examined, both as to its position and construction. It consists of an embankment and a trench, the trench being formed from the earth dug out to make the embankment. This ditch being placed invariably on the Welsh side affords a proof, if one were needed, that the Dyke was thrown up against the Welsh and not by the Welsh against the Mercians. The average height of the earthwork is ten feet, and the ditch has a depth of six and a width of twelve feet. Another very strong proof that this extraordinary piece of military engineering was directed against the Welsh is afforded by its situation. The line of country traversed by it is almost wholly composed of high hills and rugged uplands, and advantage has always been taken of a particularly lofty hill, or other strong strategic position, to include it just within the pale. This is clearly seen at Long Mountain, a bold and lengthy natural bulwark in Montgomeryshire, where the Dyke runs at some distance below its westward slopes. Where the Dyke has been taken along the side of a hill it is always the Welsh side that has been selected, and in these cases its character changes from that of a fosse and mound to an acute scarp, difficult to surmount. Descending a hillside, it takes another form; that merely of a ditch without an embankment.

These different forms of a barrier set between nations consumed with a lively hatred of each other were designed to prevent, not invasions, but the petty border forays that harassed and unsettled the frontiers, and usually resolved themselves into nothing more serious than the raiding of cattle by small bands, and the pillaging of homesteads. An army of invasion would have had little difficulty in overpassing the Dyke, but to marauders returning from a foray, laden with spoils and encumbered with the cattle they had driven off, it was a serious obstacle. Plunder might be taken across without very much delay, but the raided herds and flocks, which were always the chief of their booty, were not so readily driven across mounds and deep ditches. To leave the cattle behind would be to fail in the foremost object of their raid: to remain meant certain death at the hands of Mercians already in pursuit.

Death, sudden and terrible, lurked in the shadow of the Dyke. Intercourse between the peoples of either nation was forbidden under the severest penalties, and the capture of a Welshman found on its hither side meant the shortest shrift for him. Intermarriage between Angles and British thus became impossible through a long series of years; for a Welshman who went a-courting into Mercia lost his head a great deal more effectually than such modern phrases for infatuation would imply, and the Saxon who crossed into Wales on a similar errand would have met with no more gentle handling. It is a curious but obvious reflection that to Offa's Dyke we owe, more than to anything else, this continued isolation of the two races, and that to it is due the almost exclusively Welsh character of the population of the Principality to this day. The *Clawdd Offa*, as the Welsh called the barrier, was regarded by that choleric people as a standing menace and insult; it may nowadays with equal truth be regarded as the bulwark of that nationality to which the modern Welshman clings with such sorry tenacity and mistaken pride.

In the reign of Edward the Confessor, 1055, the wild Welsh broke from their inaccessible mountains, notwithstanding Offa's earthworks, and they invaded and devastated England beyond the eastern banks of the Severn, burning and slaughtering all before them. Duke Harold was sent to expel them, and with the edge of the sword he reduced the borders to peace and made a law that any Briton soever found thenceforth within the English bounds of the Dyke in possession of any weapon should have his right hand cut off by the officers of the Kingdom. The transition from death to mutilation shows the advance of a comparative civilization which remained at this stage until after the Norman Conquest. Then the Lords Marchers arose, and in their continual encroachments upon the Welsh, the Dyke ceased to exist as a boundary of any significance.

Offa's Dyke is naturally, from its size and antiquity, and from its remote and isolated position, the wonder of the simple peasantry of the borders. Shropshire folk-lore has it that the Dyke was a furrow turned up by the Devil in a single night with the aid of a plough drawn by a gander and a turkey, and at one time this belief of its supernatural origin was widespread. To-day, however, it is become almost forgotten in the country-side, and great stretches of the embankment have been obliterated in the progress of cultivation of waste places, and under the plough. In others it is difficult to follow, plunging as it does amid thick underwoods and coppices in enclosed lands and private parks.

LVIII.

WE had intended staying at Oswestry, but found it little to our liking; and as Whittington village was only two miles distant, we added to our long walk from Shrewsbury by strolling into it after a tea taken at a convenient confectioner's in the town. There is a beautiful park and mansion at Park Hall, on the way, a fine specimen of a black and white building of Queen Elizabeth's time, with a domestic chapel, and just beyond comes the village, populous, and with two railway-stations to itself.

Whittington Castle, whose ruins still stand beside the road, rising from the borders of a marshy brook that once served as a moat, was at one time the property of the Fitz-Warines, who held Ludlow as one of their lordships, and here that Fulke Fitz-Warine, of whom we have already heard, is said to have played a most memorable game of chess with King John. The King, who had apparently lost the game, broke Fitz-Warine's head with the chess-board in a fit of rage, but Fulke, nothing daunted, returned the blow, " and," says an old writer, " almost demolished the King."

This scene of Fitz-Warine's notable exploit is very beauti-

WHITTINGTON CASTLE.

ful. The great gatehouse towers remain, partially covered with ivy, and stained with the mellow lichens of five hundred years. The little brook that flows under the stone bridge of the approach is thick with duck-weed and tangled masses of aquatic plants, and expands into the dimensions of a lake near the village church. The gatehouse is inhabited by a caretaker whose leaded casements look down upon the brook and command the quiet street, and the vistas are closed at either end by an inn: the White Lion at one extremity, the Boot at the other, over against a hideously-rebuilt church, repellent with windows and dressings of a peculiarly livid terra-cotta. The Boot (whence that singular sign?) could not receive us for the night as they had a party staying in the house, and so the landlady found cottage lodgings for us up the street, where we shared a bedroom, perched crazily on the summit of a corkscrew flight of stairs that creaked and cried aloud with every step.

But the night was young, and we hung awhile over the garden gate with the cottager. A traction-engine came down the road, filling the air with smoke and rattle, and a tourist's caravan followed, with a weary horse refusing to "Gee-up" under the persuasions and the whip of a sunburned young man in flannels and a striped blazer.

"Ah," said the cottager, knocking out the ashes of his pipe against the gate, "he's a bit of a gawby. 'It 'im on the stummick, mister, that'll make him gee-hup, I'se warrand."

He turned to us with a puzzled smile.

"I canna understand the ways of you gentlefolks," he said; "some of ye goo trampin' round the country wi' gert packages on yer backs, and ye calls it a holiday; an' there's a gentleman, as I suppose he'd call himself, taking a gipsy caravan along the road: an' I'll be bound he sleeps in it o' nights on some common, like those Rummies as comes about here and steals our fowls sometimes. 'Tisn't the most comfortable way o' livin', I should reckon, nor the most respectable likewise."

Oh, Respectability! we had fondly hoped you were left behind in town; but here we hearkened, with a thrill of terror, to the rustle of Mrs. Grundy's skirts. The cottager himself was under her ban; the pigeons cooed propriety; the little birds on every bough whispered scandals, and the cows in the fields chewed the cud of questionable reminiscences!

The horrid thought flashed upon us, Were *we* respectable, who carried knapsacks on our backs and tramped the country until our boots wore down at heel? Were not our stubbly chins eloquent of the very converse of respectability, and our very appetites, sharp-set through pedestrian exertions, were they not earnest in the eyes of these country folk of a condition in which a good meal was a rarity?

But the variety of methods in touring is surprising. There be those who walk, who drive a four-in-hand, who go a-boating, and others, as we have seen, who take the open road in a caravan. The democratic cycle has let loose an army of pedallers upon the highways, and the ancient hostelries that decayed with the decay of the coaching era, have taken a new lease of life by reason of them. Ways the most ingenious have been contrived that make for novelty in peripatetic holidays, but no one has yet bethought him of the steam-roller or the traction-engine as an entirely novel and unconventional conveyance a-wheel! Look to it, my friends.

LIX.

WE stayed for a few days at a remote Shropshire village where old friends gave us a hearty welcome and a warm hospitality.

"You'll be finding this rather dull," said our host one morning, as we pottered about the garden with him; "but we have an entertainment, of a sort, on to-night which may amuse you. I go because it is expected of me as a supporter of the Church, but nothing is expected of you, you know, so you can stay away if it pleases you to do so."

"What is it, then," we asked, "which may amuse us, but apparently bores you?"

THE VILLAGE CONCERT. 317

"Listen, then," he replied, "and tremble. To-night"—here he produced a tinted programme from his pocket, and read, in a doleful voice—"'An amateur concert will be held in the schoolroom in aid of the organ fund for the parish church. The Glee Choir will sing,'"—here he groaned dismally—"'the handbell ringers will give their inimitable performance,' — inimitable, I truly hope," he said in parenthesis, "for others' sake. 'The Vicar—' but there," said he, "read it for yourselves; let me steady my nerves with a pipe. Excuse this agitation, but this concert is the sixth of the series. I have attended five already, and—and—"

We wrung his hand in silent sympathy, and read the programme to the bitter end.

Our minds were soon made up.

"Dear fellow," we said, "we have experienced these things before, and they do not amuse us. But this ordeal cannot well be worse than others of the kind that we have endured ere this. Never fear, we will stand by you, or rather sit beside you, in the hour of trial."

"Heaven bless you," he said in broken accents, "and should occasion arise, I will do the same for you that you do

A SUGGESTION FOR UNCONVENTIONAL TOURISTS.

for me this night. Meanwhile, let us to lunch, and we will strive throughout the day to fortify ourselves against the rigours of the evening."

Evening came, with autumn chills, and the village was alive with groups proceeding to the schoolhouse under the lee of a neighbouring hill. We took our seats in the foremost row and gazed at the educational posters on the white-washed walls which told us that "the Horse is a Noble Animal, the Friend of Man"; that "the Cow is a Useful Animal: She gives us Milk," together with other trite and deadly-informative statements. A platform had been improvised, and furnished with a cottage piano from the vicarage, and a few potted plants were set along the front to hide the unfashionable extremities of the performers from the critical glance of the crowded audience. For the room *was* crowded, thanks both to the persistent canvassing of the daughters of Moor Court Farm, and the frugal nature of the country folk, who, having been cozened into buying tickets, would have thought it a shame not to have had their money's worth.

Entered then a lady with a portentous roll of music which she unrolled, and forthwith began to violently assault the piano, the unfortunate instrument responding with loud and terrible outcries. Then Celia came tremblingly upon the platform—her first appearance on any stage—and sang with an untrained sweetness that did us good to hear after the arid performances of Monday Pops. Bravo, Celia! But this, alas! was only a respite, for a dreadful quartette succeeded to her, and sang with unction and utter disregard of time a glee called *The Chafers*. The vicar's brother recited a piece of Calverley's which brought down the house and the dust off the rafters, setting us all sneezing at the lines—

"Oh! drat them rheumatics,
Which comes of damp attics,"

for damp attics and rheumatism come home to the village mind with the more or less fond recollection of everyday experience. For the rest, let us in pity refrain from re-

THE VILLAGE CONCERT.

counting the items of that entertainment; and let us hope that the organ fund has been nearly made up, so that no more concerts will be found necessary.

By invitation of the vicar, the "artists" were present at a kind of informal gathering at the vicarage, when the tourney was done. Mrs. Sandibags, wife of the eminent grocer of the neighbouring town, was there, the Moor Farm girls, and the egregious young men of the evening. These provincial youths were not at ease in that pretty drawing-room. They gathered in a body round the door, conversed familiarly with the servants, and did not breathe freely until they were well on their way home.

William, the gardener (why are all gardeners called William?), was more appreciative of these musical efforts.

"Did I goo to concert last night? why, yes, sure," said he, when we met him weeding out the few surviving flowers the next morning. (William blows the bellows of the organ at the parish church, and so considers himself something of an authority on musical matters.) "This here place is so unked that 'tisn't often the likes o' me gets any reckeration. Now you London gentlemen, I make so bold as to say, didn't care nohow about the singin' last night—you'll be hearin' so much of it up there; but we'uns thinks a deal of these things. I were to play the flute last night, but the vicar's brother, he came down and recited instead."

WILLIAM.

But concerts are not the true pleasures of the country-side. How sweet it was to rise in the early mornings, while the dew was yet heavy in the fields and radiant in the glistening hedgerows. The farmers and their hands are here the earliest risers, then, after a while, the village shop-keeper and the landlord of the Pig and Whistle, yawning, get to business, and soon the whole community is astir, with the exception of the leisured classes, here represented by Squire Barnes, the Vicar, and the Policeman.

O! happy representatives of Church and State, how lightly your duties fall upon your shoulders. Yon slumbering policeman of the County Constabulary, happy in his cottage of three rooms, recks not of robberies with violence, nor of loiterings with intent: rather does he sleep the stertorous and house-shaking sleep of the human animal; dreamless and content.

He is a gentle soul, this guardian of the peace, yet it must be confessed that it was with some surprise that I found him one morning, seated in the shade of a great tree, soothing his spirit with the tinful (not tuneful) strains of the penny whistle. O! happy Orpheus of the County Police.

But this protector's reputation has suffered severely. It was in this wise. We celebrated the golden-wedding of Squire Barnes, with much rejoicing, at Langstone Park, and all the village was there, so that the village street was even as an habitation of the dead for quietness. All had gone to the Park, where a spread, such as the Briton loveth —rich, greasy, and plentiful—was provided upon a lengthy series of tables. The Vicar and his wife took the head of one, and Squire Barnes, an Anglo-Indian of gouty tendencies and portentous aspect, presided at another. Bates, the Policeman, was, by reason, it should seem, of his position, given charge over the ale-barrels, but alas! what a fall was there; for, from distributing the drink he fell to partaking of it so freely that he presently arrived at a state of hopeless intoxication. Not another drop would he serve, for he imagined that the whole assemblage was in his own condition, and himself the only sober man present. Overcome by a grave sense of duty, he endeavoured to take the whole gathering into custody, and was gently but firmly removed, offering loudly to fight any man present for twopence.

How the people enjoyed themselves at that *al fresco* feast, and with what zest did the young men and maidens join in the country dances, not omitting even those kissing games so deplored by the unco' guid! As dusk fell, bonfires were lighted, and blazed up redly into the starry night, while rockets drew groans of admiration from the crowd.

And so the bonfires blazed and the fireworks flared into the small hours of the morning, and it was not until the first faint signs of dawn had broadened into distinct heralds of day that the rustic swains wished their beloveds an inappropriate "good-night."

William was the son of a small farmer who lived at a wonderfully old-fashioned farm-house near by, and we visited the place at his invitation. The farmer made us welcome and dismissed with abuse a tramp who had come to the door, all in one breath. "'E's a gallus bird, that is," said the farmer, "by the look of 'um. You've no idea how many o' they fellers comes along begging; an' if you give 'um anything, they'll send others. Starving? not they; the lazy passel o' 'ell-'uns. We're not scrimmity, leastways, hadn't used to be, but 'tis best to send 'um all away when you know that giving to one means a reglar string of rascals to follow after him. Why, daze my 'oons, one came t'other day when only the missus were in the house, and said he were hungry. She gave him some pie-crusses, an' he went outside an' hited a stone through the window because she wouldn't give him no money. The missus give sech a scrike, an' I come runnin' in from the orchard jest in time to see him goin', ding-dong, down t'other side of the leasow. No, 't'aint no good givin' information to the policeman, because 'tisn't likely he'd be catched, an' besides, if ye are found to be givin' to beggars ye're liable to be persecuted, same as they for axin' of ye. But come in, come in, an' have a bit an' a drap with us. My son Will'm, tells me that ye're takin' pictures round here, an', sure, 'tis a sweet pretty place, though we don't take so much notice of it, bein' bred an' born here; but I've heern the gentlefolks say 'tis a most pictorious neighbourhood."

The room, which opened directly from the garden, was kitchen, parlour, and dining-room, all in one. A great yawning fireplace, fitted with a modern range, took up all the space on one side, and above the mantel-shelf hung a number of little photographs and old-fashioned silhouettes, while on the shelf stood brightly-burnished brass candlesticks, china ornaments and tobacco-jars. All the steelwork of the range was polished to the brightness of silver.

"Ah," said the farmer, "you look at our large fireplace. 'Tis warm here in summer, but nation cowd in winter time, an' we'd be 'alf clemmed if we didn't always have a good large log on it then."

"Now," said he, "sit ye down an' have some apple-gobs, if ye won't take nothing else. There's one there all burnt to scratchings: don't take that." (Apple-gobs, it should be said, are, in the Shropshire speech, apple-turnovers.) "And some cider; don't 'ee say nay."

"Yes, I'm a Oddfellow," said the farmer, when we asked him, seeing a framed diploma of that society hanging on the wall. "'Tain't much of a picture, though. Here's the best picture I've got," and he slapped a great side of bacon hanging behind him. "Nine score, that, if it's a pound, and worth ninepence a pound," said he.

It is astonishing how heartily country folks eat. The farmer put away immense quantities of food before he was done. But Sunday was their grand field-day, devoted as it was to continuous and extensive feeding from morn till dewy eve. The truly British dinner of roast beef, Yorkshire pudding and many vegetables filled the house and garden with a rich and heavy smell and conquered the scent of the flowers round about so thoroughly that they seemed rather to emit the odour of hot gravy than their proper perfumes. The Sunday one-o'clock dinner was a solemn rite and not to be approached with levity. Thus it was that the farmer, who had donned a suit of glossy black in honour of the day, sat down at the head of the table in his shirt-sleeves; his way of dressing for a meal which another stratum of civilization takes at a different hour, but none the less specially attired. We were not fastidious, but digestion and appetite both boggled at this heavy meal, and, for another thing, our tastes had not been educated up (or down) to the point of assimilating home-made wines with any degree of pleasure. The farmer's wife was,—as the country-side had it—a famous brewer of these things: cowslip wine, blackberry wine, and metheglin; but her prowess seemed to our sophisticated tastes rather matter for notoriety than fame, so fearful were her choice decoctions. Yet it is undeniable that the other folks enjoyed them, while we, martyrs to politeness, told unblushing fibs in praise of the several wines she pressed us to try: which we *did* try, to please her and save her pride in her Old-English housewifery.

The metheglin we sipped for experiment's sweet sake, and so constantly do Mr. Thomas Hardy's Wessex folk grow mellow and jovial under its influence that we readily sought to make its acquaintance. Mead, or metheglin, is made of honey and cider. It has the appearance of rum, is very sweet and heady, and very nasty. The honeymoon, as the country folk have it, was so called from a custom—now obsolete—of drinking metheglin during the month after marriage. It is identical with that "sack" over which so many generations of our forbears made merry. God rest them for a hardy and courageous race!

Our hostess opened her last bottle for us and filled our glasses. She intended to make some more, she said, in a few weeks, terrifying us with an uneasy sense of impending dissolution by her conditional promise of "please God I live so long." We tasted, and acknowledged her compliment with fearful travesties of smiles, for to those who have not carefully educated themselves to the point of appreciation, metheglin is everything that is sickly and horrid. We thought that, as this was the conclusion of dinner, we would take our glasses into the garden and sip her admirable metheglin in a leisurely manner. " Yes, do," said she; and we went forth into its most secluded corner and there emptied our glasses among the currant-bushes. I hope the Recording Angel will make no great matter of this pious fraud.

LX.

In the neighbourhood of this rustic seclusion lived, in the early part of this century, when Corinthianism was rampant, the well-remembered Jack Mytton, one of those hard-drinking, hard-riding, and hard-swearing squires who made Shropshire so proverbial a county for sport and extravagance, in times when aristocratic families scorned trade and had not yet felt agricultural depression. The memory of Mytton lives solely by reason of his mad pranks and the reckless folly which dissipated an estate worth £10,000 yearly, together with a lump sum of £60,000 which had accumulated during his minority.

The Myttons of Halston were an ancient family who had been settled here for many centuries, and as early as 1373, Reginald de Mutton (as the name was originally spelled) was a member of Parliament for Shrewsbury. The last of the Myttons of Halston, was born in 1796, and died in 1834, penniless and a prisoner in the King's Bench. He had gambled and drank and expended the whole of his patrimony in those few years, including a sum of £80,000 which he received for the timber of his park.

That admiring biographer and friend of his, "Nimrod," tells us that Jack Mytton was left fatherless in his second year, and that before he was ten years of age, he was as finished a Pickle as his own disposition and the indulgence of his mother could possibly make him. He was expelled from Westminster and Harrow, and after knocking down an unfortunate tutor who had been engaged to din some learning into him, this unlicked cub was sent to Cambridge after being entered upon the books of the sister university at Oxford. His college career was of the shortest, and at the age of eighteen he was sent for a tour upon the Continent. In his nineteenth year Mytton was gazetted to a cornetcy in the 7th Hussars, and joined his regiment in France with the army of occupation that held Paris after Waterloo. Four years of extravagance were followed by his selling out and his marriage, at Shrewsbury; and then he settled down (if the expression may be used) to a life of riot and blackguardism, diversified by attacks of delirium tremens and arrests for debt. Some of his odd notions and harebrained exploits compel a smile, as for instance, his reply to a relative who was endeavouring to dissuade him from selling an estate, and bewailing the probable loss of land which had been so long in the family.

"How long?" inquired Mytton. "About five hundred years," was the reply. "Then," said Mytton, "it is high time it should go out of it."

But his exploits at Shrewsbury show the manner of man he was. He successfully contested the borough in 1819, and while he was being chaired home from the hustings by his enthusiastic supporters, he threw himself through the window of the Lion Inn, upon Wyle Cop, for pure devilment.

It was at the same inn that the incident of the foxes, narrated by "Nimrod," occurred. "On going into the bar of the Lion Inn, one evening, when somewhat 'sprung' by wine, he was told there was a box in the coach-office for him, which contained two brace of foxes. He requested it might be brought to him; when, taking up the poker, he knocked the lid off it, and let the foxes out in the room in which the landlady and some of her female friends were assembled— giving a thrilling view-holloa at the time. Now it cannot be said they 'broke cover' in good style; but it may safely be asserted that they broke such a great quantity of bottles, glasses, and crockery-ware as to have rendered the joke an expensive one."

It is difficult to understand the admiration of the biographer who records these things and complacently chronicles an occasion on which Mytton was driving a friend in his gig whom he upset wilfully. He was rather a nervous friend, too, and had been hinting at danger. "Were you ever much hurt, then, by being upset in a gig?" inquired Mytton. "No, thank God," exclaimed his companion, "for I was never upset in one." "What," replied this brutal squire, "*never* upset in a gig? What a d—d slow fellow you must have been all your life," and, running his near wheel up the bank, over they both went!

The Squire of Halston has no fellows now: the squire as a class is as extinct as the iguanodon. Democracy and the franchise first cut his claws and afterwards killed him. He has not been evolutionized; he is, like the feudal Barons of the Marches,—dead. Poor Squire! have you not some happy hunting-ground in the Beyond; where Port is still the favoured drink, where jolly purple-faced fellows ride to hounds and halloo lustily when the fox breaks cover? There should be no heel-taps in that shadowy country, and ghostly toasts to the First Gentlemen in Europe should still be honoured, with the breaking of airy glasses.

It is astonishing to read with what genuine grief the peasantry and the shopkeeping class of Shrewsbury received the news of Mytton's death. He had kicked some of them, had fought more, and sworn heartily at all. He had played objectionable practical jokes upon them, and lorded it assiduously over everyone beneath his own station; all this done, as "Nimrod" says, with a bluff good-humour. But a kick is still a kick and a curse is a curse, whether administered jocularly or in anger, and the sorrow of these people for the death of a man who pummelled them to a jelly and gave them a five-pound note afterwards, as a sticking-plaster, is rather staggering to any belief in the manliness of those men.

LXI.

WE came into Chirk one morning, through the uninteresting modern hamlet and railway junction of Gobowen. Here, crossing the pretty bridge of the Ceiriog, which comes tumbling in a series of little cascades from the famous Vale of Llangollen, one crosses into Denbighshire. Certainly this was Wales, for the County Council notices posted on the bridge were couched in bi-lingual fashion. Welsh weather, too, greeted us as we set foot upon the soil of Denbighshire, so that we had to retreat into the Bridge

Inn, there to await the favours of the Lady of the Weather, that fickle feminine who, in the *Daily Graphic*, at least, has supplanted the proverbial clerk. But this was better, at any rate, than the more usual experience of being caught in a storm on some wind-swept moor, away from shelter of house or tree. But O, Lady of the Weather! would that you were more reliable:—

THE LADY OF THE WEATHER.

You have been, ma'am, playing larks
  With the elements ; how dare you ?
Stay and hear these plain remarks
  On your weather ; lady clerks
Shouldn't interfere, so there, you
  Flighty person, sooth to say
"Lady of the Weather," *vice*
  Clerk of that department, eh ?
You who prophesy a day
  Bright and warm that's wet and icy.

Here's a sorry trick to play :
  Look at me, ma'am, see ! I'm soaking ;
And your forecast for to-day
  Sent me from the town away :
Here's a pretty sort of joking !

> I would learn, ma'am, why this pother;
> Why, when you predict the weather
> Will be thus and thus, 'tis other
> Than you prophesy; another
> Kind of weather altogether.
>
> Woe is me, unlucky wight!
> See, I shiver, willy-nilly;
> For this light attire is quite
> Right for 60° Fahrenheit;
> But for 30°, all too chilly.
> So, I ask you, seek some aid,
> And pray study, when at home, you're
> Fahrenheit and Centigrade,
> Aneroids; Fitzroy; Reaumur!

The neighbourhood of Chirk is rich in engineering works of monumental character. The Ellesmere Canal has two great aqueducts, and the railway between Preesgween and Cefn is carried across the valleys of the Ceiriog and the Dee by two greater viaducts. The Ellesmere Canal was planned and constructed between 1792 and 1805, when the rage for inland waterways was at its height, and so eager was the public to share in the dreams of wealth which the undertaking aroused, that the capital required was subscribed four times over. Telford was engineer to the company, and his task of carrying the canal through this district was by far the heaviest that had yet been encountered in that young profession of engineering. The Chirk aqueduct crosses the valley of the Ceiriog at a height of sixty-five feet, on ten arches, each of forty feet span, and the canal flows along the summit in a bed of iron and masonry; the whole constructed in four and a half years. But the Pont-y-Cysylltau aqueduct across the valley of the Dee is a greater achievement, and was thought by Sir Walter Scott to have been the most impressive work of art he had ever beheld. The greatest height above the valley is one hundred and twenty-seven feet, and the length of the aqueduct is not less than one thousand and seven feet. Nineteen arches carry the canal across the vale, supported upon giant piers that straddle across the meads in long and impressive array.

Mr. Richard Myddelton, of Chirk Castle, laid the foundation stone on July 25th, 1795, and not until eight years afterwards—in 1803—was it completed. Several new features of construction were adopted by Telford in this great work, and amongst these the most striking was the designing of a cast-iron trough through which the canal runs. The cost of this aqueduct, together with the earthworks of the approaches, was over £47,000.

The two railway viaducts are even finer than the canal works, but they have not earned the fame of Telford's designs, simply because when they were built the world had grown familiar with such great undertakings, and the proverbial philosopher never uttered a more trite truism than his dictum of "Familiarity breeds contempt." So that passengers ride easily in express trains upon loftier and more massive engineering works than those of Telford's, and they look forth of their windows upon Pont-y-Cysylltau and its fellow of Chirk with an admiration and respect that belong in greater measure really to these latter-day feats of skill and enterprise.

Chirk Castle stands within sight of these modern innovations, and the shriek of the railway-train reverberates through the woodlands of its delightful park, where echoed the trumpets and battle-cries of the picturesque—if somewhat blackguardly—ruffians who, in olden times, infested these regions, and were the holders of baronies and lordships innumerable, and held men's lives in the hollow of their bloodstained hands. Life was rich in surprises in those days: something too crowded with happenings in the untoward.

LXII.

THE greatest castle-building era in England was the reign of Stephen, for at that time the authority of the Crown was probably weaker than it had ever been. The internecine wars of the time that divided England between the partisans of Matilda and her cousin, gave the barons the first inkling of the power they held over the throne. They had been held in a vice-like grasp by the first William, which had not become appreciably relaxed under the rule of Rufus. His brother, Henry I., although more of a student and philosopher than his predecessors, had no less firm a hold over the lords: and, moreover, by the astute policy of which the Statute of Liberties was an outcome, he endeavoured to raise up from amongst the people (that conquered race) a class whose sympathies should, on emergency, lie with the Crown. But all this firm rule was overthrown during the nineteen years of Stephen's reign. The barons held, and exercised the balance of power all over the distracted kingdom of England, and none was strong enough to veto their lawless courses. No less than twelve hundred castles sprang up in these years, and with their rise fell for a time the young liberties of the English.

The English chronicle of that dreadful epoch has preserved to us the thoughts of the oppressed masses, and their just hatred of the alien barons :—" They filled the land with castles. They greatly oppressed the wretched people by making them work at these castles, and when they were finished they filled them with devils and armed men." Not since Pharaoh's oppression of the Lord's People had such a terrible time been experienced as this, and so insatiable was their desire for fighting and bloodshed that they fought continually, these savage lords, one with the other. " They fought among themselves with deadly hatred, they spoiled the fairest lands with fire and rapine ; in what had been the most fertile of countries they destroyed almost all the provision of bread. They hanged up men by the feet and smoked them with foul smoke. Some were hanged up by their thumbs, others by the head, and burning things were hung on to their feet. They put knotted strings about men's heads, and writhed them till they went to the brain. They put men into prisons where adders and snakes and toads were crawling, and so they tormented them. Some they put into a chest, short and narrow and not deep and that had sharp stones within, and forced men therein so that they broke all their limbs. In many of the castles were hateful and grim things called racheteges, which two or three men had enough to do to carry. It was thus made: it was fastened to a beam and had a sharp iron to go about a man's neck and throat, so that he might noways sit, or lie, or sleep, but he bore all the iron. Many thousands they starved with hunger. They took those men that they imagined had any property, both by night and by day, peasant men and women, and put them in prison for their gold and silver, and tortured them with unutterable torture; for never were martyrs so tortured as they were. I neither can nor may tell all the wounds or all the tortures which they inflicted on wretched men in this land; and that lasted the nineteen winters while Stephen was king; and ever it was worse and worse. They laid imposts on the towns continually, and called it 'censerie'; when the wretched men had no more to give they robbed and burned all the towns, so that thou mightest well go all a day's journey and then shouldst never find a man sitting in a town, or the land tilled. Then was corn dear, and flesh, and cheese, and butter; for there was none in the land. Wretched men died of hunger; some went seeking alms who were at one while rich men; some fled out of the land. Never yet had more wretchedness been in the land, nor did heathen men ever do worse than they did; for everywhere at times they forebore neither church nor churchyard, but took all the property that was therein, and then burned the church and all together."

It is when we read such vivid descriptions as this of the "good old times" that we begin to appreciate more fully our own prosaic era. It is better to lead a humdrum and prosaic life to a green old age than to end your existence suddenly in a vigorous youth by being romantically hung up by the heels and smoked to death, like a ham. If we can purchase immunity from these things at the price of picturesqueness we may call that purchase cheap. And so throughout the centuries the merry game of Might went on, with rack and stake, and *oubliette* into which one might thrust an enemy and forget all about him, while he starved to death in darkness and despair.

> In olden times when Might was Right,
>   And undisputed held the land,
> Who wished to hold his own to fight
>   Was forced, to 'scape from thievish hand ;
> Yet those were times that poets praise
> As Chivalry's most glorious days.
>
> And none then for themselves might dare
>   To think on creeds in thoughts their own,
> Or if they did, were hurried—where
>   The rack or stake gave martyr's crown ;
> But then they all deserved their fate,
> Those martyrs were so obstinate.
>
> We oft deplore the "good old times,"
>   And say, "'twas merry England then" ;
> And poets sing to jingling rhymes
>   Of lovely women, val'rous men ;
> Those "merry times" of fire and sword ;
> Of serf, and rack, and Feudal Lord !

I wonder if the picnic parties who make the ruined castles echo with their laughter and with the popping of corks realize to anything like an adequate extent the terrible doings of other days, and if Messieurs the archæologists who discourse so learnedly upon ancient architecture, have a right understanding of the scenes those old stones have witnessed. It is doubtful, for a knowledge of the dry facts of history is rarely accompanied by a true understanding of their inward significance.

The process by which these twelfth-century hell-hounds were at length turned into nineteenth-century gentlemen, with frock coats and silk hats in place of tabards and hauberks, was not only lengthy, but complicated. A very great change has been wrought in the space of seven hundred years, but the type still survives in the needy ruffians who use the handles to their names as baits with which company-promoting sharps furnish their nets to the same end as of old—the plundering of anyone and everybody.

Chirk Castle stands on a height at some distance from the village. It occupies a site which has been fortified as far back as history goes, and was in olden times known as

THE MYDDELTONS.

Castell Crogen, celebrated as having been the place where Henry II. met with one of his numerous defeats at the hands of the Welsh. The Park, beautifully wooded, and rich in ancient oaks and elms, extends to the Berwyn Mountains, and from the Terrace thirteen counties are supposed to be visible. Certainly, when the fates are kind and the weeping skies of this mountainous land have cleared, a vast tract of country lies spread out beneath this hill; but thirteen counties is too long a list for belief, except to the most credulous of tourists.

The early fortresses erected here are quite vanished. They were, most probably, only rude earthworks, defended by strong and spiked palisades. The present building is the much-repaired and modernized survivor of the Edwardian castle, erected by Roger Mortimer of Wigmore, who murdered his ward, Gruffydd ap Madoc, in order to obtain possession. It is a great quadrangular structure, with low, but massive, angle towers and a thick curtain wall enclosing an extensive courtyard. The Castle is occupied as a residence and contains some excellent paintings, chiefly portraits. The interior was restored by Pugin in a manner much admired at the time, but which seems somewhat academic and expressionless to us who have witnessed the revival, not only of the dry bones of Gothic architecture, but of its living and breathing spirit.

The Myddeltons were owners of Chirk at the outbreak of the Parliamentary war. Sir Thomas Myddelton, who then was in possession, took arms against the King, and in his absence his castle was seized by Colonel Ellis, in 1642. Sir John Watts was placed there as governor, and on Sir Thomas Myddelton appearing before his own house he found admittance denied him. He lay siege to the Castle but was unsuccessful. Subsequently he changed sides and held Chirk for the King; but here misfortune followed him, and he was compelled to surrender. The repairs to the Castle, subsequently to the Civil War, cost £80,000.

The famous Sir Hugh Myddelton was a brother of the Sir Thomas Myddelton, Lord Mayor of London, who purchased these estates from Baron Saint John, of Bletsoe, in 1595. He is better known than the Myddeltons of Chirk, but was less fortunate than they were, for his great undertaking of the New River Company which supplied, and still supplies, London with water, brought him only a tardy fame and a paltry stone statue on Islington Green. He died, if not in poverty, at least in sadly reduced circumstances, in the North Shropshire town of Shifnal.

Mr. R. Myddelton-Biddulph now represents the Myddeltons and the Myddelton-Biddulphs in this feudal dwelling. When Colonel Myddelton-Biddulph's eldest son came of age in 1858, an after-dinner speaker, divided between a devastating waggishness and an archæological erudition which reminded him that "Crogen," the old name of Chirk, signified a shell, took occasion to say: "We are told that this is a shell of a castle, and we can well believe it, for it contains a most excellent colonel." Now, could after-dinner oratory conceivably sound a deeper depth than that?

The queer little church of Chirk seems to have been converted into the mortuary chapel of the Myddeltons, so large and numerous are the monuments of that family. The largest, of white marble with life-size statues, is to Sir Richard Myddelton, Bart., and his son, Sir William. Sir Richard, we are told by the flatulent epitaph, was "Heir to the Vertues as well as the Estate of the Illuftrious Houfe of Chirk Castle." Sir William "Survived his Father juft long enough to tell the world Whofe Son and Succeffor he was: being a Gentleman of such Singular Rectitude of Manners, such strict Probity, unaffected Meeknefs, difinterefted Charity, and exalted Piety, as qualified him early for that Place, whither he haftened to receive the Rewards of his Vertues."

Oh, my goodness, what a Phœnix!

LXIII.

This brings us to Cefn and into the domain of the "Prince *in* Wales," Sir Watkin Williams Wynn. The Wynns are the most notable family, and the most thoroughly representative of the Welsh, in Wales; and the great mansion of Wynnstay, seated on a knoll in the Park of Wynnstay that stretches for five miles between Cefn and Rhuabon, is nothing less than princely. The late baronet was the last of his line who commanded so greatly the reverence of the Welsh people, and during the present generation that feeling has grown rather into a jealousy of the great wealth and traditions of the Wynns. The days are past when these baronets were received on their progresses through the Principality with almost royal honours. They were all-powerful, and this old verse records the sort of way in which the peasantry regarded them:—

> "If God Almighty were to die,
> Who'd be God Almighty then?
> To this the Welshman made reply
> 'Sir Watkin Williams Wynn!'"

Sir John Wynn, of Gwydyr, was the founder of the family and the first of this long line of baronets. He was a member of Parliament for the county of Carnarvon in 1596, a member of the Council of the Marches, and a man of business, shrewd and successful in his dealings. His hard bargains and his good fortune earned him an ill name amongst the people, who supposed themselves oppressed by his undertakings, and a superstition was current that his spirit had been condemned to lie under the great waterfall of Rhaidr-y-Wennol, near Gwydyr Castle, "there to be punished, purged, spouted upon, and purified from the foul deeds done in his days of nature." He died, aged seventy-three, in 1626, leaving his estates to his kinsman, the grandson of that notorious and unscrupulous lawyer, Sir William Williams, who undertook the prosecution of the Seven Bishops in the reign of James II. This celebrated barrister, Speaker of the House of Commons in the reign of Charles II., had married the daughter and heiress of Watkin Kyffin, of Glascoed, near Oswestry, and thus originates the traditional name of successive owners of Wynnstay.

Wynnstay was at one time known as Wattstay, from the ancient Watt's Dyke, which runs through the Park from north to south. This park is the largest in Wales, and measures eight miles in circumference. The principal entrance, situated in Rhuabon village, is beautiful, with a fine avenue nearly a mile in length, while the Dee flows through the grounds in a winding course amid wooded dingles and pebbly beaches. The old mansion of Wynnstay was entirely destroyed by fire on the night of March 6, 1858, when guests and servants sleeping under its roof had a narrow escape of being burnt to death with it. So swiftly did the fire spread that the inmates had only sufficient time to rush, undressed, from the house before every room was in a blaze. A number of valuable Welsh manuscripts were destroyed, together with some pictures and the greater part of a fine library. Jewellery, worth many thousands of pounds, was involved in the conflagration, and much of it was recovered when the ruins had cooled down, by the careful sifting of the *débris* at the hands of an experienced officer of the London Salvage Corps.

The house has been rebuilt in the French Renaissance style, with high Mansard roofs and long array of windows fronting towards the opening of the Vale of Llangollen.

Cefn is a busy village, built on a hill beside the Dee, which here makes a great bend in a deep valley, and doubles back again on itself. Collieries, iron-works, terracotta, and brick manufactories make busy the valley and the ridge[1] on which the village is built, and great perpendicular scars show curiously against the hillside, where stone-quarries are worked. It is a busy scene, viewed from where the railway viaduct spans the valley, and both

[1] *Cefn* signifies " a ridge."

RHUABON.

beautiful with natural advantages, and interesting from the dignity of industry, whose hammers and anvils clang and reverberate from hill to hill. This viaduct was completed in two and a half years, and cost £72,346. Close beside it runs a branch of the canal, and across the two goes the highway: road, rail, and river all in one comprehensive glance; with dignified leisure seated in full view at Wynnstay, and many-handed labour toiling where the chimney-stalks of the collieries send trails of thin smoke across the sky. Express trains rush in thunder across the viaduct, canal-boats crawl along the waterway, and laden waggons are dragged by sturdy horses up the dusty road, to crack of whip and loud gee-whoa.

The road from Cefn to Rhuabon is uninteresting, when once the valley is left behind. Five miles intervene, and all the way the railroad follows near by, with many stations and sidings leading to and from the collieries of the Denbighshire coal-field. On one side runs the railway; on the other, the park wall of Wynnstay; and then comes Rhuabon—spelled variously Ruabon and Rhiwabon—a stony, coaly place, thriving from the wealth underground, and frankly utilitarian. Miners with safety-lamps, and faces black like the devils of childish imaginings, passed us, on their way home from work, and coal-grit took the place of the flour-like dust of other highways.

All the way between this and Wrexham, collieries alternate with brick and tile works, and the productiveness of this coal-field of nearly fifty square miles is immense. Over two millions of tons are brought to bank every year.

Rhuabon church stands in the centre of this increasing village, and is interesting from its containing some monuments to the Wynns, together with an alabaster altar-tomb of the Eyton family, on which are recumbent effigies of a knight and lady, date 1526; Lancastrians, evidently, for the knight wears over his armour the collar of SS; that mysterious Lancastrian badge over which antiquaries have disputed so continually. It is a most singular circumstance that no record of the origin of this distinctive order has come down to us. It is considered to have originated with Henry IV., whose motto was "Sover-aygne." Others hold to the opinion that, while still a mark of the Red Rose, the double S stood for "Sanctissimus."

The beautiful Gothic of this ancient memorial contrasts sharply with the cold classicism of the marble monuments of the Wynns. Henry Wynn, tenth son of Sir John Wynn of Gwydyr, tops in effigy a great pile of marble, whose front bears an inscription in Latin, of inordinate length; Sir William Wynn, who was thrown from his horse and killed, in 1749, also is Latinized as "generosus mæstissimus"; and a beautiful marble effigy, by Nollekens, of a Lady Wynn, a girl of nineteen, daughter of the Duke of Beaufort of the time, who died three months after her marriage, occupies the centre of the north chancel aisle. For the rest, there is nothing worthy of notice in Rhuabon church except an old, elaborately iron-bound chest in the vestry, with the names of some bygone churchwardens inscribed upon the iron bands in very, very large characters.

We had some slight refreshment at an old-fashioned inn before we left Rhuabon, in a room half kitchen, half parlour, the floor paved with red bricks, and a table, covered with black leather, in the middle of the apartment. On it a gong, a match-box, glasses. A wide-yawning, capacious fireplace, filled with a modern range of generous calibre. Spittoons, filled with sawdust, about the floor, and settles ranging round, with sides of bacon and hams hanging from the black rafters, maturing. A coloured portrait of one of the Sir Watkins hung on the wall.

"Good afternoon," said a man who was reading a newspaper by the fire, "is business good?" "Pretty good," we said, "and how do *you* find it." "Bad, bad," said he, "this here coal strike has kept nearly all the colliers idle, and that don't do me no good."

We supposed this was some small shopkeeper of Rhuabon, or a neighbouring village, but when we asked him, he said "No. A man as 'ud want to set up business in Rhuabon 'ud find an 'orld of trouble onless he had a great

A NOVEL TRADE.

deal of capital; yess, indeed. Are 'oo thinking of doing any business here to-day, whateffer?" No, we were not. "Well," he replied, "there's nothing doing, and the shopkeepers have given already, look you, as much, and more credit to the colliers than they can afford." "Have you, then, given too much credit?" we asked, seeing him so despondent. "No," said he; "when the men are not working they don't want me, and when they are at work they pays me reg'lar."

"What sort of business may that be?" we asked him.

"Why, I'll bet you a quart o' beer you don't guess in a dozen tries," said he.

We accepted the wager and tried all trades, from a tallyman to a maker of safety-lamps, but without success.

"Well," he said, "you've had a good try, and now I'm going to drink your health." With that he called for a quart.

"But," I said, "now you must tell us what this mysterious trade of yours is." "Yes, I will," he said, withdrawing his face from the mug of ale and grinning; "I'm a knocker-up."

"And what on earth is that?" "Why," said he, amused at our ignorance, "*you* don't know much about early risers. I knocks up the men who've got to go to work in the pits at all hours. *That's* my business. I've got a good many customers, and they pays me threepence a week each for knocking 'em up in time to go to work. And now you see why a strike hurts my business."

The information was worth the price. We called the landlady, paid for his quart, and asked the way to Wrexham.

LXIV.

"THE road to Wrexham?" said the landlady; "yes, that's it, and a good enough road, too, if it warn't for them colliers." "Why," I asked, "what harm do the colliers do to it?" "Well," she replied, "they're that rough, that folks don't care much about meeting 'em, when they've got e'er a drop o' liquor in their insides." "Why, as for that," we said, "so long as we have fists at the end of our arms, and while there's a law in the land, we're not going out of our way, colliers or no colliers," and so departed.

And, certainly, such colliers as we chanced to meet seemed inoffensive enough; but, for all that, we had an adventure on the Wrexham road. We had not proceeded far when a trap overtook us, driven by a stylishly-dressed woman. The road was more than sufficiently broad for us all, but she, apparently from insolent intent, drove so closely to our side that we had to spring smartly into the bank to avoid the wheels. Even so, the mud from them caught our clothes. But she drove on, without a word of apology. This was too much for endurance, from either man or woman, and we ran after her, overtaking the trap at an ascent up which she was walking her horse. We seized the bridle and brought the trap to a stand. "Now, madam," said I, "before we let you proceed, you shall apologize for trying to drive over us away up the road."

She reached forward, with a sudden impulse, for her whip, but the Other Man snatched it away and jerked it over the hedge. She sat still, in a pale fury. "I perceive from your speech," she said, when she had found her tongue, "that you are gentlemen. When I tell you that I am sorry to have caused you any inconvenience or injury, perhaps you will hand me my whip and allow me to drive on." "Let her drive away," said the Other Man, "but as for her whip, why, I think, as the woman cannot offer a more robust apology than this for a wanton insult, perhaps she had better get the whip for herself. And now," said he, "we will wish you a very good morning, and, in future, better discrimination." And then we turned away and left her to do as she thought fit.

For the greater part of those five miles between Rhuabon and Wrexham, the road runs past collieries and brick and tile works. One hateful modern village lies midway—a straggling out-at-elbows place called Johnstown—and for

THE WELSH. 343

the rest of the distance a single-track tramway occupies one side of the road. The approach to Wrexham is heralded miles away by the lofty tower of the parish church, and presently the mushroom suburbs of this rising town come, dry and gritty, and primly new, upon the eye. Their pin-new aspect, however, belies the general appearance of Wrexham, for it is rather a grimy, sooty little place, where nine breweries, some zoedone works, and a variety of tanneries and other offensive places go to defile the stone of the public buildings and the towers and spires of the extraordinary number of churches and chapels with which Wrexham is blessed. The dissenting chapels are especially numerous, and vie in size with the breweries, and, moreover, are generally well filled, while the great parish church remains too large for its meagre congregation.

For, indeed, neither Wales nor its Borderland are strongholds of the Establishment. Dissent rules the roast, for good or ill; but, even so, the modern Welshman is not, whatever his forbears have been, a religious creature.

The typical Welshman is a curious and repellent compound of many and varied traits. These Fluellens are moved by nothing so much as music of a martial character, wedded, it must be confessed, to words vainglorious and (considering the history of the Welsh people) unwarrantably braggart. They are given to empty-headed enthusiasms, and yet they have a cold, calculating side positively appalling to anyone but a Scot—and then the moral nature of Taffy is familiar in that old rhyme that needs no repetition in this place. Again (since I would be not less than frank) it must be owned that the Welsh are deceitful, and that the faithless Tudors—magnificently, monumentally untrustworthy—are true examples of the racial character. Indeed, the Welshman's true field would appear to be the profession of diplomacy, in which lying is reduced to a fine art.

Still, it is pitiful to observe how jealously this people clings to its poor, paltry, tattered rags of a worn-out nationality, and an obsolescent speech. "Gallant" little Wales is the epithetical style and title conferred upon the

Principality of late years by Radical politicians, but the epithet is not discriminating: how should it be when discrimination means the loss of votes, and fulsome flattery their gain? "Frenzied little Wales" would seem nearer the truth, or "frantic," indeed, would be not farther removed from it. For indeed, Wales is not a nation, any more than Devonshire, and not all the windy Eisteddfoddau from north to south will make it one, even though many persons speak the language and though some have no Sassenach at this day; and it is utterly beyond possibility that the work of the First Edward shall ever be set aside to gratify the notions and stop the mouthings of Welsh members returned to Parliament by the Nonconformist Vote, to the end that they may first disestablish the Church and then presently set up a politico-religious vestry within the Principality. Dissent, as I have said, overtops the Church in importance in Wales, and if one might believe the caricaturists and the satirical writers (but one may not do so!) that particularly objectionable creature, Stiggins, of the Brick Lane Branch of the United Ebenezer Grand Junction Temperance Association, would be typical of its exponents in Cambria. But, (how very remarkable!) these Schismatics do *not* wear bad hats, nor do they carry umbrellas of a fearful and

DISSENT.

WREXHAM CHURCH. 345

wonderful antiquity, neither do they, as a body of men, wear stubbly chins, ragged black cloth gloves, nor clothes ridiculously ill-fitting—all these things as per margin. They may be fanatical Sabbatarians, and possibly many of these pastors are on week-days and in private life little peddling grocers; certainly, as a class, they have little learning and few of the graces of life, but it may be taken for a truth that Stiggins is not a race but only a personality, or more truly still, that Stiggins has plumbed a deeper depth, has doffed his black "doeskin" frock-coat and his silk hat, and donned the flagrant scarlet jersey of the Salvation Army. Yet the respectable Dissenter, as apart from the disreputable Salvationist, has his characteristics by which all who will may recognize him on any day of the week, whether in the pulpit, preaching condemnation and a painful eternity, or behind his counter selling chicory and coffee. That is to say, the Mark of the Heterodox is the clean-shaven upper lip that goes with a bearded chin. I know not of any Ordinance by which these latter-day Levites agree amongst themselves for the wearing of this distinctive sign, but it is one that rarely fails to discover the Chapel-goer: an outward sign of inward grace, so to say.

LXV.

But at some time the Church must have been powerful at Wrexham, for the great parish church-tower remains at this day one of the seven wonders of Wales. It is 135 feet in height, with elaborate panelling, and niches filled with statues from ground to topmost pinnacles. The architecture of the church is of the Perpendicular period, the tower being of somewhat later date than the main building. The most singular feature of the interior, however, is the eighteenth-century monument, by Roubilliac, to Mistress Mary Myddelton, of Chirk Castle, who is represented as rising from the grave at the sound of the last trump. In the north porch stands an ancient stone effigy discovered many years ago, buried in the ground of the approach to the church.

It represents a cross-legged Welsh knight, who, *more Cymru,* bears his shield in front of his body, unlike the Normans, whose effigies show their shields always at one side. An inscription runs round the shield, by which it seems that this was the monument of Kenric ap Howell.

There is a singular epitaph upon a former parish clerk of Wrexham on the inner wall of the tower. It states :—

> " Here lies interrd beneath the's stones
> The Beard, ye Flesh, and eke ye Bones
> Of Wrexham Clark, old Daniel Jones."

In the churchyard lies Elihu Yale, the benefactor of Yale College, at New Haven, Connecticut, U.S.A. He was born at Boston, Massachusetts, in 1649, and died in England, 1721. His tomb was restored by the authorities of Yale College, in 1874. The inscription runs :—

> M.S.
> Elihugh Yale, Esq.,
> was buried the twenty-second of july
> the year of our Lord MDCCXXI.
> Born in America, in Europe bred,
> In Afric travell'd, and in Asia wed,
> Where long he liv'd and thriv'd ; in London dead.
> Much good, some ill, he did ; so hope all's even,
> And that his soul thro' mercy's gone to Heaven.
> You that survive and read this tale, take care,
> For this most certain exit to prepare :
> Where blest in peace, the actions of the just
> Smell sweet and blossom in the silent dust.

Yale "liv'd and thriv'd" in Asia as Governor of Fort Saint George, Madras. In "some ill" that he did we must include the murder of his groom, whom he hanged for taking his horse without his leave and riding it for two or three days for the benefit of his health. Yale escaped with a heavy penalty from the consequences of his act.

But there are very many curious epitaphs at Wrexham, not the least singular among them being a little engraved brass plate on one of the pillars in the north aisle, which says :—

> " Here lies a churchwarden,
> A choice flower in that garden ;
> Joseph Critchley by name,
> Who lived in good fame ;
> Being gone to his rest,
> No doubt he is blest."
> Died 10 Mar., 1673-4.

Wrexham folk seem to have had charitable minds, for a notorious baby-farmer, still remembered as "Old Bob Knox," but whose name was Robert Samuels, is dismissed mildly with—

> "Judge not too rashly, men are apt to halt ;
> The best of men die not without a fault,"

and probably this charity covers a multitude of sins in the laconic inscription :—

> "Here lies John Shore,
> I say no more,
> Who was alive
> In 'sixty-five."

Probably 1765 is meant.

We were at Wrexham upon a fair day, when it seemed that all the country-side had poured into the town. Stalls crowded the streets, and in the waste places swings and steam merry-go-rounds did a roaring business; literally as well as metaphorically in the latter case, for the bellowings of the steam-organ could be heard above all the din of the fair. The wooden horses went round and round again at a headlong pace, while the women shrieked with excitement, and the rustics looked sick with giddiness, even while they endeavoured to appear proud of the privilege by which they were permitted to use an entertainment "patronized by all the crowned heads of Europe."

Crowds of gesticulating Welshmen poured forth a torrent of words that formed a horrid orgie of consonants with scarce a dozen vowels in a lengthy conversation, and some of these excited Cymry were exceedingly drunk and quarrelsome. O, the sputtering and snarling of a heated Welsh crowd! It must be heard to be appreciated, and then, one can quite agree with a waggish fellow who once said that the three chief qualifications for properly pronouncing the Welsh language were :—a cold in the head, a knot in the tongue, and a husk of barley in the throat. The Welsh themselves say with, I think, no little pride, that no Saxon's tongue is long enough to pronounce their language.

Certainly, the proper way to enunciate the Welsh "ll" and "dd," and other queer combinations that occur so commonly in Cymric place-names, is not readily learned by the Englishman. The sound of "ll" is commonly said to be "thl," as who should say "Thlangothlan" upon the spelling of "Llangollen"; but the sound is really the (to the Englishman) guttural and more difficult "chl"—as "Chlangochlan." The "dd" is pronounced "th," as in Llanymynech, which a Welshman would call "Chlanymoneth."

This day in Wrexham was a liberal education in the mouthing of Welsh, for " Cwrw da "—or good ale—had loosened the tongues of all.

"Down in Wales"

(as an imitator of Ingoldsby observes)

"They don't talk of their ales,
But spell it as though 'twere on purpose to trouble you,
With a C and a W ; R and a W—
A word to pronounce which you'd have some ado ;
But the nearest approach to the sound is ' cooroo ' ;
For to learn the Welsh language if e'er you should choose,
You'll W have to pronounce like two U's."

Teetotalism had its hardest fight in the Principality, whose people resented the new movement very bitterly indeed. The stronghold of Dissent, Eisteddfodau, pennillion, and Rebeccaites was prejudiced from the first against tea and cold water, and Oswestry, in especial, was turbulent against the Apostles of the Pump. The campaign of the teetotalers (the expression Blue Ribbonite was not yet invented) was disgraced by some very unseemly doings of their opponents, who broke up their meetings and circulated derisive "hymns." One of these is called "A Hymn to be sung by the Teetotalers at their ensuing meeting, to be held on the 1st of January, 1838," and this is a specimen of its verses :—

"O ! ye highly gifted Ranters,
 Ye who take high heav'n by storm,
Bray with zeal, ye howling canters !
 Sound the hee-haws of alarm.
If you push your standards forward
 Then the wicked foe must yield,
For each Ranter's skull is a hard
 And impenetrable shield."

THE WELSHMAN AS POET. 349

What think you of that specimen of local poetry?

The Welsh think themselves great in poetic efforts, and even while we were at Wrexham, we came upon great bills advertising an Eisteddfod to be held in the neighbourhood at which poems, written for the occasion, would be recited, and music played, by the bards of the country-side. Any grimy collier you may meet upon the road may be a poet, or "pyrydd," as he would say. How different from the Englishman, whose poetry comes to him chiefly as wrappages of his butter. But really, poetry is so little read because the greatest verse, blank or rhymed, that has ever been written is as nothing beside the unexpressed poetry that abides within us all. The greatest poet who ever lived never wrote anything that compares with the unwritten poetry in men's minds; poetry which the coarse and clumsy medium of words is incapable of expressing, and would infallibly destroy.

Superficially, it seems strange that the horny-handed miner should have so strong a sense of poetry and music, but it certainly is very true that the sense of beauty either of sound, colour, or form, is developed most readily in the midst of ugly and even hideous surroundings. It is thus perfectly logical that the painter of rural scenes, the pastoral poet, the descriptive writer who describes the country-side, the field-naturalist, and the novelist of rurality should be town-bred and born, or domiciled even in the blackness of Birmingham or the howling wilderness of Wolverhampton.

LXVI.

AND now we came to the last stage of our journey. Wrexham explored, we set out for Hawarden on foot; for though this had become uninteresting country, we had determined that nothing should break the continuity of our walk from Chepstow to the Dee. Coal-mines continued along our way from Wrexham, through Gwersyllt and Cefn-y-Bedd (the Ridge of Graves), at whose little railway-station beside the road, waited, solitary and weary of waiting, a girl, obviously unsophisticated, with a black jacket, smart hat, cotton print frock, and great lace-up boots. The effect was like that of a man who should wear a bowler hat, a frock-coat, white flannels, and marching-boots.

Next to Cefn-y-Bedd came Caergwyrle, where the roads branched, one to Mold, the other to Hawarden, which name we met for the first time on a finger-post. Caergwyrle (pronounced as nearly as possible Cargully) is said to derive from the Welsh *Caer gwyrle lle*, that is—The camp of the Giant Legion. This is by no means improbable, as the great Roman Twentieth Legion whose headquarters were at the city of Deva—since known as Chester—seems to have had an outpost on the hill where the scanty ruins of the Castle of Caergwyrle still lift their crumbling walls against the sky. Near by, a hypocaust and other remains of a Roman villa have been found, together with inscribed tiles which bear the number XX. Caergwyrle Castle has no outstanding history, and looks more interesting from a distance than a closer inspection warrants.

Here, between this village and Hope, flows the river

"OBVIOUSLY UNSOPHISTICATED."

CAERGWRLE.

ASTOR, LENOX
TILDEN FOUNDATIONS

In Flintshire.

Alyn, to join the Dee. Hawarden lies five miles distant, along an unkempt roadway which presently declines suddenly upon the flat lands that border the estuary of the Dee; themselves once forming a part of the shallow sea that still gives the name of Sealand to the levels in the neighbourhood of Chester, and the title of Ince—*Ynys,* an island, to what is now the peninsula of Wirral.

The country grows more and more uninteresting as one approaches Hawarden, only the backward view from the hamlet of Pen-y-Ffordd having any distinguishing feature:

"UNKEMPT ROADWAY."

where Hope Mountain rises up in a great wall and worthily closes the prospect. Roads grow stony and dishevelled, and roadside hamlets look poverty-stricken, and the factories of Buckley, Flint, and Mold pollute the horizon to the left. A level crossing of the London and North-Western Railway runs athwart the road, with notices in English and Welsh that remind the traveller that he is in Wales. It looks strange to a Londoner to find his native place spelled in Welsh "Llondain," but that is how the Welsh versions of these notices ended.

To the bald scenery of the last few miles succeeded the wooded parklands of Hawarden, with the roadway running through them until the village was reached. It brings one into the centre of the village, by the park gates and opposite the Glynne Arms. Here a fountain stands, sculptured in stone, in commemoration of the golden wedding of Mr. and Mrs. Gladstone.

Hawarden is a large village of little beauty or interest beyond the sentimental feeling which all good Radicals bear for it as being the residence of their prophet and leader. They come hither in brakes and waggonettes, and drink and shout in the enclosure set apart for them opposite the Glynne Arms, where gaudy poles with gilded finials and red and blue stripes combine with crimson bunting to make beanfeasters believe they have spent a happy day. Near by is the entrance to the Park, free every day, where rapturous Radicals gather and peer over the terrace wall of the new Hawarden Castle in hopes of catching a glimpse of Mr. Gladstone. Sometimes they club together and present him with an axe, at others a walking-stick is offered for acceptance, but always some gift is being proffered, and few Radicals are there in the neighbourhood who have not bowed their heads in the house of Rimmon.

Great is the name of Gladstone at Hawarden. Photographs of him, woodcutting, speechifying, standing up, sitting down; full-face, profile, full-length, half-length, and in every conceivable posture, are for sale at every turn. Photographs, too, of Mrs. Gladstone, and all the Gladstone relatives and friends grouped around the statesman in the ecstacy of hero-worship are to be had; and the enthusiastic Radical is tempted to the aristocratic extravagance of embossed notepaper with " Hawarden " printed in colours upon it. He can also approve himself a thorough-going partisan by purchasing walking-sticks with the Grand Old Head carved upon their handles, and can butter his bread at breakfast from a pat bearing that same ubiquitous countenance. When he wants a wash he can use Gladstone Soap. You only wonder that the Hawarden people don't endeavour to persuade their hens to lay Gladstone eggs.

As for Hawarden village, it is grown to that size when, like an awkward growing youth who is neither man nor boy, it has become something indefinite: neither village nor town. Its growth into the importance of a township is hampered by the nearness of Chester, whose towers and spires are plainly visible from the last ridge above the levels of the Deeside pastures. Chester is only seven miles away, and its clustered roofs are inimical to Hawarden's expansion.

Whether Hawarden takes its name from *Haugh wardine*, or "high village," from its situation upon the first rising ground near the estuary, or whether it derives from *Y Garthddin*, "the hill fort on the projecting ridge," as some topographers have it, let us leave those learned folks to discuss. The Welsh called it *Penarlag*, as who should say "Lake-head," and this ancient title reveals to us these lowlands under waters which stretched to the foot of Hawarden heights. When the Norman surveyors came hither and noted down the size of the vill and the number of carucates under the plough, they heard the name of the place pronounced in very much the same manner as we heard it to-day, and they reproduced the sound as nearly as they could in the Doomsday Book as "Haordine." Phonetically, the country pronunciation is "Hordeen," as near as may be: not the sound of "Harden" which we constantly hear in London when folks speak of Mr. Gladstone's home.

Hawarden stands in Flintshire, within bow-shot of Cheshire, that county of dairy-farms and wondrous timber-framed houses in black and white alternations of timber and plaster. The name of Flintshire is not prepossessing on the map, and the county is hardly more attractive than its name; while Hawarden is rather a sad coloured place and wanting in that appearance of ease and comfort which one usually expects to find in places similarly situated, outside the pale of an ancestral park and within the grasp of a landed family. No village green nor any generous width of street marks Hawarden village above the common run of places where the land is held by little freeholders, whose rule generally produces a settlement where the graces of life are conspicuously absent.

We lodged in a little cottage in the village street, where a bootmaker plied his trade, he and his wife enthusiastic in praise of Mr. Gladstone. When night came, the bootmaker practised the bugle fitfully in the wood-shed at the end of the garden, and his hideous gurglings and stifled bellowings mingled in an indescribable charivari with the noise of a neighbour who played " When other lips " in spasms on an accordion.

LXVII.

It is a singular irony of fate which has made a demagogue of the owner of so beautiful a demesne as Hawarden Park. You who chance to pass through the lodge gates and adventure upon the lovely lawns and deep delightful dells of this woodland estate cannot but feel surprise at the mental and political attitudes of a country gentleman and rural squire who damns privilege and has thumped metaphorical tubs any time, and all the time, during the last fifty years, in anathema of class and glorification of that superlatively virtuous noun—the People.

It was by marriage that Mr. Gladstone became possessed of Hawarden, which had been the property of the Glynnes for two hundred years. The history of the manor and castle goes back very far indeed, for when William of Normandy came, he found both possessed and held by a Saxon Thane, Edwin of Mercia, who himself had wrested them by force of arms from the Welsh. Hawarden was then held for two centuries by the Earls of Chester, and afterwards by the Lords of Mold, styled variously Barons de Montalt, de Monte Alto, de Mouhaut and de Moaldis. Thus it is evident whence derived the present-day unlovely name of Mold. The Mons Altus which gave these Barons

HAWARDEN CASTLE.

THE NEW YORK
PUBLIC LIBRARY

ASTOR, LENOX
TILDEN   TIONS

a territorial designation is still to be seen at Mold town, and was the site of their castle. It is now known as Bailey Hill. But the records of Hawarden are somewhat involved and obscure, and these Barons are merely names and historical will-o'-wisps to us of the nineteenth century who essay to reconstruct their lives from the tattered contents of mouldy muniment rooms. Robert de Montalt, the seventh Baron, who died without issue or near kindred in 1329, bequeathed Hawarden to Isabella, Queen of Edward II. Subsequently the manor came to the Stanleys, and remained in the possession of that family until James, Earl of Derby, was captured by Cromwell's troops after the Battle of Worcester, in 1651, and beheaded at the market-cross of Bolton, in Lancashire. His property at Hawarden was confiscated and sold by the Parliamentary Commissioners to Serjeant Glynne, a law-officer and a friend of Cromwell. Mrs. Gladstone's father, Sir Stephen Glynne, was descended from the purchaser of this estate. I wonder if the late Earl of Derby, Mr. Gladstone's sometime colleague, ever meditated upon the spoliation of his ancestor and this purchase of what was really not the property of the Commissioners to sell.

The architectural history of Hawarden Castle goes back to the reign of Edward I., to which period the remains of the keep belong, having partly survived the attack of Dafydd, brother of Prince Llewellyn, who surprised the garrison on the night of Palm Sunday, 1282, slaughtering many of the knights and esquires whom he found in their beds. In 1643, it was taken by assault from the garrison who held it for the Parliament, and the Royalists, in their turn, were ousted in 1645, when the stout walls were shattered by a mine sprung in the principal doorway. There would still have been a respectable ruin remaining had not Sir William Glynne, who succeeded his father, the Serjeant, been a determined foe of feudal buildings. What Cromwell's men had left he destroyed, and the picturesque fragments of the keep and sallyport that now rise amongst the trees are the careful restorations of the late Sir Stephen Glynne. Thus had the hatred of Gothic architecture veered round to appreciation in the course of years. But Gothic had already been admired at Hawarden before the last of the Glynnes restored the fragments of the keep. Sir John Glynne had built a typical Georgian manor-house of red brick in 1752, and, a matter of fifty years later, one of his race conceived the idea of making this box of bricks look as much like a feudal castle as he could. He cased the building with stone and plaster and ran up sham battlements and paltry machicolations with this object, and the preposterous result he called Hawarden Castle. That building, with some later additions, is what we see to-day. Age cannot make it venerable, and its pretensions to Gothic architecture are enough to make the archæologist gasp with dismay.

Hawarden Church stands in its very large and extremely crowded churchyard just across the village street from the Park. It is an Early English building, constructed of the red sandstone of the district and dedicated to Saint Deiniol, presumably the Welsh variation of Daniel. When Mr. Gladstone is in residence at Hawarden he attends service regularly, every Sunday, and reads the lessons, standing at the lectern; and on those occasions the church is crowded to an extent far beyond its proper capacity by people from far and near who push and scramble for entrance, not for the love of God, but in worship of an Old Parliamentary Hand.

LXVIII.

THIS was the last day of our tour. We had reached the sands of Dee, now spanned by the great girders of the Hawarden Bridge, built to carry the Wrexham, Mold, and Connah's Quay Railway across to Wirral and to its junction with the other lines to Liverpool. Another railway runs along the estuary from Chester to Flint and the sea-coast, and the coal-mines of Buckley and the chemical works of Flint Town smirch the sky, viewed from Connah's Quay, with thick trails of black smoke.

When the tide is in, this broad channel presents a magnificent aspect, but at the ebb only sands and mud-banks spread out over the scene of Kingsley's beautiful song in *Alton Locke*, the sands mentioned in the lines

> "O, Mary, go and call the cattle home,
> Across the sands of Dee."

The scanty ruins of Flint Castle stand upon the shore, washed by every tide and melting gradually away. Architecturally, the castle is of but little interest, but historically it commands attention as having been the scene of Richard II.'s meeting with Henry of Bolingbroke. Shakespear has it in *Richard II.*—

> "Go to the rude ribs of that ancient castle;
> Through brazen trumpet send the breath of parle
> Into his ruin'd ears, and thus deliver:
> Harry Bolingbroke
> On both his knees doth kiss King Richard's hand."

Bolingbroke had returned to England after his banishment, and, with a large following at his back, demanded the restoration of his estates, and a revocation of the decree of exile that had been pronounced against him.

The King returned from Ireland, whither he had gone to crush the Irish rebels who had slain his kinsman, the Earl of March. Had he used a reasonable expedition in his movements, it seems likely that the course of events would have been very different from what now followed. Richard's faithful partisans of Wales and Cheshire assembled in great numbers at Conway in answer to the call of the Earl of Salisbury, but, instead of appearing in the course of six days, according to his promise, it was not until the eighteenth day that the King arrived at Milford Haven. By that time the army assembled at Conway had dispersed, disheartened by the King's delay and the sinister reports which began to circulate. On his arrival at Milford Haven, Richard had a force of several thousand troops, but the greater part of them deserted almost immediately, and propositions were made that the King should take ship to Bordeaux. Other counsels prevailed: he assumed the grey habit of a Franciscan monk and crept away towards Conway. When the King's flight was known, the last remnants of his army dissolved, after plundering the royal treasure, and the chiefs of his following went over to Henry of Bolingbroke.

When the King with his small party reached Conway, he found with dismay that of all the thousands of men who had awaited him a few days before, only a hundred remained. Henry lay at Chester, and the King's two brothers, the Duke of Exeter and the Earl of Surrey, were commissioned to visit him and learn his true intentions. They approached him on bended knee who was but recently an outcast from England, and delivered their message, which incidentally gave Henry the intelligence that the King was within the castle of Conway. Having learned this, he detained the envoys, and sent his friend and fellow-rebel, the Duke of Northumberland, with a thousand archers and four hundred men-at-arms, towards Conway. The Duke's instructions were to dispose his force in ambush, lest the King should take alarm and escape over sea; to proceed then to Conway Castle and by fair promises induce him to leave the shelter of that fortress; when he was to be at once taken prisoner. The Duke departed from Chester and faithfully followed his instructions. He lay hands upon the castles of Flint and Rhuddlan on his way, and concealing his men in a dingle, appeared before the gates of Richard's retreat, accompanied by only five esquires. On his being admitted, the King's first inquiry was for his two brothers. Northumberland replied that he had left them safe and well at Chester, and that he was the bearer of a letter from the Duke of Exeter, in which that nobleman was made to say that full credit should be given to the offers of Henry of Bolingbroke's messenger. These offers were that Richard should promise to judge and govern his subjects by the law of the land, and that Henry should be appointed Grand Justiciary of England. Richard, unsuspecting, expressed his approval of these terms, and consented to accompany the Duke of Northumberland to Flint, in order to meet Henry.

They came, in the course of their journey, to a steep road near the sea, overhung by a cliff, and, dismounting, the King was proceeding down the road on foot when he caught sight of Northumberland's ambuscade. "I am betrayed," he exclaimed, in despair. "God of Paradise, assist me! Do you not see banners and pennons in the valley?" He turned to the Duke. "Duke of Northumberland," said he, "if I thought you capable of betraying me, it is not too late to return." "You cannot return," replied the Duke, laying hands upon the King. "I have promised to conduct you to the Duke of Lancaster."

They had now arrived within the ambuscade, and it was clearly impossible for the King to escape. "May God reward you and your accomplices at the Last Day," said he, bitterly. "We are betrayed," he exclaimed to his friends, "but remember that Our Lord was also sold, and delivered into the hands of His enemies."

The party reached Flint that evening. The following day, Henry of Bolingbroke's army came in view and surrounded the castle. Henry appeared in the courtyard in a complete suit of armour with the exception of his bascinet, and approached the King with outward deference and protestations of loyalty!

"Fair cousin of Lancaster," said Richard, "you are right welcome." "My lord," replied the Duke, "I am come before my time. But I will shew you the reason. Your people complain that for two-and-twenty years, you have ruled them rigorously; but if it please God, I will help you to govern them better." "Fair cousin," replied the King, rage and bitterness gnawing at his heart, but fair words needfully on his lips, "since it pleaseth you, it pleaseth us well." The next day he was sent, under guard, to Chester, on "two littel nagges not worth forty frankes," and from thence to London, a prisoner.

Stowe says that Richard's downfall was perceived by his favourite greyhound, Mathe, who left his side and fawned upon Bolingbroke. "Kynge Richarde," says he, "had a grayhounde called *Mathe*, who always waited upon the Kynge, and wolde knowe no one else; for whensoever the kynge did ryde, he that kept the grayhounde did let him lose, he wolde streyght rune to the kynge and fawne upon him, and leape with his fore-feet upon the kynge's shoulders. And, as the kynge and the Earle of Derby, Duke of Lancaster, talked togedyer in the courte, the gray hounde, who was wont to leape upon the kynge, left the kynge, and came to the Earle of Derby, and made to him the same friendly continuance and chere as he was wont to do to the kynge. The duke, who knew not the grayhounde, demanded of the kynge what the dog wolde do. 'Cosyn,' quod the kynge, 'it is a great good token to you, and an evyll sygne to me.' 'Sir, how know you that,' quod the Duke. 'I know it well,' quod the kynge; 'the grayhounde makyth you chere this day as kynge of England, as ye shall be, and I shall be deposed: the grayhounde hath this knowledge naturalye, therefore, take him to you; he will follow you and forsake me.' The duke understood well those words, and cherished the grayhounde, who wolde never after folowe King Richard but folowed the Duke of Lancaster."

From the stormy and blood-boltered politics of that time to the poetic strains of *Lycidas*, Milton's mournful elegy, is an abrupt transition; but the sands o' Dee offer no outstanding history between the deposition of Richard II. at Flint and the drowning of Milton's schoolfellow and college friend, Edward King, off this treacherous coast on the 10th of August, 1637, as he was voyaging from Chester to Dublin. That was, of course, only a domestic loss, but Milton's pastoral lines have rescued the name of his friend from an oblivion which had certainly been his lot had not he been so fortunate in his misfortune as to count a poet as his friend. The ship in which King sailed is supposed to have struck upon a rock in mid-channel of the estuary, and all on board, say some accounts, perished. Milton calls his poem a monody, in which "the Author bewails a learned Friend, unfortunately drowned in his passage from Chester on the Irish seas, 1637; and by occasion foretells the ruin of our corrupted clergy, then at their height."

It is cast in a peculiar convention in which the poet and his friend move as shepherds in an Arcadian landscape, where the friends do not

> ... " Sport with Amaryllis in the shade,
> Or with the tangles of Neæra's hair!"

but

> "Scorn delights and live laborious days."

This idyllic life of study and sweet learning is rudely interrupted by a message from the sea. The poet

> ... "Asked the waves, and asked the felon winds,
> What hard mishap had doomed this gentle swain?
> And questioned every gust of rugged wings
> That blows from off each beakèd promontory.
> They knew not of his story;
> And sage Hippotades their answer brings.
> That not a blast was from his dungeon strayed;
> The air was calm, and on the level brine
> Sleek Panopè with all her sisters played.
> It was that fatal and perfidious bark,
> Built in th' eclipse, and rigged with curses dark,
> That sunk so low that sacred head of thine."

We turned away from the Dee, and made our way back to Hawarden, passing by that fatal dell of Ewloe where Owen Gwynedd and his sons, Conan and Dafydd, at the head of a wild mob of Welshmen, attacked Henry II.'s army and almost annihilated it in 1156. Ewloe Castle, a very fragmentary ruin, stands here, amid a wild tangle of underwood, and shows a wreck of featureless walls to the traveller. Their history is unknown, their builders, their old-time owners forgotten. The very place is difficult to find, and when found the ruins are as difficult of access, so that not one of twenty tourists, nay, nor ninety-nine of every hundred, ever see them; and as they are not worth seeing, why, we need not deplore their inaccessibility.

"PHYSIQUE OF THE SUFFOLK PUNCH."

Our last day was drawing to a

close. Evening fell in subtle gradations of light and temperature. The sickle moon rose in the sky, wan and pallid against the flaming sunset; the cattle lowed in chorus from the meadows, and the milkmen came homewards with their pails.

The milkmaid, apparently, belongs to a decayed order, for everywhere at this time the man has supplanted her. That short-skirted buxom wench, with the print frock and straw hat, and the physique of the Suffolk punch, who (somewhat conventionalized from her state of too, too solid flesh) has been the central figure of idyllic poems and poetic operas, has passed away with so many other old-world figures. She lives, like the Welsh peasant-girl of opéra-bouffe, only on the stage; for not even in the remoter parts of the Principality do we find the latter, with her steeple-crowned hat and general aspect of the bypast centuries. Alas for convention! Modernity has become the slayer of pleasant customs, and the last half-century has been the death of

THE CONVENTION OF OPÉRA BOUFFE.

many interesting things. Only the sordid and commonplace remains to the end of the chapter, like the disreputable Welsh harpers who, with unsteady hand, twang their strings to the tune of "Ar-hyd-y-Nos," for the coppers of the Sassenach in the hotels and railway-stations of the Principality.

We returned through scattered villages from the sands of Dee to Hawarden. A strange rumbling sound pervaded one of these village streets, and we stopped to listen and discover whence it came. It proved to come from a church in which the village choir was practising. We walked in, on tiptoe, and sat there, listening to them, while the yellow gas-jets lighted up the interior and the daylight died out, and the gorgeous saints in the easternmost window, in their tabernacles of silvered glass, faded away into the gloom of night, and the blazoned shields of arms sank out of view.

"SEA-GULLS."

It had long gone dark when we again reached Hawarden, and our little sitting-room, lit up with a lamp, seemed quite dazzling as we came out of the gloom of the village street. Its light fell upon the open harmonium which was eloquent of "most musical, most melancholy" Sunday afternoons, and upon a portrait of the Hawarden Idol, painted upon a terra-cotta plate, which gave him china-blue eyes and a terracotta countenance, the colour of salmon. O! Thomas Carlyle, of Ecclefechan and Chelsea, were you but among us to-day to write anew upon windbags and Hero Worship, I would direct you, and I might, to this Flintshire village, for the preparation of an *envoi* to your work.

And so to close this chronicle. We left Hawarden on the morrow, for Chester and London, and came upon town once more with all the feeling and awkwardness of country cousins, so long had been our pilgrimage, and so far removed from the bustling centres of commerce.

THE END.

Lightning Source UK Ltd.
Milton Keynes UK
UKHW022047080622
404084UK00003B/217